GIVING
UP THE
GHOST

GIVING UP THE GHOST

A Writer's Life Among the Stars

by
SANDFORD DODY

M. EVANS AND COMPANY
New York

Library of Congress Cataloging in
Publication Data

Dody, Sandford.
    Giving up the ghost.

    1. Actors—United States—Biography.
2. Ghostwriting.   I. Title.
PN2285.D6   790.2'092'2 [B]   79-26016
ISBN 0-87131-142-9

M. Evans and Company, Inc.
216 East 49 Street
New York, New York 10017

Design by Ginger Giles

Manufactured in the United States of America

9 8 7 6 5 4 3 2 1

For Harriet
Who would have been pleased

Contents

The Beginning

The Greenwich Savings Bank sent me a notification of my annual interest, which I was to attach to my income tax form and then submit, along with all my worldly goods, to the Internal Revenue Service. Although this is neither an event nor a time of the year usually considered to be festive or even remotely entertaining, April indeed being the cruelest month, I was amused.

Harry, the postman, unhappily now retired, always had a sixth sense, and thereby managed to pigeonhole this correspondence, though it had been addressed to one Mr. Simpfud Dupy, a name that resembles a ventriloquist dummy's at least as much as mine. In truth there were remarkably few matching letters. Harry had always performed beyond the call of duty, but the arrival of this letter was a minor miracle. My amusement knew no bounds. If my interest, considered income, was really listed under a name so dissimilar to mine, I shrewdly deduced in a lovely flight of reason that Uncle Sam would be unaware of my connection with it. Ah, yes. But there is always the tragic flaw. I craved attention.

I have come to believe that one's good character is created solely by the priority of one's vices. In this case it was truer than ever. My venality was exceeded by my vanity, hence honesty prevailed.

"How typical!" I now philosophized. "That's the life of a ghostwriter. Not even my own goddamned bank can spell my name correctly."

And I was pained.

"I allow them to use all this cash for their devious purposes and this is my reward, a measly five per cent and the capital belongs to a ventriloquist's dummy. They may call this interest! I call it neglect."

Neither the telephone company nor Consolidated Edison—both formidable enemies, to be sure, and therefore, one would logically assume, committed to an efficiently aimed missile—has ever spelled my name correctly; but the loss of one letter now seemed exemplary beside this utter defacement.

The Helen Hayes book *On Reflection* had received excellent reviews, and as the ghostwriter I was mentioned in a manner of speaking by a few kindly critics—to no avail. They almost uniformly mutilated my name. Even with credit, I was evidently doomed to anonymity. Anonymity was my karma.

When against my better judgment I was prevailed upon by my then agent and my present publishers to lunch with Stella Adler, actress, dramatic coach and poseuse, we all met at The Running Footman. I was not interested in doing a book with the lady, though her family and her life are doubtless good copy. I was there as a favor to friends —to pursue the possibility for *them*. We were introduced for the thousandth time in our lives. She knew all about me.

"Miss Adler, may I introduce Sandford Dody?"

The still-beautiful woman tilted toward me and extended her hand—it seemed for kissing.

"Mr. Ferdoti!" she purred, baptizing and stabbing me at the same time.

The Running Footman froze in his tracks. It was not a successful luncheon although I dined out on it often enough. Now I could no longer be amused with such as this. *The Greenwich can bank on it,* I decided gravely.

I dropped all work and planned a frontal attack on the banking establishment. My irritation grew as I warmed to the outrage. Did the Bowery Savings Bank have a bulging account for Normand Mauler, Citibank a Bore Vital? Ghost or no, I had solid loot in that bank—to others perhaps a modest amount, but to me considerable. I was carried up the avenue on a wave of loathing—for the Greenwich Savings Bank, for my various publishers and subjects, and for all the famous who can add or subtract letters at will, like Barbra, or in a different and lower case, reduce them like e.e., only to have the entire world to a man jump at attention in immediate recognition and retention of the peculiarity. What had I done to my life?

I had chosen this particular branch because of its stylish location on Fifty-seventh Street off Fifth Avenue. I am a great walker, and considering myself something of a boulevardier, I had been diverted by the fancy that one afternoon, surrounded by other beautiful and accomplished arrivés, all of us carried up the avenue by the brilliance of our chatter and the head-turning elegance of our style, I would suddenly find myself on my way to the Plaza without sufficient funds—nothing new to be sure, but now a gilded detour on smart Fifty-seventh Street would lead me to my bank. There in my fantasy, I saw potted palms and inlaid floors and the high and mighty depositing and withdrawing shamelessly in front of everyone while fawning clerks, pronounced *clarks,* greeted me by name and opened their coffers so that I could satisfy my fugitive appetite for Dom Perignon. For everybody!

This delirium, prompted by a modest account at the Greenwich Savings Bank, was now destroyed. As I sailed up Fifth Avenue, I conjured up a fleet of other unhappy depositors who now convoyed me to my destination. They were morose company. Filip Broth, Harold Hinter, Grayish Greene, and bringing up the rear, P.S. Eliot.

When I reached the bank, I forgot I was in blue jeans and high dudgeon. I was my haughtiest. I had made up my mind to be composed, cool, and calm. All the things I am not. I now approached one of those desks that house pink-and-white fatherly gentlemen in gray. They are cast rather than hired. It was a quiet day and the gentleman asked me to sit down. Calmly I placed my correctly titled passbook and my mutilated notification side by side. I thought my tone had exactly the right combination of hauteur and mockery.

"I am a new depositor and it is essential that I have faith in those who guard my funds. To misspell one of one's names is inexcusable. To obliterate one's identity should be punishable only by masked robbery."

I now smiled and elaborately placed my hand in my breast pocket—even more gaudily leaving it there. Would the dough be legally mine, owned as it was by that idiot, Dupy? This bread that was swelling the Greenwich ovens was earned mostly by my Helen Hayes and Bette Davis books. *They never misspell their names,* I reflected bitterly.

After much throat clearing and an artificial smile, the man departed, to return almost immediately with a retyped form for Uncle Sam. He was as proud as the winning schoolboy at a spelling bee. "There you are, sir," he beamed. "Spelled perfectly."

And there is was. S-A-N-D-F-O-R-D D-O-D-Y.

"That's right," I marveled. "Thank you, sir. And all my future mail will be addressed thus?"

"When are you moving, Mr. Dody?" was his reply.

I quickly pushed my seat back, thinking that I was resting on the gentleman's toes.

"No, no! I mean when are you moving from your present residence?"

"When hell freezes over. Why?"

"Oh dear," he said.

"I don't understand. I'm rent controlled and extremely happy where I am. I haven't the remotest intention of— by why do you ask?"

His logic made my sentiments sound foolish.

"The computers are changed only once annually, and *unless* a depositor moves, of course, the records have to remain the way they are for the fiscal year."

"Do you mean to say," I sputtered, half crazed, "that I must pull up my roots—walk the streets seeking another home—alter my entire life—in order for the Greenwich Savings Bank to spell my name correctly?"

He was clearly annoyed.

"Well," he said, "there's been very little action on your account, and does it really matter if . . ."

I removed my savings from the Greenwich Savings Bank and after I closed the account I sat down and took stock of my life. Despite their stupidity, I laid the entire blame for the birth of Simpfud Dupy on my chosen career. It came as a flash. One should never ignore these illuminating streaks of lightning wisdom that cut through the murkiness. I had been begging for anonymity.

Fifteen years ago, I stopped smoking, not out of fear but anger. The surgeon general's grave warnings had not been convincing enough to break my habit. But my brand's TV advertisement, which anticipated the report, was so slick and of such amoral nature, so revealing of a lack of caring that I snuffed out the weed—swearing first that I would never touch another, and second, that I would outlive the copywriter. This was a like decision. I knew that no longer would I allow myself to be used and unloved.

After *All My Sins Remembered,* my book on John and Elaine Barrymore—the only time I ever got equal billing—all a reviewer could say was that Elaine Jacobs had exacted the last pound of flesh from the corpse of John Barrymore. The literary criticism was, in reality, a judgment of poor Elaine's alleged sins. Not a mention of mine.

Damn it! If I die of starvation—if I fail as a flesh-and-blood writer, I shall at least personally be attacked by the powers. If so, the ghost will be finally laid, the tombstone, I would hope, proofread and correct. Mourners will grieve at no other patch of ivy but my own. Imagine the ignominy of *Here Lies Simpfud Dupy.* That would really be the end.

And that is why I have written this, my own ghost story.

For years I have been asked what it is like to be a ghost to such immortals as Bette Davis and Helen Hayes, what it is like to be alter ego, confidant and shadow to such lofty figures, indeed, what it is like simply to be a ghostwriter.

Is there anything, could there be anything madder than an autobiography written by someone other than oneself? It is, of course, a contradiction in terms. Can one imagine a surrogate patient, with complaints freshly supplied by the sick man, now relating them to a doctor? There is a world of difference between a fact and the presentation of it.

But I have tried in that limbo to convey, and not obscure the truth. It has been, one after another, quite an experience. When the ghost's job is done, he wanders, unheeded, unseen in a half-world and in circles now too grand for him. Unseen by everyone—except on rare occasion by the subject who pretends blindness but winks conspiratorially when the unfamiliars are looking the other way—I have been able to slip through closed doors and between locked mortals as they engage in their earthly affairs. Impossible to be heard, I for one have cried out in protest, in joy, in vain. Isn't that what death is all about finally? One is no longer listentoable. One can no longer affect the smallest change in direction or script, but is bound and gagged and relegated to a balcony seat to endure the endless melodrama. Impossible to be contacted, the actors play out their lives without my cosmic counsel. When the work is done, the worker vanishes. Such is the nature of this medium. I have written on the wind and I have been lost in stardust.

After all, how does one become a ghost without dying a little? And if it is undeniably by one's own hand and therefore (to the Catholics certainly) a deterrent to paradise, isn't it also true that there has been the all-too-willing collaboration of the haughty, the vain, and the powerful? Couldn't that militate in my favor, and is suicide less touching than murder?

If my tone is self-pitying, let me hasten to say that I have used others as they have used me. With every stake through my heart, I have haunted those who have tried to exorcise me. I may be specter at the feast, but I have sung for my supper and rattled the china along with my chains. It has been a gay and mutual destruction of a human spirit. My own masochism has astonished me.

The indignities of the ghost are endless, and I have at last faced my mad acceptance of them, or rather the madness of my acceptance of them, which is something else again. In self-examination I find it less likely that my once-believed need for security, my love of people, chance, luck, or the fascinating challenge led me into ghostwriting. I somehow slipped and fell into this literary graveyard.

Having started my career as a playwright with the encouragement of knowledgeable powers, fortified with a scholarship, a grant, the faith of a great literary agent, and the protection of and assistantship to one of the pundits of the drama, for whatever reason, I evidently lost confidence in my own ability to project my rocket to the moon, and I hitched my wagon to the stars instead.

I suppose I found it easier to hide behind another's psyche. Easier! The frustrations are the devil's own punishment for squandering one's gifts; and, like a not thoroughly committed masochist, I ungraciously bridled at the rules of the game while joining passionately in their perpetuation. What did I expect, I often wonder? How could I have trafficked in such a business and not anticipated the cost?

For someone whose ego does not ostensibly suffer from arrested development, how could I so have threatened my own identity?

In front of Sardi's, an aging stargazer, autograph book clutched in his hand, a man with skin like beefsteak and eyes like a child, invariably stops me. He is feverish with expectancy. "Are you anybody?" he always asks. An entire book is in that pathetic question and its answer.

After my first of such books, which was, by contract, a job with no billing whatsoever, I felt that while I was doing my serious writing I could earn my keep and build a modest reputation working in this genre. I felt that linking my name to the celebrated couldn't hurt me.

One doesn't reasonably expect disproportionate fanfare when a household name is one's subject. Or even fanfare at all. One simply wants the recognition necessary to survival and the protection of one's work. One rarely gets it. The stars and the starstruck see to that.

Now the most sensible way to view the stars is from a long way off. It is the nature of my work that I have trafficked with them. There have been countless times when I wish I had kept my distance—at a point where they again would look divine and point the way.

Just as a star is a leading man or woman in life and destined in his or her excesses to advertise and exalt that species, the actor, to me, is Adam—the first combination of cells that became conscious. The first form of life to contemplate itself. The first creature to move intransitively simply for effect, with no object whatsoever. The actor is excited by the spectacle of his own being—actor and audience merging and producing the first communion. Unlike everything else which *is,* the actor *appears.* He is a series of contradictions possessed of breadth of observation and narrowness of vision, inexhaustible passion and fugitive feeling. His generosity of nature is almost equaled by his thrift with himself. Flamboyant and shy, he is the symbol of his trade—two-faced: one grinning, the other wretched. I adore actors.

At work or—so terribly often—between engagements, the actor's precarious life is still lived with high style. He seems the very abstraction of man, proving by his pretense that he can be what the rest of us only wish we were.

The constant need for role playing and applause makes most actors creative lovers but preoccupied mates and co-workers. You may start out co-starring in an emotional production with an actor or actress, but it's a cinch you'll soon land in an aisle seat—creatively participating perhaps—but assuredly not onstage.

While playing, every sigh is noted and checked for decibel strength, the audience reaction being essential to the continued performance. Now no one denies the importance of response, but it should be the dynamics of a fellow player, a co-star, not a fan. With the actor's tech-

17

nique fairly gleaming, abandonment is impossible, and I say *ars est celare artem*—though I confess I don't say it often.

If you insist on making the scene with them, be prepared to take your curtain call with grace. At their worst, actors still have a talent for building castles in the air. They inhabit them with grace and entertain with hospitality, although if you accept you may find, at your hungriest, that the whole damned place has vanished—never having been. But that's show business.

The detachment so vital to the actor's work can be disaster to his partner's pleasure. With that invisible spotlight or camera always framing him, the jockeying for position would make the *Kama Sutra* seems to reflect the tragic limitations of a paraplegic.

This awareness never leaves him, and even in the throes of genuine emotion, he is wont to simulate it, perhaps in the belief that it is not being sufficiently projected. Always there is the superimposition of art over reality. Not a tracing, but an improved version—a second draft, as it were. It is all so reflexive and immediate that the untutored eye cannot detect the white on white.

Laurence Olivier, in rejecting my petition to play John Barrymore in a possible film based on my third book, *All My Sins Remembered,* told me that he would never play an actor again. He had found that in doing so, "One doesn't act, luv, one only acts at acting!" Well, why not?

My father was an actor, and in my youth, I watched him during genuine grief, choreograph my own mother's funeral—arranging his stalwart sons on either side of him, shrinking ever so slightly to heighten the contrast and, in so doing, touching the mourners and earning my eternal contempt. It was only later, at the cemetery, that my father, really bereft but automatically acting the bereaved, happened to meet my gaze. The sight of my grief reinforced

18

his, and I saw the naked emotion through the sackcloth and ashes. I was sobbing, a boy of fifteen whose loss was immeasurable and whose contact with reality had been broken, who was now the newest working member of a theatrical family, pressed into service as the juvenile in the melodrama of its life. My heart was broken but as an actor and writer I saw and recorded all of this. I was beside myself.

One only acts at acting? It seems to me a challenge worthy of an Olivier. To simulate the simulation of an emotion which in itself is impure is—for such an adventurer as he—the last frontier.

Yes. Like my father before me and before him back to the Greeks, I—God help me—had also become both actor and audience, spectator and chronicler who, by the simple act of noting a fact, alters it forever.

It is unreasonable to expect those unique qualities that make an actor great on stage to vanish when the theater is dark. It would be like asking caviar to lose its salt when not being eaten.

The actor's habit of exaggerating his emotions, better to reflect the human predicament, may thrill us and illuminate our own experience, but offstage much of this degenerates into narcissism, extravagance of gesture, and simple bad manners. But with the professional dissipation of his enormous energy and accommodation of his passions —with a showcase for his attitudes—what is then extravagant once more can become ennobling and gorgeous on stage. An actor's life never ends but, like everyone else of flesh and blood, the actor himself eventually tires, so that a full day of paid employment can somewhat relieve his intimates of the burden of his gifts.

Madame Godowsky, my first lady, had been a silent-movie actress and unfortunately hadn't worked for over thirty years when I entered her life and recorded it. She was

19

that most dangerous of creations—a star without a vehicle.

I, in turn, was still a shy and unassertive ghost with that first book, *First Person Plural*. The Godowsky wanted sole credit and I needed a job badly. It was ghastly, but I agreed to it, and I was to receive fifty per cent of all earthly rewards. I called the extremely plump Madame and myself "body and soul." In reality we looked like the nineteenth-century illustration of the portly capitalist and skinny mendicant, which bore the legend: "I sold for cash; I sold for credit." And I wasn't even getting any.

I wasn't happy hiding my light under this bushel, but I was resigned to the devil's own bargain and couldn't have been more delighted when the reviews were kind and the lady's surprising literary style was noted. I was secretly pleased that all of Madame's lofty friends were convinced that she had written the book. It was the cream of the jest. Evidently, I had so caught her personality that, as the saying so rudely goes, I had hoist myself by my own petard.

That was the game I was playing, and I had to play by the rules. Subsequently I wearied of it. With publication, the goal reached, the road forgotten, and the bridge burned behind the subject, the peripatetic ghost is now a mere skeleton in the closet. As a lesson in abject humility, this work beats the order of St. Francis. I've done with it.

The series of autobiographies started with Dagmar Godowsky and I not only wrote that book but I had to read it to her, every word—on her insistence—lingering lovingly over passages I knew would please her and choking over those self-deprecating observations I felt necessary in order to make her, if possible, rounder.

Admit I must, that my subject predicated changes. Her wonderful, almond eyes, always seeking out a nugget of gossip or a crumb of food, would squintingly search the air in momentary thought. "No! No!" she would yell. "I loathe that. You must change that sentence. It has no

grace. I am free and that is corseted. Terrible, terrible!"
And change it I would—and for the better as well. Dagmar
had an ear as well as that mouth. And her style was her
own.

Now what was that style and who was Dagmar Godowsky? It was both her curse and blessing that she was
the daughter of the once-famous pianist-composer, Leopold
Godowsky. A beautiful child entering the glittering,
chandeliered, waltz-and-pastry-ridden Vienna of Franz
Josef, she was adored, pampered, and filled with false
notions and real whipped cream.

Life was ever to be a charlotte russe to Dagmar. Coming to America where, incidentally, she had been, to her
eventual irritation, Chicago-born, she was nonetheless truly
Vienna-bred, and grew into a raving beauty and an early
film player, reaching her flood tide as Valentino's leading
lady and her ebb as lady friend to the musical greats of her
and other generations.

Though her need for her father's love predilected her
to composers and musicians, she by no means restricted
herself and was often engaged *a capella*.

When I met her, she had already become a grande
dame who looked for all the world like an Aubrey Beards-
ley sultan. Like exiled nobility, she dined out on her past
triumphs since, as an intimate of the haut monde, she was
an often discreet confidante, and as a raconteuse, she was
unequaled. Highly comic, always outrageous, with the
attention span of a French poodle, she soon convinced me,
amidst my laughter, that the fragmented material torn
from her past would allow me to create nothing more than
a swatch book. I sat at my typewriter with the absurdly
few notes I had gleaned, wondering how I was going to
start the book. How was I going to submerge myself in
another human being? How could I write a first-person
book? How could one person possibly convince a third

21

that a second person has been speaking? And then it came to me. It was so simple.

Wasn't I a playwright? What was I so damned worried about? I would simply write a three-hundred-page speech—the longest soliloquy in theatrical history. Hamlet's role would be dwarfed by this multi-milli-sided part. Of course. I made believe I was starting a play.

> ACT I
>> The curtain rises. The scene is a penthouse on Park Avenue. The apartment is in disarray. The French doors to the terrace are open. Several phones ring in different keys, creating a studied dissonance.
>>
>> The barking of a dog is heard offstage. Added to the visual and audible confusion we now hear a woman's voice. The accent is European, perhaps Transylvanian.
>>
>> *OFFSTAGE VOICE:*
>> Toy-toy-toy. It's the telephone. They haven't stopped all day. No! Don't stop, Charlie darling. It's bad for the bladder to change horses in midstream—and you can't answer them anyway. Zut! People have no sense of timing. My God, it must be the Countess Tolstoi.
>>
>> We hear a crash on the terrace followed by a squeal.
>> *ENTER DAGMAR GODOWSKY*

Dagmar
Godowsky

"Hello. Pronto! *Un moment. Ach,* these phones—will they
never stop? Who is it, darling? . . . Who? Sandya Dodya?
Should I know you, my dear? . . . The night of the
audition—the musical [*Excitedly.*] But, of course. I was
so amusing that night *I* should have been produced. You
and the other young man couldn't stop the laughter.
[*Philosophically.*] But it is always like that. Yes, my dear.
[*A pause.*] Darling, just a moment—I cannot reach my
chocolates and I need energy today: Harry Richman ate
them on that nonstop flight to Europe. Who would think
that chocolate could be so good for you. [*Dreamily.*] You
have a very soothing voice, darling, and I wish I were
wretched so that you could soothe me. Well, I will be
again, God knows, and then we shall see. But today I am
happy—happy to hear from you, happy even to be able to
be wretched. . . . *Ach.* Of course I remember. My
memory is a *scandale* but I always remember being adored.

You and your friend did adore me. Is the truth? No? [*In mock anger.*] Charlie! Stop being so jealous. It is only an admirer. *You* are my life. Go. There are some sautéed chicken livers in your bowl with the rest of the *pfundkuchen*. [*With a great sigh.*] So, Sandya Dodya, you are calling to invite me to dinner. . . . No? You are not? What? . . . A book? *My* book? My *memoirs? Random House?* But, of course, I am interested. I shall be sued by the entire *Almanach de Gotha* and what's *left* of the *Social Register.* Our world is crumbling, my dear. [*Sharply.*] Are you attractive, darling? Are you the handsome one with the green eyes and the hussar's mustache or the other one? [*Resigned.*] Ah! The other one. Well, you were slim, and that is a virtue that has eluded me, and you have humor, a vice which has not. When can you come to see me? . . . But why tomorrow? Why not now? Seize the day! I could die of overeating at any time. [*Businesslike.*] At three o'clock *sur le point.* I am looking forward and then we shall look backward together on my life. You won't *believe* it but is true—*all* of it. I am thrilled. [*A telephone rings.*] Hello-hello-excuse me, *liebchen.* It is business. At three o'clock, Sandya. You call me Dag*mar.* I cannot wait, but must. [*Another bell is heard.*] Zut! Imagine if I were *thin,* I should be *trampled.* Au revoir—[*exuberantly*] Darling. One moment, the phones haven't stopped."

Dagmar could be foolish, but she was never a fool. Her exposure to the greats of the world had doubtless not only revealed in her youth her best qualities and immunized her to the common cold, it had also refined her tastes. To my knowledge, she was never vulgar. Dagmar might not have been the most distillate of brandies in a Baccarat cordial glass but she was certainly an overflowing baronial goblet staining the linen, reddening one's hands and altogether conveying an unmistakable opulence.

Dagmar Godowsky was more than physically larger

than life. All of her foibles were oversized. I wouldn't say (although she would) that she was too much of a good thing, but I would admit that like the rest of the stars she should have been viewed from a considerable distance, where that squint of hers became a twinkle.

Her appetites and satisfactions were all excessive. Quick to tears and slow to feeling, Dagmar had, I was to observe, great heat and little warmth. Her passions were surface—today's arch-enemy possibly becoming tomorrow's most diverting escort. The Sicilian vendetta takes on the profundity of a sacred covenant compared to such conviction. Dagmar could not even—after my fury at her infamy and several classic battles—sustain her hatred and fear of me. I amused her too much and loved her not enough. This was a thorn in her side.

After some absurd injustice she had perpetrated, she would outrageously ask me if I loved her. I would quite reasonably answer no, which drove her mad. Like the small child who must prove her lovability and test it endlessly through punishable naughtiness, Dagmar Godowsky would find it unthinkable that—despite an endless list of misdemeanors—she could be, at any juncture, resistible. Since she had been, since Franz Josef's lapdays, adorable, how could I *not* adore her? "You lie," she would then accuse me. "How mean you are! You know you love me. *I* love *you!*" she would add shrewdly—knowing that most people do not easily reject such a declaration and are wont to pay it back in kind—and then, as the final fillip, the quintessential Godowskian touch: "Liar! Your taste is too highly developed *not* to love me."

And then I would have to laugh and she would too. She would rock with mirth. "I knew it—you do love me and why not?" To find Dagmar amusing, which was easy, was—in her eyes—almost as desirable as to love her, which was difficult. When one is unique, there is no yardstick, no general rule that is applicable. Despite all reason and without one, I had affection for her.

Dagmar was unique—I'll give her that—and with a sense of the ridiculous that bordered on madness. Behind her foolishness lurked cunning, but she was too poorly organized to use it. Caught in the act, her eyes would narrow merrily, her shoulders would shrug helplessly in a gesture that asked, "But who in nature, darrling, would not filch the sweetmeat, the last morsel, the mate one wants? It is only nahturelle." Not who indeed, but *what* indeed, and that is the categorical subtlety that escaped Madame. She was a jungle thing who could not endure without an income. Like a pretty whining cub, she might momentarily get her own way, but charm is not enough in the jungle. She wouldn't have lasted more than a few days, her interest even in her own survival being too fleeting. With no attention span, one cannot be cunning with any appreciable result.

And so, beneath the guile was finally an ingenuousness that prompted her, in inevitable defeat, to throw herself upon the mercy of the victor—her very surrender by its nature bringing her excitement and a genuine curiosity as to the final outcome. Dagmar was curious about everything, including defeat, her appetite so ravenous and eclectic it included humble pie. A little drama is diverting, and if one is starring in it, so much the better.

Dagmar Godowsky was always a spectator at her own life, watching it from a box seat that commanded, by design, a far better view of the theater than the stage. Munching *marrons glaces,* waving and gossiping about the rest of the audience behind her fan, mopping her upper lip and base of her throat with a kerchief which she would impishly drop on some bald head below to attract attention to herself, she added another scene, creating a distraction from her own drama. She recklessly, noisily interrupted her own life with nonsense. Barely following the play, she missed most of the plot and the entire theme. Glancing briefly at the sets and costumes, she retained a few quotable lines and then went on to the important business—to join in the laughter and posturing between the acts. Dagmar Godowsky—an original.

Knowing all of this, I now had the job of ghosting the life of a woman who hadn't lived it, who had been given a bowl of cherries at birth and had threw them all at passersby. I had to get my material from my subject, get the material for a book from a woman who only traded in gossamer and could barely sustain her interest even while yelling fire!

To write about such a woman was a challenge; to write her book in first person seemed an impossibility. Her eagerness to do the book degenerated quickly, becoming (or always having been in reality) a desire simply to fill her datebook. Her empty days would now be filled, and how better filled than with the custard of her endless self-advertisement? What bliss—to sit, not too far from the stuffed refrigerator, her dog on her lap, her thrice-told tales now being recorded by an official scribe who, after doing his job like a good little genie, would vanish into thin air, but who for the present was presentable enough to be an escort if it were necessary, who would never become bored with her life, his survival depending on it, and who would always sweep the terrace and water the plants.

I wonder what his family's like. What bliss, to smoke and fume and spark endlessly and have it all eventually take shape and put between covers, proof positive that she may have really existed. And if the book never came to pass, the afternoons would fly with all that laughter—*he's so amusing*—and good talk and *such* good listening on *his* part and there needn't be any guilt about overeating because *he* can almost eat her under the table.

*How in God's name does he stay so slim?—and he
does know good cuisine and appreciates my sense of humor
and damn it, he looks like Igor did back in the Paris days
and even more important, those eyes see everything and
he still loves me I can tell—despite everything he's heard,
I've told him, or worse that he intuits—and he'll walk
Charlie and anyway he is so amusing!*

I can hear myself now, begging Dagmar to stop fluttering about, to stick to the story she was telling me about
Stravinsky or Lin Yutang or Rudolph Valentino. She did
get about. I begged her to stay put or I'd pin her to some
mauve velvet like the butterfly she was. I would practically
run around her penthouse apartment with a net. When
she wasn't floating off somewhere she was cooking something delicious for us. I wondered if I'd been wise to get
involved with her at all.

We had met at that audition of some long-forgotten
musical play, and, thrown together as we were, an im-
movable object and irresistible force, something had to
give—and Dagmar was a taker. Along with a friend,
Stanley MacDonald, I convoyed her up Park Avenue to
her home. This destroyer in mink never stopped talking
and was never, for a moment, less than amusing.

Dagmar had once been a great beauty, but now was
shipwrecked and lost in a sea of fat, only an occasional
remnant of the trim craft miraculously afloat. The finely
bred nose and brow, the delicate ankle, were evidence of
the past. One felt that at any moment this flotsam of the
S.S. *Godowsky* might drift off and sink forever, leaving
only the bubble of her laughter.

The lady's weight was remarkable for her less than
medium height. It was a source of wonder that her tiny
feet could carry the burden of her. Any thought of path-
ology was fleeting. One only had to note the hungry eyes
and ardent mouth to understand. Dagmar loved to eat.

Without humor and wit, both of which she also possessed in abundance, she would have been grotesque. But Dagmar could laugh at herself.

There was no denying her enthusiasm for life, her happy acceptance of her now-unphotographable image, and her gifts as a raconteuse. For sheer name-dropping, Dagmar Godwosky was second to none. From the crown prince of Germany and England's Prince of Wales she moved up or down to Franz Josef or Adolf Hitler, whom she suspected was once the family chauffeur. Her range was unequaled. She knew everybody worth knowing and avoiding. With her gimlet eyes, she sought out the singular quality in everyone and made it work, incorporating it as she did into her endless routine. She was the sit-down, lie-down comedienne of all time and, even when walking with her on that first meeting, Stanley and I were convulsed with her tales.

Somewhere amidst her monologue she extracted from me that I was a writer and confided in hushed tones that she was working on her autobiography and had been for a long while. I wished her luck, accepted a nightcap, and we were off.

Not too long later, Belle Becker, the then chief editor at Random House and assistant to Bennett Cerf, happened to be at a dinner to which I had also been invited. A warm and interested woman, she asked what I was up to. She had known me for years, but only as a playwright struggling in the theater. I told her briefly of a play I was working on and quickly changed the subject, since we were at table and I wished to speak less personally. I recalled meeting Dagmar at that audition and related some entertaining impressions of the Godowsky.

"Dagmar!" Belle marveled. "What an incredible character. Do you know, Sandy, if you would ever get her to write those memoirs she *claims* to be doing—if you would write them for her, I'm sure I could get Bennett to publish them." And that's how it all began. The road to purgatory is paved et cetera et cetera!

I called Dagmar and suggested that we work together, insisting that if we could hand in a sample chapter and a synopsis, we could become household words. I later arrived at her invitation with the one perfect rose that gentlemen on their uppers always bring ladies of quality.

We kicked the idea around a little bit and Dagmar couldn't have been more pleased. When her dusty dog, Charlie, an old and lovable cocker, found me physically exciting, the deal was clinched. I decided to gamble a month or so of my time to gather material and hand Random House a presentation. This was the spring of 1955, and I still had months to throw around.

Her charming flat was as disorderly as her mind, and a couple of weeks passed seemingly to no avail. Dagmar Godowsky fluttered from one deathless bon mot to another. She lived her entire life in italics. I have never known anyone so self-centered. Her conceit was of such proportion that I never heard her say that she ever met anyone. Everyone greeted *her*. She was always the object of every compliment, the subject of every sentence.

"Guess who rushed over to me on Fifth Avenue!" Déclassé streets and avenues suffered the same fate as their denizens. Dagmar lived out her life in the very best neighborhoods.

"Lloyd George caught sight of me. Jesus, with the finest view in all Calvary, called, 'Dagmar! darling!' The Prophet Isaiah, strolling with Mrs. Stuyvesant Fish, was delighted to see me back in town. While blessing the dear masses, the Pope stopped everything when he spied me in my red Chanel crossing the piazza. 'Ave, Dagmar.'"

Where she was was dead center of the universe. Where she was not was not worth a cartographer's tumble. She wanted this book, it was true, and being between covers took on new meaning for her, so she let out all stops. In those two weeks I heard her entire routine, the act that made her a coveted guest in one half the world's shooting boxes and persona non grata in the other. It wasn't a life but a toastmaster's speech, lovingly delivered at her own testimonial dinner. There was no material, only sequins; no cake, only icing. Utterly unrelated epigrams, petty triumphs and menus filled the room like colored balloons, floating out the window and leaving not a trace of their former presence. As for chronology, sequence, or order, these were as unheard of to Dagmar as cause and effect.

I discovered to my horror that the events of her life had no pattern for her. Each development in her life was a fresh surprise. Eating an entire two-pound box of chocolates had absolutely no relation to the stomachache that followed. Like the primitive tribe that has yet to associate the act of sex with the epilogue of childbirth, Dagmar sowed the seeds of her own destruction directly at her feet and then lashed out at the fates when she found the undergrowth an obstacle in her path. She intrigued, but never planned. After all, to plan is to choose a goal, establish one's direction, and then proceed step by step until one reaches it. The placement of a fork into a dish of food and its eventual voyage to the mouth, its cargo intact, was achievable by Dagmar only through instinct. It was an atavism, not a learned procedure. Dagmar remembered nothing. She admitted to having no memory at all.

One of Dagmar Godowsky's greatest charms was her enthusiasm for life. It was genuine and completely understandable. She never had the remotest idea what was going to happen five minutes hence. I am certain that had she, in a fret, flung herself from the tower of Neuschwannstein, while on the way down, tumbling in space, she would have toyed with the idea of making a luncheon appointment at Sacher's the following afternoon—her current fancy for a

31

torte mit schlag demanding satisfaction. It would never for an instant have occurred to her that she might even have been late, no less beyond such earthly appetite.

"Was it Ernest Boyd who used to say 'Dagmar is my dogma'?"

It was just this kind of remembered encomium that filled her head, displacing sequential facts that might help me build a life story. Uncharacteristically, she wasn't organized enough to have kept a scrapbook. Even her vanity was unframed.

"Letters! Pictures! They are all lost, darling. I have lived in the eye of a cyclone, and you expect me to have a neat little parcel with everything in place. Please! Even Helen cannot find anything and she knows my life better than I do—*I* have only *lived* it!"

Helen was an old friend who lived nearby. She was gay and pleasant and devoted to Dagmar—omnipresent—doing her errands, arranging her appointments, walking her dog, and refreshing her memory. The reward for her devotion seemed to be simply one more job to do. She was a tiny, slender thing and my sympathy was doubtless unfounded, since all these relationships are two-way, satisfying needs at both poles.

At about ten in the morning I would arrive at her house—usually fortified, by a bakery right near my house, with some "marvelous" coffee cake she'd heard about, and my empty notebook; and we would fritter away the day. First there was the extended ritual of the streusel cake and then some of her own ("So we can compare, darling, for the next time. A good bakery is like a good gynecologist, except not so fresh.") and then I would thumb through magazines while she kept promising that we would "work, work, work!" while instead she kept making or answering phone calls. She had three phones and was never happier than when juggling all three simultaneously, proving that she was loved and wanted and also not responsible for the disgraceful delay in our project. Each telephone call, she swore with eyes to heaven, was the last she would accept. But she really could not stop. Each time the bell tolled she was sure that it would herald a magical change in her life —an invitation to the White House, the winning of the Sweepstakes, or as the sum total of all her cardinal sins, her election as pope.

The fact that the rings were never of gold or even of smoke escaping from the Vatican chimney, that these phone calls brought nothing but dinner dates and not mystic appointments, never discouraged her from tripping over all the wires as well as Charlie to get to their source. To be alone was death, unless on rare occasion she was forced to be, in which case it became the pleasantest of experiences and, anyone else that night who was shallow enough to have gone out missed the delight of "reading and reflecting and recharging one's batteries, darling." Anyone who was out when she was *in* was a boor. Her every caprice was interpreted as a call, her every prejudice a universal truth to be shared by the world.

Dagmar lived in a perpetual state of self-adoration and would accept nothing less from others. Her need for constant proof of this adoration kept her on a merry-go-round, whirling to the screeching calliope. If one keeps going round faster and faster, one doesn't see the poles that impale the ridden and driven. One may even forget that one isn't going anyplace at all. "The phones didn't stop ringing all day!"

"Darling!" she would scream excitedly to someone to whom she hadn't spoken in twenty minutes. "How divine of you to call though I'm working and shouldn't be talking. . . . On what? My *book!* Darling. My *book!* . . . Thank you, *liebchen*, I *was* in great form last night. It was the full moon and I am at my most lunatic. Igor used to howl

at dusk every day. When you're *sensitive,* my darling—
wait a second, the phones don't stop ringing. Hell!
Mischa, yes. You caught me working, *working.* I'm *exhausted*—the *book!* . . . What? One moment, Lisa . . .
Yes, Mischa, the Colony."

Her eyes would now dart to me—to observe my annoyance and/or my envy.

"The Colony? *Zut, alors.* Can we make it dinner at
Twenty-One instead? I can eat more at night . . . Divine!
There goes the doorbell. The bells haven't stopped all day
. . . roses from an unnamed admirer . . . what taste he
has! . . . a small box from Monsieur Cartier and my
darling, the A and P is at the door, not that I *ever* dine
at home unless I'm entertaining . . . it's all cleaning things
. . . ugh. Toy-toy . . . there goes the other bell. It is a
madness—Hello . . . Poopsie! . . . No. I'm lunching with
the Princess Flavia who insists that I come up for air.
She's from *such* a nice family . . . I've been working,
working, working . . . What have I been up to, darling? I
just told you—work, work, work! But I *love* it. Strange?
No. I am talking about myself. How can one tire of that?"

In desperation, hoping the quick movement would
break the lyric flow of drivel, I would jump up from my
seat, point my chin toward the French doors with terribly
contained and lip-chewing fury and march myself out onto
the filthy terrace, where dear Charlie, not any better
organized than his mistress, also made me hop.

"Toy-toy-toy!" she would mutter. "Darling! I'll be
right there, Sandy. *Auf wiedersehn, au revoir, chérie.
Liebchen,* I must work. How did Thomas Mann and Count
Leo ever do it?"

And then she would waddle out, the sun creating
maroon highlights in her soot-black hair and so harshly
penetrating her makeup that her face became a demented

drawing of the moon in a George Melies film—grinning and welcoming nineteenth-century space travelers.

"I swear, darling—on Charlie's life—that we will work as we have never worked. I swear it. I should never enjoy another meal—but first for strength I'll fix us a little lunch—fuel! Fuel for energy. What oxes artists have to be. Igor was a tubercular. He worked in a fever always —the energy, the *energy,* and you know in sanitariums, doctors will tell you, the *libido* in those consumptives! Zut! 'Find me a consumptive,' I used to beg in the old days. Darling, the blender has been fixed. Do you feel like potato pancakes? I have sour cream and some caviar left over from the party. Toy-toy. How I used to swim in great, big, battleship-gray caviar. What they pass off as caviar now. That color! One can dye one's hair with it."

"One has, my dear," I observed.

"You are angry with me—and *mean!*"

"Now, Dagmar, we have just so long to make our presentation. We have *got* to work and we haven't done a damned thing. If you'd like to forget it."

"*Forget* it? Daaaaarling! It is my *life.* On Mutzie's grave and Poppa's. But it is painful to remember and I must fortify myself first—and then I will spill *everything* and you will be *shocked . . . .*"

And then she would make the potato pancakes, which were the best I ever tasted, and while we gorged ourselves and Dagmar blew up like a balloon, I would try to ballast her. But it was impossible to bring her down to earth. Answers to my questions were answered with a roll of the eyes and a licking of chops, though some information willy-nilly would dribble through the smacking of lips. The staggering revelations!

"Caruso was a marrrrrrvelous cook. What spaghetti he made, and that sauce of his mother's. Ah! Those Italians.

Rudy Valentino, too. He loved to cook for me when I worked in pictures with him. He bobbed my hair, you know. Such a sweet boy. I never understood the brouhaha in the whole country, my dear, *zut,* the whole world. He was just my dear friend Rudy."

All I seemed to have in my notebook after so many days were foodstains and compliments paid to Dagmar by famous people and capitals.

"Prokofiev dedicated his *Dance of the Witches* to me . . . Caruso found a hairpin of mine and saved it in a little envelope . . . all New York was at my feet . . . James Huneker called me the girl with the Iberian eyes . . . Paris was made for me . . . Papa called me his Poppy . . . Jimmy Walker always sang 'Will You Love Me in December' to me . . . and DeMille begged to meet me . . . Charlie Chaplin loved me, not the girl he married . . . Dagmar is my dogma . . . Leopold Seyffert did twenty-one oils of me that summer . . . Noel Coward was so delighted to see me he picked me up . . . Lon Chaney said I was a real trouper . . . Artur Rubinstein would have rather lost an arm than my friendship . . . All Vienna smiled when I was seen leaving Demel's with a sweet . . . and, I swear it, Helen Keller felt my face and then said, 'How lovely you are, my dear.' . . ."

At this rate, it was clear that I was not going to be able to write a synopsis, much less a sample chapter, with this flibbertigibbet, who was now having a seamstress come in to construct tents for her. I was being presented with a continuous pageant of grunts and cackles and postures, curtain lines punctuating no acts whatsoever. Her days were filled with aimless movement, involuntary motion as in shuddering and shivering. *My God!* I recalled *even the dead move* in rigor mortis.

Daily I watched this delirium and I thought, *this is like palsy. Animation without purpose is palsy, which is simply shimmering paralysis. I will go mad.* But I was fascinated by the variation on the themelessness and evidently could not resist the challenge. I had promised Belle that I would make a presentation, and the cuisine was first rate. And of course I had my own problems, or I wouldn't have been there in the first place.

The telephones kept ringing and Dagmar kept answering—her datebook being the one piece of literature in which she could presently be engrossed. I was her only bridge to the Vulgus—who introduced her to the West Side and Ritz Crackers. She was incorrigible and the situation hopeless. This combination of facts has not always stopped me from continuing a relationship, and I was still there a couple of days later reliving the same nightmare. No matter what path I chose, in what direction I led her, all roads led to the kitchen.

She now wiped her mouth, threw the napkin across the little table and sighed deeply.

"Dagmar! I have had it—you cannot except me to waste my time—"

"Toy-toy-toy! I am miserable," she moaned. "The unhappiest of moments is when I cannot eat anymore—not because I am full, darling. I am never full. How can I be full? I am simply not hungry any longer. I'll bet you can eat more? No? *Please!* I am wretched. To lose one's appetite is terrible. Perhaps a little ginger ale. Thank God, there is always the thirst when the hunger is sated. Do you like Canada Dry? It is my favorite—the best there is. No? Don't you agree? Listen, Sandya. I have been invited to a wonderful dinner tomorrow and you must escort me. Terribly chic, and we need the change. All this work is too much for us. It is not good for you—you look too thin. We will go, you and I, and look like a circus act. And I swear! We will work in the taxi. Please, Sandya!"

Obviously she needed an escort. That was clear. The

Count of Monte Cristo or the Archduke Rudolf or Ivan the Terrible was busy and couldn't make it, hence this invitation. Sometimes when she telephoned the voice dropped lower and she would imply that it was a life-and-death communiqué while she, in actuality, would pursue her dance of the mayflies. It was now my time to sigh deeply.

"Dagmar. I am here to glean enough facts . . ."

"Darling! You have to eat somewhere? No? Why not deevine food and you can meet important people. I want to expose you to the best . . . ."

It occurred to me that there are times when one doesn't fight the inevitable—as with the bending bamboo in a raging storm. Of course. How stupid I was. If you can't lick 'em, bite 'em!

I went to the party and the next morning I pleaded a hangover, which I thought she might find a stylish excuse. "But what of our work?" she dared ask. It was the first day I had missed.

"I'll be at your house at ten sharp tomorrow morning."

She then insisted that the Count and Countess Dracula had asked her to lunch at the Colony and she'd refused because of me. She was bitter, her datebook having been stabbed in the heart.

"You'll do something fascinating, Dagmar, and you'll tell me about it tomorrow."

"You are cruel and selfish. Under that big, toothy smile and clever words, you have revealed yourself."

"That's more than you've done, milady. I'll see you at ten."

And I sat down on my little terrace and simply described Dagmar, a day in her life, ending it with the party we had just attended. Of course, I described it from Dagmar's vantage point, starting with her line: "It is my tragedy that the years have deprived me of my bad reputation."

I then went on. I was no longer decrying her lack of order, but luxuriating in her chaos, reveling in it. No longer fighting but yielding to Dagmar's stream of unconsciousness—picking up her tricks of speech, her use of the definite article rather than the possessive and the like. Her interspersal of "Please" or her questioning "No? You don't agree." Her exasperated and mysterious "Toy-toy-toy!" and by sundown I had my first chapter complete.

It was simply a current day in Dagmar's life, ostensibly related by her and certainly peppered with typical lines from her routine and augmented by my own. Obviously the way to write the book was to become her as completely as possible.

Names and places and half-remembered facts were served up as a mad hors d'oeuvre, a *vorspeise,* an appetizer, and promise of things to come. Would she ever give me any more? I threw names and adjectives around, establishing myself (Dagmar) as a colorful, literate, scatterbrained, snobbish, conceited, warm, witty, urbane, obese woman who was resigned to her latter-day sainthood, being both lovable and insightful. Only the last of these descriptions can I reserve completely as my own contribution. But it made all the others work in first person. She could only be seen clearly through the writer's perspective—not her own.

It occurs to me that it is very much like portrait painting. The picture of her was so accurate that everyone believed she painted it herself, but if she had it would not have looked like her. Any portraitist knows the blindness of the sitter who thinks he knows his features and from the first view of the painting, starts to make suggestions that are ignored by the real artist but have driven lesser ones to destructive flattery or surrogate careers. No less an artist than John Singer Sargent knowledgeably described a portrait as a painting in which there is always something wrong with the mouth!

The morning I arrived at Dagmar's with that first chapter in my hands, I wished I'd been fortified with a pint of Scotch instead of orange juice. I knew that if the book were to work at all—not only for me to sell to Random House but to make it a work from which I could derive satisfaction if not credit—Dagmar Godowsky was going to have to present herself as she was: an overweight, over-indulged, overbearing, overcivilized woman whose sense of humor and honest self-appraisal allowed her to reveal the tragic flaw I had yet to discover, A few minutes of her supreme vanity were diverting at a cocktail party, but in an entire book, or even a chapter, it would be insupportable. Conversely, to diminish the self-love would be fraudulent, rather like a portrait with a nose job or a face-lift.

But I felt, one could be honest and complimentary, showing one to better advantage. Two unretouched photographs of the same person can be utterly unalike though taken at the same sitting. One simply threw another light on the matter. If I were to be—as Dagmar again—even vainer (if possible) and thereby, through hyperbole, make the reader smile corroboratively, if I were to be outrageous but aware, if I were to be in a sense mute witness to my own folly, helpless to stop it but willing to share my astonishment with the reader, mightn't I have something?

This all demanded, of course, that Madame Godowsky go along with the brutal self-appraisal of this first chapter, which I knew could sell our book. I had to convince her that it was the only way to write a *chef-d'oeuvre* and not a self-serving goulash. I had little interest in writing anything other than a special book, since I was to receive neither fame nor fortune from it. It was an act of renaissance and a labor of love. Above all, it had to be honest and now that I was better acquainted with this jumbo lepidopteran I wanted to capture her in black and white and nail her to a page.

Madame Godowsky was as nervous as I that morning and had a pot of steaming coffee ready. She knew something was up. Certainly she was trying to please. It was a glorious morning and the terrace was bathed in sunlight. I noticed that the little glass-and-wrought-iron table was set for *petit déjeuner*. Her apartment was always stuffy, and knowing how I loved air and sunlight, she was evidently making a sacrifice this morning.

"Well. How have you been, darling?" she asked accusingly, the implication being that I had been neglecting her for months.

"Exactly as I was two days ago when last you saw me, Dagmar—except that I have a surprise."

"A surprise? I *adore* surprises. Is it a gift? Sandya! You shouldn't have!"

"I didn't."

"Ah," she parried nervously, looking at my manila envelope. "The world has changed—or I have. Breakfasts were different in the old days. Men used to hide diamonds in my grapefruit—under the maraschino cherry. Now the cherry has arsenic in it—not from the men, darling, but the manufacturers, and there is nothing—not even calories. It *isn't* a gift?"

"In a manner of speaking it *is*. I have our sample chapter."

She was visibly shaken and I saw the chill race through her. It started in the instantly congealed eye and departed through her cold feet. She was far more frightened than I, and I was petrified. This was the moment of truth, a commodity for which there was little or no demand at this door. I could lose the chance to do the book—and I needed money desperately—if I earned her disapproval. And so I was deeply concerned. But to Dagmar, this reading of chapter and verse was traumatic. For the first time in her life she was going to see herself reflected not in her own mirror, but through the detached eye of someone who was neither lover nor petitioner, and with luck was going to commit his findings to print and posterity.

"I thought I'd make us chocolate today instead of coffee—a *desayuno,* but you—"

"Dagmar. Coffee is fine and I want to talk to you."

I then nervously explained that I had written these pages with a humorous and self-damning honesty that I thought would help her.

"Remember, darling, if *I* were to call you a fat woman, that might be considered unkind, if accurate. But *remember.* This is *first person* and *you* are calling *yourself* fat, and therefore the reader will adore you if you admit to being generously endowed in every department."

Dagmar wasn't buying a word of it. Her eyes narrowed further, doubtless in an attempt to blind herself to any truth. She looked like a samurai in fancy dress. She wasn't buying anything but a mother's or Vonnegut's "uncritical love." And she even wanted that for nothing. I am reminded of a close friend who forewarned me with a sweet smile as we became closer that she could not tolerate criticism of any kind, to which I replied that under those conditions we would never have a problem since I expected from her absolute perfection. Dagmar Godowsky obviously wanted a premature eulogy from me, and she was shrewd enough to know she wasn't going to get one. The coffee was served and the cake was forgotten. She was about to lose so much, she lost her appetite as well.

I handed her the neat pages that had taken hours for me to type and retype—I'm so bad at it—and she refused them.

"Read to me!" she commanded. "My eyes, this morning, they are not verrry good. It is the glare from the klieg lights in Hollywood so long ago."

And so she refused to look at what I had done. I had to face her and read aloud the shocking portrait that I had written. It was a terrible time and my heart broke for the two of us. I poured us some coffee and we got as comfortable as possible as we lay on long terrace chairs, a table between us. Dagmar covered her eyes with her left hand, the gesture of someone in pain. If she could have covered both ears with the right hand I believe she would have. I took a swig of coffee and a deep breath. This was it. I read with the vaguest accent, simulating her voice.

"It is my tragedy that the years have deprived me of my bad reputation. At one time my notoriety assured me of a marvelous evening. Now, Euclid would be fascinated to know, my circle has been squared . . . I love life anyway. . . the phones don't stop ringing all day. Even as I write, I see me glancing obliquely at myself like a self-portrait of the Dutch school. I am my favorite creature and what I see is a joyous Buddha with a Fu dog named Charlie on its august lap, a bowl of rice within easy reach. Quite marvelous really. The next best thing is to awe them, darling. I have become venerable . . . I didn't know then that tragedy wasn't always Grecian, poetic and applauded by a fashionable audience . . . that tragedy was a lonely, wretched red-eyed thing—a horror . . . I was draped in yards of material I brought home from India, looking like the Taj Mahal camouflaged for an air raid . . . the mistakes I made, the mistakes! . . . Lisa and I had a bite and I'm afraid so did Charlie. The handyman is livid . . . The phones never stop ringing! . . . I lifted my chins and sailed into the room like the *Queen Elizabeth* being tugged by the hostess . . . 'I need a very dependable chair, darling. Once I sit down it will take twelve flunkies to get me up!' . . . 'Of course I met you with the de Lesseps . . . delightful people though their father was a ditch-digger.' . . . There were great skillets—four feet round filled with breasts of hen floating in wine and capers. The eggplant was a symphony . . . Then came my most unhappy moment. I couldn't eat anymore . . . May I have some waxed paper? . . . But it's for my dog . . . they handed me to my doorman like a precious gift . . . the sculptor's voice echoes in my ear . . . you should have seen her years ago. She was incredibly beautiful. It was impossible not to fall in love with her!"

The beginning and the end, with a few moments that may give the feeling of the chapter. Dagmar's hand had not once left her eyes. There had not been any reaction at all, no laughter, no screaming, no coconut oil. I put the pages down and picked up my now-cold coffee. I waited and there wasn't the slightest movement. It must have been dreadful for her. She obviously felt that by not opening her eyes and thereby confirming my presence, I might not be there—it might all not have happened— making the entire experience simply a nightmare from which she had awakened, shaken but regenerate, depressed but soon buoyed up by heaping plates of blintzes with sour cream and apricot jam. I waited. I was still smoking in those days and must have resembled, on that rooftop, one more chimney. At last I could not wait any longer.

"Are you dead, Dagmar?"

Madame Godowsky never missed a cue in her life. The tableau came to life.

"God knows you have tried. I *detest* it. It is terribly written. It is not *me*. It is ugly. You cannot *write*. I have lived amongst and read the greatest writers. I read *everything,* as you know, and this is *terrible. Terrible.*"

"I know how shocked you must be, Dagmar, but—"

"I am never shocked. I cannot be shocked except by

myself, and if I am shocked it is because for the first time I have misjudged someone. You! You are *awful!*"

I allowed her to explode. I realized that she could not conceivably compain that she was furious that she hadn't emerged as a combination of Garbo and Madame de Staël—that there in black and white was her admission that it was over—the free ride. She had to attack me and the gods, so I sat strapped to my chair like the second half of a vaudeville act, my cigarettes being lit and extinguished by the lashes of this amazon's whip. It was not a pleasant morning for either of us, but it was, of course, the most important one. The ice was broken, we both got our feet wet, and Dagmar slowly got used to this truer reflection of herself after she sensibly accepted my motives. It is fact that not one word of that first chapter was ever changed and was so printed when eventually we sold the book. But it wasn't that simple.

Miss Becker at Random House had asked for a sample chapter and a synopsis, and the latter seemed impossible altogether since Dagmar had never known, nor could she now remember, not only where she was going but also where she had been. It had worked once, and I believed it could again. In a telegraphic style with plenty of ellipses between them, I rattled on, dropping names and places with absolutely no shame, but with a chronology and crescendoing desperation that might lead the reader to believe that I knew where the book was heading.

"*Alt Wien und* Franz Josef and Lehar . . . New York with Rachmaninoff and Caruso . . . Paris *avec* Maurice Ravel et Stravinsky . . . Hollywood with Chaplin and Valentino . . . Berlin *mit* Goering . . . London with the Prince of Wales . . . the gaming tables of Monte Carlo . . . *rouge ou noir, faites vos jeux.* One played for the thrill, not for the money . . . The twenties. Little feet running in circles and I never bumped into myself . . . *le duc* and *la duchesse* de Richelieu . . . Sergovia, Whitneys, Vanderbilts. I lived only for pleasure and spoiled my own fun . . . love, marriage, divorce, death and transfiguration."

Not allowing the reader's mind to stop and consider, I went on breathlessly, scattering paillettes that glittered and hinted that there might have been some light nearby. It was champagne on draught—unbottled, uncontained, flowing freely, endlessly, a stylish sample of what was in the big barrel—and probably could never really be emptied. But, my God, I was going to try.

"The hangover was as much a ritual as morning mass . . . Why couldn't the merry-go-round go round forever? The universe did . . . My heart broke a thousand times and still it was never touched."

I was convinced I could make it work. If it didn't fall I might concoct a black soufflé. Into an envelope it all went, chapter and synopsis, and it was delivered to Random House and Belle Becker who called me almost immediately. It was exactly the kind of material she had expected. It was Dagmar Godowsky to a "T" and she had already placed it with a glowing note of recommendation on Bennett Cerf's desk. "Relax. You've done a splendid job and Bennett will fall for it completely."

Dagmar was carried away by the news. She saw herself in the immediate future as a literary celebrity and darling of the TV talk shows. She mischievously insisted that the chapter "Needed worrk, darrling" but had to confess that perhaps I had caught "a certain *je ne sais quoi* and it *was* amusing." I was over the hump. From then on, I realized, with the approval of subsequent work by professionals and Dagmar's own acceptance of her image, it would all go well. Belle Becker's recommendation, plus the fact that she had practically commissioned the work, would insure its publication and the much-needed advance that would pay my bills for the next year while I wrote it. The Godowsky and I toasted each other with her watered Scotch and gorged ourselves on her pot roast and potato pancakes.

A bit prematurely. The intangibles are endless. I should have known that Dagmar, who knew everybody and who talked to only half of them, also had known Bennett Cerf who, it seemed, wasn't talking to her. Dagmar had been a friend of Sylvia Sidney, the actress, who had once been Mrs. Cerf and whose suit for divorce was aided by the generous Dagmar who thereby earned the gentleman's eternal enmity. Mr. Cerf would not even read the chapter and synopsis, but brushed it off his desk at the sight of her name.

"Sandy, dear, I'm so very sorry. Who would have dreamed that Bennett would hold this against her, or that they even knew each other? There just isn't any way of getting around it. But the material is great and I don't have the slightest doubt that another publisher will take it on. Good luck, dear, and I'm terribly . . ."

So it was. Careers and empires have been built and shattered by such resonations. When I questioned Dagmar she amusedly recollected that period in her life. Her story, with the proper embellishments, momentarily blinded her to the problem at hand. She now had one more tale to dine out on. She was not in the least depressed, simply furious that the gentleman was unprofessional enough to allow such nonsense to divert him from his prime duty, which was to publish fabulous things of which this, her life, was (despite her opinion of it a few days before) the most fabulous. She slapped her thigh and shouted, "Vee must not give up, darrrling."

I had no intention of giving up, but I had now run out of money and could no longer speculate. Fat chance! I would, of course, try other publishers with the work already done, but I couldn't give another day to the project without money.

"You mean you aren't coming here in the mornings anymore? We are not going to worrk?"

There was a squinting of eyes that made all other squinting of eyes just nothing at all.

"Dagmar, my dear. I am, it is true, independently poor—but that only allows me the privilege of extravagance. What of my daily bread?"

"You writers take such a long time to say what is on your mind. I am—like most sensitive people, without monya. I haven't a penny but we must write this book. How much do you need a week to keep you so disgustingly thin and sheltered from the elements? We get along, you and I, despite our fights, and a great book will come that will make Bennett sorry for his bearing the grudge because I was a good friend to his wife. How much?" she asked. "You can pay me back when we are rich!" Her thumb and forefinger tapped on her teeth while she awaited a reply.

I was reminded of friends who play bridge for a small sum of money, in order to keep themselves honest, in order to insure that they will not go crazy, the possibility of indemnity giving them a prudence they might otherwise lack. Would the payment to me of a salary make this woman work? Or was the willingness to advance me the wherewithal to continue the book merely her reluctance to give up her days filled with companionship and chatter about herself?

"But would you work, Dagmar? I mean, really work? This last five or six weeks, I only got a small introductory chapter. Do you know what a whole book entails?"

"What a marvelous time we shall have working working working. I swear on Mutzie's grave, I should never enjoy another meal, on my father's life if he were alive, I will give you so much material you will beg me to

48

stop. I will get a tape recorder wholesale from an admirer."

"I'd rather you just told me—"

"But I can work even when you are sleeping at home —where you haven't invited me to dinner yet! I will never stop talking and I will give you food like you've never eaten and we will laugh and I will tell *everything* about *everybody*—especially about those who are dead and cannot sue us—and I will bring you luck in your career like I brought to Stravinsky and Jascha Heifetz and we will sign papers through lawyers—you have a lawyer, yes?— and we will go fifty-fifty and only *my* name is on the book and I swear it will be published and become a best seller. If only my *friends* buy it, we'll become rich, there are so many, and you know you love me and will miss these days with me and Charlie."

There wasn't a friend who didn't think me mad to pursue this any further and out of my own madness I did. Now that Madame was going to have to pay me—no matter how little—she looked upon me with suspicion and resentment. Now that I was actually to be legally involved with Madame Sans Souci, my own paranoia was awakened. I can only assume that Dagmar resented her need for me along with my distressing *lèse majesté,* but I remember vividly my instinctive fear that unless I guarded against it my brains would be picked and the rest of me thrown to the fish.

This was my first experience, and in my innocence I had made the mistake of discussing business with my partner instead of her representative. It was an error I was never to repeat with subsequent subjects. I was to receive no credit whatsoever but be allowed a stipend each week— simply to cover my expenses for the duration—to be repaid to Madame out of any future royalties. I was to share equally in any and all expenses like typing and publicity, though these obligations as well were only to be discharged once the book was a profit-making reality. It was fifty-fifty down the line, although Dagmar at my request played with the idea of sixty-forty and a credit line. She decided against it, vanity triumphing over parsimony.

In this climate of mutual mistrust but bizarre conviviality we ignored all the storm signals, and with the help of an agent—who never spoke to either one of us again—along with lawyers who drew up a simple contract and witnessed our signatures, Dagmar and I made it official. When the lady completed writing her name, it was with such extravagance that not only did the document look like the Treaty of Ghent but there was barely room for my name. And wasn't that the whole point?

Dagmar was unregenerate. Never boring, she filled our days with merriment and haute cuisine. There was simply no way of containing her; she spilled all over the place like the contents of her bulging refrigerator. I know it is impossible, but I could swear that the refrigerator bulged at the seams. I can see it. To open it was the riskiest of businesses. Out would tumble the A & P's entire inventory. One could be maimed for life in the onrush of comestibles. At the very thought of food, her eyes would glitter, the tip of her tongue seek out the corners of her little mouth.

"But we were talking of Ostend, Dagmar, when Popsy was surrounded by all the master students—"

"Ah, those days. Pa was like the sun and everything revolved around him; but I'm in the mood to talk of Paris today—those *écrevisses,* they were *so* divine and the Dubonnets used to—"

"But Dagmar, how can I possibly do a book when you flit about like this? I can't, for a whole book, do what I did with the first chapter. The reader will go mad. I must suck the flower dry before I move on. There has to be continuity."

"And you will give it, darling. That is what you are being *paid* for! I cannot afford the monya I pay you, but it is an investment we must try. Ach, can I help it if I feel French today? My memories will come easily if I can be French today. Perhaps we will have an omelette—would that please you? And it will help. An *omelette aux fines herbes* or perhaps with some confiture. Don't be so cross. It is not so tragic, it is my monya that is being spent, and it will help my memories."

"Perhaps if you would make some *hasenpfeffer* you could continue your more Teutonic memories."

"Perhaps if you weren't so fresh and disrespectful and used the machine more."

"Darling! The one advantage to that damned tape is that I have been able to study your rhythms, your peculiar syntax; I've got it down pat now. Sitting around here fressing and listening to those same old stories is insanity. All I ever hear on that tape is the telephone ringing and you answering it between anecdotes that are already tattooed on my brain."

"I cannot bear you sometimes! It's true. I swear. Can you stay to dinner tonight?"

"No, I don't see how I can tonight."

"I can have Nita Naldi. She will fill you with tales of Rudy and Hollywood so you see how much I want to cooperate if only you weren't so mean, and not willing to work. What is this nine-to-five like a little job? It is so bourgeois. We are working on a book. You think that my dear friend Erich Remarque stops at five! I can't really afford this monya you get every Friday."

"By the way, it *is* Friday."

"*Zut alors!* Toy-toy. I haven't a penny. We must go to the bank."

"But that happened last week."

"Do you expect me to carry gold around, to remember such undignified matters as monya? If you want the cash you will walk me to the bank and then we will pick up some food for Nita and you, and I will have another man too. I must call Joe—"

I would flee as soon as I could.

As time and Dagmar went on, the weekly payments became more and more painful to her. Summer was upon us and I would go off for Saturday and Sunday, freed only by Dagmar's busy social life that took her to the Hamptons or to Connecticut for the weekend. If she had been at liberty, she would have found my two days at the beach sheer treachery, but her own hedonism allowed me this respite.

In those days I used to visit friends at Ocean Beach on Fire Island and in order to get there before midnight I would have to catch a four-something at Penn Station that linked up with a ferry at Bay Shore, which my hosts would meet. Every single week I would race through the gate and jump on the moving train because Dagmar would count out the money like Madame Scrooge and hand it to me at the bank. Somehow it was less painful to her to pay me there on the dot of three at the teller's window—our breathless arrival two minutes before a now-familiar sight to the employees.

I suppose she couldn't help this perversity but I wanted to strike her every Friday—not really for this dramatic reminder that I was simply in her employ and beholden to her, that she was the *Marschallin* and I a shabby petitioner (this was almost amusing), but that in the terrible heat of these July days I was forced to sweat and strain and stand all the way to Bay Shore because the great exodus was on and the rest of New York was already on the train and every seat and lap taken. And if I left without my money, I wasn't certain when and if I would ever see it. The Chinese say that to give with joy is to give twice. This is doubtless why there was no delight in her giving.

And yet, when she was in the mood, Dagmar could be expansive. She gave of herself very freely, and this was no small thing. She was always extravagant with Dagmar. Her charm and naughty delight in observing and contributing to the world's madness were not altogether unendearing. I remember distinctly escorting her to one of the endless dinners she was invited to and imploring her, after our day's work, to rush or we would be late. She was deciding on which tent to wear and what jewelry, and she was being impossibly disorganized. I was arranging my day's notes when I heard her impatient, "Sandya!"

"What is it, Dagmar? Look at the time."

"The time? I cannot go without my hair."

"I am!"

"That is not funny. I cannot find my hair. My God! It is a tragedy!"

Dagmar often wore a braid that crowned her classic hairdo. It was, she had once told me, real hair, not hers but her sister Vanita's, which matched hers perfectly. Like everything else she had, she had thrown away her own, when she'd had it bobbed years before, so she always wore Vanita's switch when she was all gussied up.

"Oh, my God!" she now moaned as if she had lost her firstborn. "I cannot be *seen* without my hair. Darling! Don't just stand there. Please! My God—*look* for it."

"What do you mean look for it? Shall I call all the Third Avenue bars? Where *could* it be? Don't you keep it in a drawer or a box or something. It didn't leave home."

"Are you going to preach to me at the eleventh hour like a Virgo? Are you insane, Sandya? Don't be impossible. If I were a switch, where would I be? I don't know. I have asked myself that question over and over—I am bereft of reason. Where—where?"

I searched the living room and the bath and the bedroom and was about to give up when, as a joke, I got on my hands and knees and looked under the bed. There against the wall was little Charlie, who now glared at me with the nearest thing to a snarl his sweet nature could muster. In his mouth was Dagmar's hair. Between the dust and the spittle, it was in hopeless condition.

"I found your goddamned hair, Dagmar. Charlie has it under the bed."

"Charlie, Charlie! It is his way of keeping me home. Charlie, darrrling, give Sandya my hair."

Charlie and I had a tug of war with the braid and I eventually won. When I offered it to Dagmar, deploring the fact that we would now be delayed another hour while she cleaned it, she swept the hair from my hand, put it on her head, securing it with a pin all in one gesture.

"Ach! We can go now. Thank you, Charlie. I promise —on my health—that we will not be too late."

And we were off for the evening.

Dagmar was hopeless. Her deafness to my supplications, her blindness to her own motivations and her mental untidiness, plus the heat of summer, all contributed to the inevitable deterioration of our relationship. Her demands became greater and greater, my five-day-a-week incarceration suffocating. There was a new wrinkle, if I may continue to be ungracious. Now she was so tense that she wished me to massage her.

One more irritation was piled upon the other. As for work, I barely had Dagmar in Hollywood in 1919. I was appalled to realize that there were over thirty-five years to go. The prospect was becoming as unattractive as it was increasingly improbable. It wasn't enough that I had my own emotional difficulties, I was now an equal partner in milady's self-destruction. She'd never finished anything in her life and so why would she allow me to finish the book? Like a witch in a fairy tale she would strew my path with obstacles each day, challenging this prince to win the princess's hand only by overcoming them all—an impossibility because the obstacles bred like dividing cells, insuring their immortality and my frustration.

"Where is the work?" Dagmar demanded one day, after I declined her dinner invitation, pleading a previous engagement. "I am paying you the monya and you do not work. You live for pleasure alone and I do not believe that you love me—and I am sick of this one-sided partnership."

"Dagmar!"

"You are mean and spiteful and selfish and lazy; and you go out too much—but *not* with *me!* Louis Bromfield was such a worker and Fanya Hurst—"

"They weren't dependent on you for material."

"You always have an excuse. Fanya—don't sneer, Sandya Dodya. She might not be George Eliot, but she's famous, not like *you*. Who are *you?* A saucy boy and a failure with a flair and you are *bleeding* me. Every week the monya and where is the work? Such a little bit you have because you are always with that sick friend of yours who is dying, dying and you *bore* me and depress me with her dying. And you have never asked me to your house for dinner."

I was now up to my neck and almost out of my mind. I also believe that Dagmar was precipitating trouble because she wanted to accept an extended holiday in the country. She could throw away her birthright for an invitation to dinner, no less for a fortnight with the Guermantes—even if it were Seymour and Sylvia Guermantes.

I cannot, in truth, recollect why—midst all the *Sturm und Drang* that could materialize immaculately with no collaboration of man, God or this unholy ghost—but one dusk, Dagmar perhaps inspired by Stravinsky's alleged lycanthropic attacks, turned on me viciously. She accused me, this time without a trace of her usual humor, of exploiting her, and I counteraccused her of not fulfilling her part of the bargain.

She now demanded all the work I have done up to that point, since she had paid for it, and I gladly gave it to her, having, in my sensible paranoia, sent myself the original by registered mail. The copy had hidden evidences that it was written by me, and I almost welcomed a court procedure in which all of my Nabokovian clues would be revealed along with my long suffering. Hand in hand we had for some months been gaily figure-skating on the thinnest of ice and this was our reward.

Dagmar Godowsky! I learned to sigh during this period in my life and started for the first time to use profanity. Working with Dagmar was like going to war, or being in a plane crash. If one survived it at all, one was changed forever, never the same, all innocence gone.

That afternoon Dagmar had had it with me. She threw me out of her apartment. Short of stature but formidable in her width, she came at me, eyes flashing, fangs bared, hands poised for choking, chest forward, and she wheezed and she puffed and she mowed me down. I had never experienced anything like it. She was like a child's toy tank that once wound up, sparks and flashes red lights as it senselessly attacks anything that happens to be in its path. I was petrified. As if afraid that she might kill if she used her hands, only her awesome chest was used as a weapon, and with it, I had been hustled and jostled through her door and into the tiny vestibule outside her apartment. Then came the necessary curtain line—the malediction.

"I hope, you disgusting man, that God gives you what you deserve."

"I hope so too, you maniac," I replied.

She slammed the door in my face and I was free.

There was a suitable intermission in which I could take a smoke and stretch my legs and Dagmar could repair her makeup and then the curtain rose on Act Two.

> Some weeks later.

> It is autumn. Leaves and soot are falling on my terrace. I am getting the last of the September sun and read the *Times*.

> The telephone rings and I reach through the window and answer it.

VOICE:

"Sandya? Sandya Dody?"

My heart fell.

"Yes. This is he."

"You will *never* but never guess who this is—please! —never in a million years."

"Edith Sitwell?"

"Come, darrrling. Try harder. Out of the blue. Someone you really love despite yourself. And someone who loves you though you are an impossible and saucy boy."

"How are you, Dagmar?"

"Sandya. I am *marvelous*. Rested. I was under such a strain. You and I, we understand each other. That is why we fight so much but will always be friends. No? I am right? You didn't miss Dagmar—even when she was naughty with you? The truth, darrrling."

"I don't believe you, Dagmar. I really don't. What can I do for you?"

"Your voice is cold. Why? Because we had a little scene? What is that between artists—friends? Listen, darling. I must see you. It is important. We must rise above the trivia. You are working? I have an idea and you will not be sorry you came up. I will fix us lunch on the terrace. It is gorgeous today. You have a good summer? I missed you. I missed my fresh *schreiber*. *Mon dieu!* A little excitement in one's life keeps the circulation going. Can you come up today? It is important. I swear on my life."

"Dagmar."

"Do not be a deacon now, darling. You know you become less attractive when you look down the nose at the mortals. You know I am what I am and our book *must* be done. And impossible as you can be, *you* are the only one who can do it. It is Kismet. I have some cold chicken and home-made potato salad. Sandya! On Popsy's grave, you will not be sorry you came up. It is important. The agents wants for us to talk and I cannot on the phone. Toy-toy. We have a *contract* . . . but what is that? To me, a handshake is more strong between friends."

I was curious. What could Dagmar possibly have to say? Four chapters were done that at least looked good to me and it riled me that this was unfinished business. But the revival of our disastrous relationship was so chilling a consideration that I resisted—despite the mouth-watering mention of her potato salad—the temptation to hear her out. I pleaded social commitment, sexual involvement, and, as a final try, leprosy—to no avail. Dagmar had all the stops out and was being her most charming.

"Darling. I *promise* I will never be naughty again. I was wrong. Not even to lovers have I said this. It takes a big person to admit the wrong. No? Well, who is bigger?"

I dropped in to see Dagmar the next day and she welcomed me with open arms.

"Is different from the last time here, no?" she teased. "Toy-toy! Such a *crise* we had."

It seems that over the summer some of Miss Godowsky's royal and celebrated friends had read the four chapters and thought she was crazy to drop the book. Whoever had convinced her I will never know but she now insisted that we resume our work, work, work under circumstances from my viewpoint far more felicitous. She not only promised to cooperate more fully, and in as orderly a fashion as she could on pain of my immediate departure, but she raised the ante and made the weekly stipend far more tempting. Evidently, Dagmar was convinced that her dream of a book could be realized if she could only abide this man who could write it.

She was all soft curves that afternoon, and as serious as it was ever possible for her to be. She was even—for an instant—coldly logical.

"You know I will work when I am paying this much monya every week."

"I do not wish to escort you to the bank on Friday afternoon at two fifty-nine where we will draw it out together like the three cc's of blood for a Wasserman."

"I swear. Did I say 'I swear,' Sandya! It is business. I want the book. In an envelope every week, the monya. It is over if that is not so. Don't you understand? I have changed—a new woman. We will write *I Made My Bed*. Enough of this terrible practical talk. I have missed you. You have missed me? The truth, darling!"

I had missed Dagmar the way a released prisoner misses his confinement.

By Christmas, still on her very best behavior, Dagmar was so delighted with the latest chapters that she asked what I was giving her for Christmas.

"Please, something sweet, darling, and *not* expensive. It is the thought, no? When my book is the best seller you will shower me with the gifts! Now Bloomingdale's has a simply marvelous confiture. That is all I want. I already know what I am getting you. I am buying you the most deevine . . ."

Dagmar then went into a description of a Charvet cravat she had seen that was suitable *only* for me. She thrilled to the body and softness of the silk. She swooned at the audacious but elegant colors. It was quite a tie and quite a description and that's what I got as my Christmas gift—the description of the tie.

My life with Dagmar—like Ravel's "Bolero"—was an endless repetition of the theme first described. But she called me one night while I was working, hemmed and hawed, and then told me that she was about to reveal to me something that would make our book a great one. Nobody, but nobody, knew what she was going to impart to me except her family and she hadn't been certain up to now that she should uncover such terrible information; but she was "thinking of our work and what you call the red line. You will understand the burden I have been carrying. Vanita swears she will never speak to me if I tell this—but I will. It will shock the world!"

It was midnight and I poured myself a cup of coffee from the recently brewed pot on my desk. Had Dagmar murdered someone? Had she been mistress to Hollywood's Rin-Tin-Tin? Or, better still, was her life of sin and frivolity simply a cloak, as with the Scarlet Pimpernel, for her undercover work with the Salvation Army? What a spy she could make! I thought. Was she the head of the French Resistance or a secret agent from not one but all the Russias? Who would ever detect in this most disorganized of flibbertigibbets the mastermind behind the greatest of crime rings, the Mafia—or the renaissance of the Nazi party, the loathsome but still unheard of *Gadempftebrust?*

"What is it, Dagmar? Relax. If you decide you

shouldn't have told me, the secret will die with me. We needn't use anything you don't want."

"But I do want this. It's Popsy. About Pa and Mutzie."

She then, in the hushed tones of one being overheard by the secret police, confessed that her beloved father, the famous musician, was not the *mari parfait* the world thought him. With all the moment and earthshaking consequences that a revelation of Cleopatra's easy virtue might provoke, Dagmar sadly told me that there had been a music student, a girl named Catherine, with whom the great Leopold had dallied. Her mother had almost been destroyed by the affair, and it struck me at that late hour that it might have destroyed Dagmar as well.

I listened sympathetically to this exposé of a forty-year-old scandal involving a man dead for twenty years and virtually unknown outside the world of music. No one cared. It would not make the book a sensation—but Dagmar cared, still. She cared very much and it would make the book better. For months, I had been searching for the red thread that Dagmar had mentioned, that line of communication that runs through a work, starting with the first word and directed toward a target, despite its apparently aimless course, which it finally strikes. She was vulnerable and adorable at this point.

When I discovered that the acquisiton of all her weight followed Popsy's death years later, it no longer being necessary to conquer the entire male population as punishment to him and herself, I knew exactly where I was going and where it would all end. Design was emerging in the work, not simply a verisimilitude of design but true order.

Dagmar, bless her for this, had reached a point in our partnership where she knew what I needed and wanted, and I hoped she'd accept my finish. She had to end her memoir as honestly as she began it.

The reader had to believe Dagmar, even believe her unbelievability. I had planted, with and without her knowledge, hints of her self-awareness throughout the book; now, after a begrudging acceptance of her aloneness and beyond-the-paleness, came—as befitted her *symphonie fantastique*—the coda.

Instead of deleting some of the famous names with which she kept mercilessly supplying me, I now encouraged their use. The more the sadder. She gave a luncheon in Hollywood for Alexander de Seversky and entertained Arnold Schoenberg, John Gunther, Emil Ludwig, Jascha Heifetz, Artur Rubinstein, Igor Stravinsky, Cornelius Bliss, Atwater Kent, Lion Feuchtwanger. On her ready admission, they all brought their wives. She was at peace. She had returned to Hollywood, the scene of her early victories, and it was a kind of Flanders Field. The Poppy, as she had once been called by her father, had been worn in so many lapels, in remembrance of so many Château-Thierrys, that she was unrecognizable.

Dagmar listened with great interest as I read the last chapter. We were by this time beloved enemies and also sometime friends. She now knew, if nothing else, that what was good for me was good for her, and she trusted me. When I arrived at the very end, I was still anxious. It was the last brutal, honest curtain lines—combining her vanity and insight—and I couldn't look at her. I took a deep breath.

". . . I was generous with myself always. I spent myself freely. That, was indeed my greatest extravagance. I let myself slip through my own fingers . . .The End."

I waited.

"Is good!" she said, with tears rolling from her Iberian eyes. "Is very good! And *true*—every word."

There is no end to life's surprises.

And so it was finished, and I put the original copy of the completed manuscript—along with our personal contract—in my vault before I handed over the copies to Madame, and to the agent whose job it now was to sell it to the highest bidder. Dagmar was confident that we had the masterpiece of the century. I thought we had a salable book. We were both wrong.

Months later Dagmar called me in great excitement. Wasn't it typical, she screamed, that not only was she everything else in the world but now she was agent as well. She had been sure that the book could be sold. It seems that at one of her dinner parties she was telling the actress Rita Gam and her husband, Tom Guinzburg, about the book when Tom—

"Dahrlingg! He *is* Viking Press. You've *heard* of it? Is a good house? But of course. Well, he is *crazy* about it. But I tell you, darling, *crazy* and I thought you would like to know."

"I should think so," I exulted. "That's marvelous news, Dagmar. I'm thrilled. When did this all—"

"Toy-toy. Wait a minute. No, darling, the phones. It is impossible today. They haven't stopped. I'll have to call you back."

I soon discovered that this happy meeting between Dagmar and the powers that were had transpired weeks before and no one had bothered to inform me that all my labors might not have gone for naught. Mr. Guinzburg, I learned, was not only "crazy about the book"—if indeed he ever was—but far better had already said that he would buy it. In the most ostrichlike and pointless act of dissembling, Dagmar apparently thought that she could sell the book, have it published, and keep it all a secret from me. It was a senseless concealment since I wasn't dead or blind and would certainly see it in the shops. But

Dagmar had never thought anything out and wasn't starting at this late date.

This very phone call informing me in mock excitement of the happy facts was made to cover her embarrassment. It seemed that before publishing Viking wanted some minor changes made (that is how far the thing had gone) and had sent someone up to see the authoress, who almost dropped dead, not having read the book. It seemed that she sat petrified as suggestions were made that she did not understand. Even if she had understood, she couldn't have acted upon them. It was then that my name came up for the first time. That I had not been informed until I was needed did not endear the lady to me. Poor Dagmar had burned her bridges behind her, and with her characteristic lunacy was nevertheless retracing her steps. Walking as she was on troubled waters, I was the rock she could use as a stepping stone. In a blur of fast talk and fancy stepping, she wasn't even going to get her feet wet.

"Darling! Call Helen Taylor. She's charming! Absolutely charming! It has to do with some technical problem —*zut*. So boring."

That took care of any contribution I might make. The bubbling fountain of which she was so proud now needed some repair and why should Madame Bernini be disturbed when Sandy the Plumber was available.

"Darling! Isn't it thrilling? That our baby is born— we made it together, Sandya and—"

"More and more I do feel as if I've been screwed, Dagmar."

"But that is vulgar. I do not know what you—you are so mean and on the eve of a best seller."

I called Viking with alacrity, and the warmth with which I was greeted by Miss Taylor can only be approximated by the welcome one reserves for an after-midnight wrong number or a draft notice. She could have been

Barbra Streisand being asked to appear at a benefit for the P.L.O. With my joy undiminished, I rattled on about my pleasure at the imminent publication and my eagerness to cooperate in every way. There was nothing I wouldn't do to help shine the script up until it sparkled. Miss Taylor's voice was still glacial. She was not impressed by my enthusiasm; if anything, she was suspicious of it. She informed me that the manuscript was sparkling enough, but simply needed a few editorial changes. She then—as if making a dreaded dentist's appointment—agreed to meet with me the next afternoon in her office. Her coldness made me ponder the difficulty some people have talking on the telephone—especially with strangers.

The next afternoon, with my compulsive promptness, I arrived at Viking and was led through the corridor to Miss Taylor's office, where the manuscript and family photographs which I had gathered lay on her desk. The woman was correct and polite. After offering me a seat —not too near her—she spoke of the book. She had made notes and asked about some remarks. Did Gaylord Hauser really give Dagmar such a concoction or was it hyperbole?

"You mean the pure-sulphur business? Dagmar *claims* that he did but does it matter? It's her hyperbole and fun."

"But he can sue if it's poison," she literally but professionally observed.

"Well, why don't we change it to a bubbling broth and say she felt like one of the witches in *Macbeth?*"

"Good!" she said, carefully making the change. "Now who is this Margaret Rutherford?"

"Just the funniest woman in English films. She was the Lady Bracknell in Gielgud's *Importance of Being Earnest* on Broadway. She's the typical English eccentric and always cycles through town and province dressed in tweeds and a slouch hat. That was the allusion. 'One doesn't arrive at Maxim's looking like Margaret Rutherford.'"

Miss Taylor was taken aback. "But doesn't that make Miss Rutherford look ridiculous, at least in the eyes of her lawyer?"

"No! Not in the least. It's her on-screen image. It would be like Chaplin's suing because we said he had baggy pants. I think she's the perfect image for Dagmar to use as an English frump."

And so we worked over the script.

"You know the book *very* well, Mr. Dody," Miss Taylor said.

"Well, of course. I mean, I should, shouldn't I?"

"I don't know what you mean."

"I mean, why shouldn't I? I did write it, after all."

"You did?" she asked, without the frigidity of tone that had up to now been accompanied by clouds of vapor emerging from her lips.

"Now, I don't know what you mean? Who do you think I am, Miss Taylor?"

"We were told her typist."

"Her typist?"

Miss Taylor held my eye. "Her typist, who was trying to blackmail her."

Poor Dagmar! She forgot we had contracts. She forgot everything.

"We apologize, Mr. Dody. I mean, I'm sorry that I acted so coolly but—well, what were we to think?"

"After reading the book—that she was not the most reliable of witnesses. Is there anything else in the manuscript that bothers you, Miss Taylor?"

We worked on, and then the work was finished. Now it was a question of the title. Helen Taylor and I had got to know and like each other. There was little need for formality.

"What about *Who The Hell Is Dagmar Godowsky?*"
I asked.

First Person Plural was Viking's choice. It was a lousy title, but I was powerless to prevail.

The book came out in February. Cleveland Amory reviewed *First Person Plural* in the Sunday *Times*. Mr. Amory was the only reviewer to detect the hand of a ghost —perhaps because he had done such work—and invented for the occasion the word "sbook," which he dubbed the work. He said very nice things about us in his witty manner and Dagmar called immediately.

"He is a friend of yours, this man Amory?"

"Never met him."

"You did not tell him you wrote the book?"

"I just told you I never met the man. Of course not. He didn't mention my name, did he?"

"I don't like what he did."

"It wouldn't surprise me, Dagmar, if others suspect you didn't write it yourself. And why or how could you have?"

And we never discussed it again.

If Dagmar could have turned a magic ring (or emptied it) or concocted for my noonday meal a hemlock soufflé or sent me smallpox germs without characteristically bungling the job and killing herself instead, she would have. Dagmar divided her time by calling Viking to find out whether we were on the best-seller list and casting the motion picture which she was certain would be based on her sensational life.

"I see Audrey Hepburn as the young Dagmar!" she kept saying.

We would speak on occasion but Dagmar wasn't seeing me now. My presence was no longer required and if she ignored me I might just possibly vanish.

One night my friend Consuelo Rubinow saw Dagmar

at a party. Since she had lived through my ordeal and often counseled Dagmar and me on the script—having once been an editor herself—she felt she knew Madame. She joined the circle of admirers surrounding her.

"Madame Godowsky? I'm Consuelo Rubinow."

"Oh? How attractive you are. Do I know you, my dear?"

"In a way. We've spoken often on the telephone."

"Oh?"

"I'm Sandy's friend, Connie."

"Sandya?"

"Sandy Dody."

"Sandya Dodya? Sandya Dodya? Who he?" the authoress queried.

"He author your book!" Connie was tempted to answer, but she didn't. Her control, I suppose was admirable.

I called Dagmar the next day to chastise her.

"You have never loved me," was her only response.

"You dare ask for love when you stab me in the back?"

"They are all lying. I did nothing. Lies. Lies. The world is filled with troublemakers and you believe them and not *me*. You are an awful man. You were a nice boy when first we met. You have become cynical and bitter and ugly. I never met this Connie. Would I have done a thing like that?"

"Yes."

"I do not like you anymore. Listen, darling. There will be need for a sequel. Let us bury the hatchet and do another book—"

"Not on your life!" I shouted.

We sold like four hotcakes. Many years have passed since Dagmar and I first worked together. Almost twenty-five. And still the entire experience is vivid in my mind.

One does not forget Dagmar Godowsky easily. Also, we saw each other on occasion. I remember visiting her when she was in the hospital having something or other removed. It made no appreciable difference.

"You do love me, after all," she squealed when I arrived with some posies. She was still on that tack.

Every few years she got the urge to write another book and called me. Every three years like clockwork.

"Sandya? Dagmar! I have changed. I swear. I will be sweet and no more wicked. I was naughty. Is true. But no more. I swear on Charlie—your friend Charlie who died. We belong together. You *know* that. We understand each other and we can laugh at the world. You have lost your hair but you are not unattractive—like Rachmaninoff—"

"Thank you."

"Or Igor when he was young. Not that you are young anymore. Who is? That's what I want to talk with you. You *must* come to my new apartment."

I eventually visited Dagmar. She had begged me to see her on a matter of great urgency.

"*Please,* Sandya," she had pleaded, "come over. It is important. About Igor. He's dead now and I am ready to *talk.*"

"But I thought we told the whole story in the Stravinsky chapter," I said wearily.

"My letters, *his* letters. A London paper has offered me a *fortune,* darling. A *fortune.* I have them and you and I, in harness again, we will work, work work! Now that you are older, are you rich?"

The idea of a book on her Stravinsky relationship did not, of course, interest me. I had told her years ago that I would never again work with her, but Dagmar was never deterred by facts. We sat sipping something that tasted like Kool-Aid. Dagmar had not changed perceptibly, though I was a different person.

"London will pay a *fortune*. They are enchanted with the idea. I tell you, the newspaper syndicate will pay much monya—"

"Then why don't you sell them your letters? What do you need me for?"

"Darrrling!" she said with that meaninglessness that was so filled with meaning.

"But it doesn't make sense, Dagmar. I thought you gave me all the material worth using . . ."

"Not the *letters*. I have *found* them. So tender and sweet and about business. It is musical *history*. And our *relationship*. The truth at last. It will be hard to have lunch again with Vera, but a writer must sacrifice, no?"

"Dearest Dagmar. You know and I know that when the time comes to produce the letters, you'll not even be able to find them. Then under pressure you will recall in a great flash that in a temper—after a battle with Igor—you burned them in the eternal flame under the Arc de Triomphe. I know you."

"You don't see value in a book about me and Igor?"

"My dear," I said, "Igor Stravinsky is one of the few authentic geniuses of our time. I respect him as an artist. It is pointless and tasteless to rehash all that business, to pick away at a corpse—and after that impressive Venetian funeral."

"Ah, Venice—how it suits me."

"Dagmar," I shouted, "do you want to be a vulture?"

"Yes!" she answered quickly and I was reduced to laughter. There is nothing one could do with this woman.

"Dagmar. You are one of the unchangeable and quite, quite beyond belief."

"When are you going to invite me to your house for dinner?" she now asked with as much passion and interest as she had asked me to write the book. I never did entertain Dagmar in my house, but I dined with her and Alice Tully and happily shared what proved to be her last birthday. Her excesses and the years had caught up with her and now the laugh was hollow. There was bewilderment and there was a cane. But she was surrounded by admirers and her engagement book was filled until Doomsday, which proved to be very near. Her friend Joe Machlis gave her a great sendoff that evening.

Dagmar slipped away from us quickly—she was never a bore. It was between meals, and all that misspent energy still hovers around us. I'm sure that somewhere she is dining at this very moment and whether it is angel cake or lobster fra diavolo, she's smacking her lips and amusing her dinner partner. Dagmar was an original, *sui generis*— to a fault.

Despite everything I have written about her, I will always be grateful that at our last meeting—in answer to her maddening and persistent question—I found myself shouting with grudging honesty:

"Yes! Yes! You lunatic. I *do* love you."

Mrs. John Barrymore

Our first meeting proved our most intimate moment. It was all downhill from there on. Elaine Barrymore was to exert her full quota of charm and consideration at that conference. The book that emerged a year later was another miracle.

Dagmar's very lack of cooperation became copy. She was ubiquitous. Elaine would vanish before your eyes. She offered me voluminous scrapbooks and a hero about whom I fortunately already knew much and felt more. That was that.

We had met through a mutual friend. I had shared my terrace for a while with a theatrical director who had watched me at my typewriter under sun, moon, and gray-cloud struggle with Dagmar. He now called me to see if I was working. If not, he had a project which might bring me satisfaction and some money. Had I ever heard of Elaine Barrie, John Barrymore's last wife?

"Now, before you scream," Hal quickly added, "she's bright and warm and there's quite a book there."

Though I was wandering around town changing the position of the Godowsky book to more accessible shelves at Womrath's and Doubleday's and God knows I needed money, I wasn't interested in Elaine Barrymore. Still, Hal Gerson was a charming and intelligent fellow as well as a talented director. He was not easy to impress. I had tried.

"I swear to you that you'll like her, Sandy. As a favor to me, just see Elaine. A publisher is already interested and I know what you think but . . ."

It has been Elaine Barrie's plight that Hal knew exactly what I thought. My whole generation thought it. Miss Barrie (née Jacobs) had—according to her "enemies" and Mr. Barrymore's "friends"—pursued the great actor in his declining years (when he was no longer fleet of foot) and exploited the dying man to her own ends. Their long, peripatetic, cross-country "Ariel and Caliban" affair and tasteless courtship had occupied the front pages for many weeks during the thirties, the Great Lover and the schoolgirl achieving a notoriety that was to outlast their eventual marriage, his previous glory, and even her ambitions. I recalled, at the mention of her name, a plain-looking swart girl, rather Near-Eastern looking, with a worldly and not unattractive mother who was, some said with glee and probably no justification, the third side of the story.

"You're going to be *very* pleasantly surprised," Hal insisted.

As a favor to him and out of curiosity, I called Mrs. Barrymore. Mrs. Barrymore! Who would change that name unless one were to become the Baroness Olivier? Her telephone voice was charming and she was eager to meet me. An appointment was made.

Many years had passed since I'd first seen the lady. I reminded her that in 1938 when as a boy I crashed the glamorous opening night of Talullah Bankhead's play *I Am Different* at the Ritz Theatre in Los Angeles, I had seen her among the famous. She and her mother, at the height of their notoriety, were standing with John Barrymore and the actress Constance Collier: they were the center of attention.

Elaine, I recalled, had seemed shy, but her attractive mother could have been Gertrude as she held forth with the greatest of Hamlets, while Miss Collier, looking down her nose, suggested that she was smelling something rotten in Denmark. She was the haughtiest of woman and had been the original Mimsy in *Peter Ibbetson* with Barrymore. Now she was one of the elder theater stars, contributing marvelous cameo performances in lesser actors' starring films. She also coached the parvenus in speech and deportment.

There were many such greats—to be joined shortly by John's sister Ethel—who played out their last years in the golden glow of Sunset Boulevard. Jessie Ralph, Garbo's Nanine in *Camille,* was another such legitimate actress who was now doing character work and happened to be with a group I knew that evening. When she heard me voice my admiration for the great actor, she urged me to ask for his autograph.

"In this whole damned crowd, he's the only one who really counts. *I* have his autograph and wasn't the least embarrassed to ask for it either."

I approached Mr. Barrymore with my program and observed the corroding matinee idol close to. He was a ruin of a man—motheaten and palsied. His autograph, which he graciously gave me, looked like the signature of a dying man on a will. It was literally John Barrymore running downhill. He who had lived with such panache and flourish had dwindled into an illegible scrawl. It was a vivid memory. Mrs. Barrymore, hardly to be faulted for not

74

remembering me, did not even remember the evening or the play. It is true it was considered by the critics to be a forgettable evening, but I was surprised. I was even more surprised by the fact that Hal had been right. She was all he had said—intelligent, quick-witted and congenial.

Tall and still willowly, she bulged round the middle like a Spy drawing. Her dark eyes were feverishly bright and filled with humor. While I grew gray during our relationship, both ladies were to turn blonde. They did everything together.

Surely Elaine Barrymore was easy to talk to. I found her immediately as comfortable as a school chum. It was easy to see why the aging actor, sick in a hospital and sated with strawberry blondes of Hollywood who were as bland as Wonder Bread, found this bright and wry little New York girl, with all her crust, a tasty morsel. Elaine could be a delightful companion—informed, articulate and zany. Elaine, like Dagmar, I discovered, could bubble— not because she was going down for the third time, but simply because she came by it naturally.

Edna Jacobs, who eventually joined us, was, though the years had gone by, barely changed. She and her daughter shared both this apartment in Manhattan and a house in Haiti where Elaine (who was incidentally also a licensed stockbroker) designed and manufactured a line of rattan objects like table mats and baskets and lived—from my point of view—a life of mystery. She was to be always rushed and pressured and in the midst of political intrigue or on the verge of business deals, without which she could not survive the season. She was forever crucial, but that first day, she was eager for my cooperation and sat still for a remarkably long period. We did get on, as Hal had said we would, and she related some exciting stories about John while I toured the cluttered living room, examining photographs of John as Hamlet, John as her idol, and John as her husband. It was an amusing couple of hours I spent there, and both women obviously were interested in interesting me in the book. I was taken with Elaine, who knew how to charm you when she wanted something. My instant impression—never to be changed—was that Elaine Barrymore, in short, was a warm and calculating woman.

It was true that she and her agent had an interested publisher. An editor at Meredith Press was only too eager to discuss the possibilities of a life story of these Barrymores with a writer. Elaine had to sell me on the book and then I had to sell the publisher.

After a couple of hours over drinks, enthused about our undeniable rapport and my obvious worship of her ex-husband, her eyes grew brighter as she promised me not only great melodrama but high and low comedy as well. Elaine sold me that afternoon. I admit it. She'd let out all stops and charmed the pants off me. I almost lost my shirt as well, but that was later. To my surprise I heard myself agree to work with her.

"Elaine," I decided, "if you let down your hennaed hair and tell me the whole truth, I'll do the book. If you let me clear your name by confirming, not denying, your sins, we'll have something great. There's a way of assembling the facts and presenting the truth to your advantage. But if you want a whitewash, forget it."

Mrs. Barrymore shrewdly agreed to my approach—perhaps, she may have thought, a bit too quickly, because she added, "Do you mean you don't believe that I was in love with John?"

"Certainly not when you met and married him, Elaine, dear. You were starstruck and had dreams of glory and were flattered beyond reason. What's wrong with that at seventeen?"

Her eyes glazed. I continued. "If you play it like

a saint we'll be clobbered—and rightfully. *But if* you tell your tale with the detachment time and maturity have given you, if you admit your *chutzpah,* your courage of ignorance, your burning ambition, the reader will understand. I want the public to see you as I do now."

"It would be the first time they would," she said.

"I walked in here, Elaine, thinking what everyone else has thought all these years and—well—I'm astonished."

"People always are when they meet me. They expect some kind of aging dance-hall hostess who sucks blood!"

"But you've got to admit you latched on to Barrymore, that you were grabbing an opportunity . . . It was only natural that you—"

There is a way of getting a subject to admit to anything. To say, "It's only human that you would want . . ." or "Jesus said, 'Render unto Caesar—'," or "I myself under those circumstances might easily . . ." or "For Christ's sake, Tom Jefferson and Abe Lincoln, in order to reach a position . . ." is to allow the reluctant one to confess his sins at a revival meeting in the Hall of Fame. Then there is the appeal to sheer vanity. I once got an acquaintance to admit to a disgraceful act of which I only suspected him by simply implying that only he would have had the style and imagination to have pulled it off. As he was taking his bows, I forced him—on pain of exposure—to rectify maters.

When I suggested to Elaine Barrymore that hitching her wagon to a star such as Barrymore had not only been enviable and difficult to accomplish but tragic as well, considering the plunge they took on his dramatic fall, she rightly bought it and dropped her twenty-year-old alibi that pictured her as a lovestruck innocent. I could with some difficulty buy her eventual submission to John Barrymore's tarnished charms, but it had to develop with the early rewards of such an alliance and not appear full-grown.

On any level, Elaine was wise to agree to my approach. It was hardly unnatural for an imaginative, romantic young girl and her vivacious, dissatisfied mother—both of them imprisoned in a milieu that crushed their free spirits—to escape it with the help of such a guide as Barrymore. One might question the wisdom, the taste, and the manner of escape, but certainly not the need. Oddly enough, these two women would have been, not as they thought, more sympathetic but absolutely monstrous, had the truth really been what they preferred people to believe. The idea that this seventeen-year-old Hunter College undergraduate could fall desperately in love with the jaded actor, ailing, drunken, on his last legs—her loving mother even begrudgingly acquiescent to the obscene arrangement—was unthinkably repugnant. The protective mask deformed the face of things.

Though I doubt it, Nurse Edith Cavell as a teenager might have fallen in love with a decaying alcoholic, but not this nice Jewish girl. That she willed herself and then became trapped in a genuine involvement with this aging Apollo and that with her romantic nature she succumbed to his spasmodic but still considerable charms were not entirely out of the question. Elaine, I believe, has always had a gift for self-delusion, and her basically pleasant character would demand that she justify her deeds through the grand passion. Certainly her life became Olympian now that she had entered her favorite mythology, but it was not Zeus or Apollo with whom she was cavorting—which she should have recognized from the start. She was an ill-suited consort to Bacchus, and her apotheosis was to become her hell. It is perhaps her worst punishment that in her Assumption and Presumption, she came to care for someone who was beyond caring.

"Everyone said I was after his money. *Money!* That's a laugh. My poor father—a traveling salesman—had more security on West End Avenue. I was sure that John would make me a great actress. What happened? He *kept* me from getting jobs. He called people and killed jobs I had got for *myself*. And the drinking, the drinking and the jealousy. There was nothing I could do right. If I called a doctor when he was ill, he was sure I was having an affair with him. And the press! While they claimed that I was burning John at both ends, they would throw another log on the fire, every chance they got to make the late edition hotter. The entire Barrymore family, whom I'd *adored* from childhood—the whole family from Ethel down to poor Diana considered me Typhoid Mary. Even John's cronies, when they momentarily stopped attacking me and admitted that John did love me, attributed his devotion to my profound knowledge of the *Kama Sutra*. Those intellectual hobos. I could do nothing right except what they felt no decent woman should have known how to do *at all*."

Elaine's eyes flashed with merriment, her head shook with disbelief as she relived it.

"Those dreadful men—those aging sophomores—sodden with booze—always pulling John back to the bottle after Mother and I had dried him out. Now Sandy, I am *not* perfect," she now revealed, "but I am not and never was Ilse Koch nor a circus performer."

I liked her. I didn't know how much I could trust her protestations of love for Barrymore but I knew she had been genuinely dedicated to his sobriety, his health, and the resumption of his career, for no matter what reason. In many ways, she had been good for Barrymore. It was true also that she could, indeed, do nothing right in the eyes of Gene Fowler, Ben Hecht and Charlie MacArthur, Sadakichi Hartmann, and the rest of the lynching mob. If she had been Little Nell, which she wasn't, these vigilantes would have run her out of town as a fraud and a nymphet. These talented, childlike men were a shark-infested moat around their Sweet Prince.

"My God," she went on, "I *did* stop him from drinking. I did get him back to work—which was more than his royal family ever did."

Also true! I was to learn subsequently much about Elaine Barrymore that I liked and disliked, and I don't believe that she was worse than I subsequently painted her. It is true that through the hindsight I provided she may have pretended to understand the mistakes she made: but by the same token I don't believe that she was as bad as even she thought. She was too defensive not to have believed herself guilty of something. She had to answer only to herself and to her god. I just had the problem of writing the book.

"If we get to work together, Elaine, remember this. It is to *my* advantage as well as yours that you come out smelling like a rose—but if you insist at any time that I make you into a calla lily, it's no dice. There will be no whitewash. There isn't any need of one. The story—your story—is too good not to let the facts and fancies speak for themselves."

Elaine was still weighing the advantages of a candor that would disarm the prejudiced reader.

"They were always calling me Elaine Jacobs."

"That was your name."

"You know what I mean."

"Where did you get the name Barrie—from Sir James Whimsy?"

"No," she laughed mischievously, "it was the nearest I dared get to Barrymore."

"Hardly."

"I mean *then*, Sandy."

She was an intriguing combination of honesty and evasion. I sometimes thought that in her wildness of spirit she ceased to know the difference herself. I examined her now as she thought it all over. Her eyes were those of a princess in a Persian miniature, a Persian princess the soles of whose feet were being tickled off-frame. There was a madness in those dark eyes. Obviously Elaine Jacobs Barrie Barrymore loved the precipitous, anything to avoid the ennui of those early bourgeois years, her dull West Side story. Perhaps that is why now that she was in trade, she would fill her days and nights with such feverish activity and audacious plans. If she were really lucky enough, she might be placed in jeopardy, and boredom would be impossible. Prudence was not Elaine's long suit. Why should it have been? It invited safety.

She may have been considered a pushy litle girl, but yes, there had always been that delicious madness in the eyes that must have refreshed the sober Barrymore as he lay in New York drying out when this wacky kid walked in with pencil and pad to interview him for her class paper. Elaine was always quick to see the irony in a situation. She had a sense of the ridiculous. Only in this was she like Dagmar. She could see the humor of her own situation if she were caught posturing. But unlike Dagmar, she would never go into contortions to get a laugh. Elaine was not a clown. She was dead serious beneath the fun, but seemed destined always to outwit herself.

Elaine had purpose and energy, but no sense of direction. She always knew where the target was, but her aim was faulty. Logical, reasonable and organized, she always set out to accomplish the wrong thing.

Editing her own life that first day or two of talk, she revealed to me what she wished, of course. They were not lies, but only part of the whole truth: the early desire to rise above the humdrum; her love of the theater; the worship of Barrymore, its prime deity; and the sacrifice of the virgin to that god who turned out to be all too human —clutching her in a death grasp as they tumbled through the heavens—he to his destruction, she to notoriety and obscurity. She had had quite a moment up there with the stars—short but bitter. Nothing ever worked the way she'd planned.

Now that the ball was over, there was nothing left but confetti, some of it caught in her hair and in her lashes. *It would be marvelous,* I thought, *marvelous to put the pieces together*. I was now interested in her life. Wanting excitement, she had generated more than she had bargained for. Obviously hoping to be a leading woman to the most famous actor in the world—even a co-star if she did her homework—she landed up nursemaid to a dying man. She had shared her young life with a hopeless alcoholic.

Women more mature and more saintly could not have survived the experience without some errors in judgment and a loss of poise. Without any illusions concerning Elaine, I must say that it seems highly likely that, despite all, she gave for what she got. Few people act purely. Man always wants something, if only the ennobling satisfaction of knowing that he wants nothing. Elaine, of course, wanted plenty, and she unfortunately got it.

Instinctively enough, somewhere along the line, she began to believe her own bad publicity. I observed that she had blacked out some of the unwise decisions she had made, but in her defensiveness she revealed a guilt I'm not certain she deserved. She had been so maligned over the years that while she deplored and never stopped battling her enemies, she (knowing in her heart she had been self-interested) was now convinced that her judges might have been right after all. It was a feeling I had and

I found the character intriguing. It struck me that this girl's love affair and marriage were far more foolish than immoral. Elaine is not the first woman to discover that the achievement of an impossible goal does not always bring reward.

As I warmed to the subject I realized that if she continued to be cooperative and really worked with me I could have a corking book about Barrymore. I was also fascinated by Edna, Elaine's mother, the dowager Fata Morgana, and her role in the epic. Mother and daughter were, as always, inseparable, highly keyed—almost the same tense woman, though one was present, the other past and future. Elaine was not only the continuation of Edna's life but she was also running concurrently with it. It was like a double soundtrack, or better still, a melody in two-part harmony. When chatting with them, I was surrounded —like having identical twins as a mistress. One was always treated with fact and editorial, joke and subsequent laugh, drink and instant hangover. All angles were observed. What a spectacle it was to see these women—originally brunettes, then redheads—turn blonde simultaneously. Bright Elaine, cheery as a department-store Christmas, and wry Edna, her face wreathed in a funereal smile that mourned late delivery and the good old days that never were. Though Elaine was better at simulating a relationship with me—and on one level, we laughed and kissed cheeks and agreed on many things—both these ageless girls were remote, removed. Rather than answers, I often received, especially from Edna, what sounded like prepared statements. Elaine had her alibi memorized by now, but with her agreement to bare all she occasionally flirted brazenly with the truth. She was a cliffhanger. She had insight, and with her help, I could have delved deeply and sorted out her life. But it proved that she neither had the time nor the inclination to accomplish this.

The Barrymore period in her early life was her claim to fame. Why wouldn't she stick to her story and her name? Elaine *Barrymore,* indeed! Her line of table mats was called Barrymore Originals. Ethel and Lionel must have been revolving in their graves. John, of course, would be amused. Why not? It's an honest business. Well, she was never again to reach such celebrity, and I understood her reluctance to part with the cachet, but I couldn't believe that so vibrant a woman could have stopped dreaming and hoping. Elaine told me that John Barrymore was an act impossible to follow or replace. That she was satisfied with her memories. Something—one of the pieces of confetti—was missing.

Elaine had a disarming and deceptive honesty. She talked turkey with you always. With all the trimmings. Her bright eyes looked squarely into yours, her expression was earnest, and it didn't mean a damned thing. She was mad, but not like Dagmar. Elaine was mad because she believed what she was saying at the time. I think her dreams became realities before the fact, which is quite a gift.

There was a mystery to Elaine Barrymore that I was never able to solve. Her loyalty and closeness to Mama were remarkable. They lived as roommates, like two young girls with their lives ahead of them, although something in their past bound them together, making them even think like one. I really knew nothing about the present Elaine Barrymore except that she never had time for me and proved so undependable that Dagmar by contrast resembled the 12:05 to New Haven.

I was never to meet one solitary friend or business associate of Elaine's, and never spent one social moment with her or her mother. I barely spent work sessions with her. Never in my entire life have I seen such a busy woman. No Egyptian slave or Siberian salt miner ever worked such hours as Elaine Barrymore. One would have thought that she was working on world peace or a cure for cancer. It was night and day, day and night. Such dedication should have been rewarded with something other than impoverished middle age and sunlit exile. One should, at least, have become president of Bloomingdale's or the New York Stock Exchange or even America. There has never been such divine industry that produced so little.

Dagmar had been idle. Elaine proved to be preoccupied, and I was her preoccupational hazard. Except at the outset—at our initial meetings that insured my doing the book—Elaine was cavalier beyond believing. For all the personal involvement or attentions I received on arrival, I might have been, on my infrequent visits, the window cleaner. Nothing interfered with this compulsive business of hers. The telephone calls back and forth would be frenzied and endless. They would continue almost uninterrupted during my stay, and I was all but ignored but for an occasional wink from Elaine that mutely spoke of her understanding, her shame, her regular dameship, and her genuine promise of early redemption, with an extended period of compensating work. Except it never happened.

As for Edna, if she wasn't out shopping, she would busy herself in the kitchen, from where I would expect an occasional platter of food to emerge. It never did. I didn't believe that either woman ever ate. I must say that I don't think Edna ever got my message. She would hoarsely greet me, offer me some magazines, and then disappear like a nurse in a busy doctor's office.

When Elaine was forced by me to do some work—and it was rare—she became peculiarly, inexplicably vague once she had given me sufficient information and warmth to have clinched the deal. It was nothing but frustration. For a fleeting moment she would tell a great tale, and then she would drift off like a bad radio and the channel would be lost, all contact gone and she would become involved with her buyers at Bloomingdale's. But how could I forget a girl who at thirteen had over her dresser an eight-by-ten glossy of Barrymore as Svengali smirking behind a filthy matted beard, stained mohair Prince Albert, and Westmore cataracts? She had to be special.

She could have these fugitive moments of hilarious self-revelation, but unlike all my other subjects, Elaine Barrymore never leveled with me. Considering that we were to be partners of the most intimate kind, and under these circumstances ordinarily, even extraordinarily close, all of our intermittent camaraderie was a sham. Elaine never told me anything but the apparent. There was a reason why she was doomed to a reputation founded on rumor and what my dear friend Helene Fraenkel calls "insinuendo." It was her absurd need for privacy when it was unnecessary. She so sequestered herself in shadows that people around her got out their searchlights to seek out the evil.

Elaine Barrymore had the unique ability to ignore successfully a question that she found threatening, as if she were stone deaf. She would just stare at me in a kind of coma until I became so embarrassed for her that I would change the subject.

Catching people in a deception or evasion isn't all it's cracked up to be. It is mortifying to both caught and catcher alike. "What are you doing with your hand in the till?" you might well ask of someone so discovered. If he throws the cash in your face, using your own legal tender as a weapon, or shoots you, or runs like hell, you can act accordingly. But damn it, if the thief freezes into a tableau, his eyes half-crazed with fear, and his very soul has departed the scene in the faint hope that on its return you may be gone, what do you do? I fear that I retreat. To press the issue at this time isn't worth the money.

Elaine would go into that kind of escape when a probing question demanded an answer that could only incriminate her and couldn't be dissembled gracefully. I never saw such a thing in my life. It was a gift that must have enraged John—creating, as much as his drinking, their tempestuous relationship. I could only infer what the truth was, use it judiciously and hope that when I wrote and she read the text that she would accept the resultant appraisal—now that it was a *fait accompli* and not a personal threat.

Elaine then was an open mystery, her mother a false clue. I could imagine what Elaine was omitting in her broken narrative. Edna was impenetrable. Since she usually deferred to her daughter in a three-way conversation and when we were briefly alone together played the wisecracking best friend, she was no help at all. Elaine's tales of her "naive" mother who was always "shocked" by Elaine's rebellions and by her yielding courtship with the famous actor made no sense; Edna Jacobs looked unshockable to me. The woman seemed cynical—her world-weariness the result of personal experience, not collective consciousness. Still, her loving daughter refused to admit that she was anything but an unheeded Cassandra as well as unwilling spectator to Elaine's recently recognized mistakes. I could not shake her from this resolve. Now that Elaine agreed that she would confess her sins, she would not share them. Although it is improbable, it is, of course, not entirely impossible that her mistakes were solely her own. In either case, it was her life. I was only going to write it and since they were one woman anyway, the division of guilt didn't really matter.

Elaine had agreed to drop all pretenses of early innocence, and Mama, though she may not have been Herodias, was certainly at the banquet table when John was served up on a platter. Though I couldn't conceivably think of Edna as the provincial, middle-class mama—passionate and quick-tongued as Elaine admitted she was—it could have been that the aggressive daughter opened doors for the two of them, all on her own. Doors that the mother gladly followed Elaine through despite her warnings. It was hard to swallow, and I knew I was going to have a problem, but I would manage. Not as with Dagmar, by surreptitious revelation, but by making her believable as the realistic, dry-humored, bluff woman she was. Her ubiquitousness in her daughter's life would speak for itself, her dialogue of such earthiness and sarcasm, such scorn and bitter acceptance that she would never be maudlin or even faintly ingenuous.

All in all I found the project a challenge.

"Of course it's fifty-fifty right down the line, Elaine. If you'll get off that wire and give me a couple of months' time I'll give you a book that will wash away the past."

We shook hands on it and I saw her agent, who, God help me, became mine as well. A rendezvous was made with Bobs Pinkerton over at Meredith Press; she was pleased that we had all found each other, and knew even less than I of Elaine's recalcitrance. We all started off with high hopes. Miss Pinkerton had read the Godowsky book and although it proved excellent credentials, she asked that I also do a little synopsis of the Barrymore book for her superiors. She assumed that I had known Elaine since childhood, someone's idea of a selling point. Miss Pinkerton, I suspected, really was eager to see how much Elaine was willing to say. I conveyed this to my collaborator and said that our presentation had to be a strong one.

I asked that we start working the next day and Elaine agreed and that was the beginning of what should have been called *Will o' the Wisp* instead of *All My Sins Remembered*. We were to start early and work through the day.

My life has always been feast or famine. Dagmar Godowsky had spoiled me. Elaine had none of Dagmar's chic *gemütlichkeit*. As a matter of fact, she had no *gemütlichkeit* of any kind whatsoever. To get a simple cup of coffee in her house was unlikely. A morsel of food —a cookie or crust of bread—was out of the question. I was gateful that I stopped that first morning at a diner on First Avenue and had a blueberry muffin. That was it until nightfall.

This was the first of those frantically wasted sessions that almost spelled the end of our book. At those isolated moments when Elaine did deliver, she was perceptive and orderly and intelligent. But then came the frenzy. Bloomingdale's was breathless for her goddamned mats.

One might think that since this was her only visible source of income, all this activity was understandable and certainly should have taken precedence over our work. I don't believe it because I begged after a day or two of this nonsense that we change our work hours to the evening. This practical alternative was greeted as if I had asked Dracula to play a round of golf after sunup. The women were not available after dark and any question as to why was greeted with impatient shrugs and four rolling eyes and a series of grunts. Cries of business and buyers' dinners fell on deaf ears.

It was the most bizarre of facts that this woman could want her book done so badly and then barely lift a finger to make it possible. She got the writer she wanted, swore compatability with him, and then made every effort to discourage and enrage him. It was so self-defeating that I became concerned. If this indeed was her neurotic pattern, then I, as her partner, would have to suffer her lot as well. Had she chosen the unavailable John Barrymore as her only object of love so she would remain loveless and then, in a quirk of fate that to her surprise won him, settled for a doomed romance to which she heavily contributed? Was she in love with failure? And, if so, how in God's name did I get involved with such a *ménage à trois* and how in hell could I extricate myself?

I talked this over with Elaine, who couldn't deny that her life was unduly hectic, but assured me all would be settled the moment we signed personal contracts, which we did shortly after—to no appreciable change in her work habits. Appointment after appointment was postponed or canceled, and I decided that she was blocked. After all, why should she be different?

This was the Dagmar story all over again, with a new twist. Suddenly I had it. I was sick and tired of waiting around her apartment and parrying questions the publishers were asking me. How could I tell them that in the three weeks since our talks began the woman had given me about two hours' work? They would doubtless throw up their hands, thinking—as is true in some cases—that the desire to do a book is not always accompanied by the will or drive to write it. I had been doing some fancy footwork with Bobs to keep the project going, but I was bored. I spoke to the publishers and discussed Elaine's lack of cooperation. Oddly, they had been conned into believing that when she was back in Haiti permanently all would be well.

Elaine always had a plan. She always had everything figured out like an intricately designed, well-oiled machine that finally wouldn't function. This was her latest design. If I could get down there ("After all, they're going to give *you* the advance.") she would arrange a cheap lodging ("I wish we could put you up, dear, but we can't.") and my meals, heaven help me, could be taken with them. She even knew of my fear of planes and could recommend a freighter. I was to join her in Haiti after her production period was over.

Meredith thought it an excellent idea, though they

made no offer that I remember to pay my fare. It was necessary to sublease my apartment in order to negotiate the trip since I could not even reasonably maintain two establishments, and in a kind of delirium I went along with the whole scheme since I had never seen Haiti and I knew that Elaine would be captive down there and would have to deliver.

The honeymoon was on again, with Elaine merry and warm as toast. The New York scene would dissolve and fade into the serene seascape of her tropical isle. She had been in raptures about Haiti and how we would work on the edge of her pool with nineteen servants hovering over us as we accomplished masses of work in the sun. Elaine's Haitian work period covered every conceivable contingency. All was papaya in the sky.

"Wait, my dear, until we are in Haiti together. John always wanted to take me there to live. You'll see how we'll work!"

I believe that I had seen Elaine Barrymore a total of five times when she suddenly picked up and flew off to Duvalier's island with assurances that she would send me information that I might need to complete my synopsis. By the time she was to return to New York, she hoped we would have sold the book, and then we would be off together to her tropical home.

Elaine, I now discovered, adored sending cablegrams of great moment signed, of course, BARRYMORE. And I adored receiving them. I was still struggling with the synopsis, a chore I have always found more difficult than five volumes. I needed some immediate information and Elaine promised to send me a long, long letter, which she did—but only after sending me a cablegram warning me of its imminent arrival. PORT AU PRINCE. DELAY APPOINTMENTS SENDING LONG LONG LETTER TODAY BARRYMORE. I saw us together a couple of months hence. We were lying under palms, Elaine looking like a Gauguin matron, I sipping rum and coconut milk and turning bronze as I filled my notebook. What a life!

I managed to whip up an outline based less on the mad facts than reasonable fancy. I tried to do an exciting portrait of Barrymore in decline and, with Elaine's partial sanction, I discussed in brutal terms the brassy young girls who—through the great actor's alchemy—eventually proved her mettle. The synopsis was filled with holes but it managed to be provocative, and it sold the book. Elaine was beside herself, which made three of them down there.

Now we signed contracts and I saw some cold cash before what would now be our first official session together as partners. Surprisingly enough, Elaine was again in New York and we made an appointment for Monday morning, which she broke on Sunday night. As quickly as she had come to New York she was now gone again—this time to arrange for my stay. "Darling, you'll adore it."

A date was set that would give her sufficient time to arrange her affairs—which I decided was really the problem—and then all would be paradise. But I no longer believed a word of it.

I had been lured by John Barrymore, who was sitting in the wings and aching to be dragged onstage again. I was eager to bring him alive. I also do not deny that I had wasted so much time up to this point that I again needed the money. Now, if Elaine refused to work, I, at least, could afford the blueberry muffins that gave me strength to sit out her marathon business calls. More and more I believed that her resistance to work—now that it promised to become a reality—was deeply psychological. She was panicked and no amount of soft soap from me could alter her schedule.

Something told me that when I departed for Haiti it would be a mistake to sublease my apartment. Something told me that after three days in Port au Prince with no work and a knock-down-drag-out fight, I would be back in town. So I made an arrangement with a friend who could expect me back at any time. I had lost faith in Elaine. I was, however, now committed and waited patiently. The rattan evidently had to be gathered and her "new line" executed by faithful workers who "adored" her and were "fiercely loyal" although the "entire island might be blown up at any moment." This was Elaine's new tack, presumably to discourage my visit.

My family did remind me that stories in *The New York Times* indicated that this was hardly the time to visit the troubled island, but this and Elaine's dark hints didn't bother me in the least. I found it exciting, somewhat like moving into Versailles to write the memoirs of the Capets in the spring of 1789. Elaine, as John's wife, had lived on the lip of Vesuvius. This was her natural habitat. I must say, I have only been a frequent visitor.

When Elaine would speak of the trouble in Haiti, her eyes would flash with some secret joke, and I thrilled to some new conjecture. I wondered, *Is her business a coverup for the United Fruit Company or perhaps the Rosicrucians? Or it now came to me in a flash: Is she the white witch of Haiti and able to destroy with macumba? Would she stick pins in a little rattan doll that resembled me and wore a bit of my clothing? Hadn't I,* I now remembered, *once torn my sleeve helping her move one of the huge cartons that always cluttered her apartment? Had she used the tattered fragment? What in hell was in those cartons, table mats or shrunken heads? My God, do I go down there on that freighter as a passenger and come back in a carton— strange cargo—a new line to be sold at Bloomingdale's in their brand-new exotic-island-boutique?*

Whatever it was, I stopped hearing from her as zero hour approached and I was making my arrangements to leave. About ten days before my planned departure, I wrote asking if she had my reservations—something, I mused, in all of her deliria, Dagmar would have accomplished with great style through one of her titled minions—and would she meet me at the dock? I told her that my place was leased and my clothes purchased and by body and soul hers. Now that it was upon me, I felt the visit would be illuminating. It would certainly be an adventure.

I shouldn't have been surprised by her immediate response, but I was. I was more than that. I was stunned. She wasn't postponing my junket. She asked that I cancel my trip altogether. Her business was in a holy mess and the government was teetering or tottering and she really couldn't say any more because she was convinced that all mail was being censored. She was absolutely up to her neck and that's exactly where she belonged. I saw her penning her note furtively as she dodged a poison dart in the garden. Had I not written that letter I would have arrived in Haiti and wandered the streets homeless; and, knowing her, she would have had no compunction to act any more graciously there than in New York. Her *sans souci* in this matter was the last straw. She and her mother dizzily cavorted in a tiny world they evidently preferred to keep sacrosanct for whatever reason. It seemed clear that I was not to see the ladies in closeup. Elaine's ducks and dodges were now to be replaced by total absence. That this made our book an impossibility was so evident that it was a wonder that she continued the charade at all. More action? More intrigue? How she adored trouble.

All of this just a week before my departure. Aside from all other considerations and lack of it, I was thrown into confusion. I had canceled or refused important engagements, spent far too much on a suitable wardrobe, and most importantly, would be without a home if I couldn't cancel the sublease (which she didn't know I had called off). She *thought* I had given up my apartment, which was what really mattered. *I won't even have a roof over my head!* I kept complaining unfairly to everyone. I wrote her a blistering letter.

With that enraging coolth she had, Elaine answered my outraged manifesto with a long self-serving note filled with affection and minutiae about her table mats and her shipments. She was living, she said, on Miltowns and returned home for lunch at 5:00 P.M. She went so far as to say that the "dream of our book is the only thing which has helped me to stay sane." It didn't seem to me that it had done its job sufficiently. She now suggested that in four months—in March—I plan to come down and work with her straight through the summer. She wasn't to be believed. She just didn't give a damn and now neither did I.

I called the publishers and unburdened myself. Meredith was curiously tolerant of the lady's behavior. She had become friendly with one of the bigwigs there, and I can only infer that she was being allowed to get away with murder. If I could help it, it certainly wasn't going to be mine.

Only Bobs Pinkerton was sympathetic to my plight. Her chief, Ted Purdy, always glacial, was faintly bored with my complaints. Mr. Bigwig was impressed sufficiently with Mrs. Barrymore or her name to accept all this nonsense and expect me to do the same like a nice little ghost. Not one person deigned to say, "How terrible this has happened. It's unfortunate that you were so inconvenienced. It's appalling, but we'll work it out."

I was simply expected to await Madam's return with patience. I raged apoplectically while Elaine now wrote that she had had an attack of nerves and was hurt that I hadn't answered her letter. "I can't understand your silence." The offense was supposedly the best defense. She just couldn't wait until we could get together and work. "If you're free in March, darling, I'll give you my *undivided, loving* attention."

By this time I was foaming at the mouth. The advance was dissipated. I came out of the whole affair with nothing but a tropical wardrobe and no place to go.

It took a full year before we could continue what could only loosely be called our work and Meredith Press, impressed with my activities in the interim, offered me a brand-new advance if I would effect a rapprochement with her.

It was a sweet sense of power I felt. I was able to report to them that after collaborating with a professional and completing an entire work in four months—albeit with hardships—a renowned book within one year of its very inception, that I would never again tolerate Mrs. Barrymore's sashaying around. I did feel, however, because of my earlier advance which remained unrepaid, that I had some obligation to the publishers, but only if the new advance was greater and I was contractually indemnified against the lady's recalcitrance. In fact, I demanded and got written assurances that my subject would *give me a minimum of twenty-five hours a week for one month.*

Elaine was now eager to refresh our bargain. She was distressed that I was receiving more money and made some vain demand that she, too, for no reason—except that she obviously needed it—also receive a consideration. Though she had signed the new contract, eyes blazing with regeneration, she was to fall back on her old ways almost immediately—again pleading business. I could count the time she spent with me in hours, rather than days or weeks, though they were spread from April 10 to May 15.

Whatever her compulsions, Elaine did try, somehow knowing that I would manage this time even without her. She gave me little material and less food. I recall vividly being asked (one luckily reserved day suddenly only made available by several cancellations by department-store buyers) if I couldn't stay on for dinner so that we would be able to make up for lost time by working through the evening as well. I was only too pleased.

"Great!" Elaine now said to me on the telephone. "Would you be a doll and bring along a tin of coffee, a quart of milk and a bread. I'm up to my neck and—"

"But of course dear. I'm delighted about the long stretch ahead of us. I hope we get a lot done. Is there anything else you need?"

"A million dollars, darling."

"In what denominations?"

"I'll see you at ten sharp!"

At last the Barrie girls were going to feed me, the gourmet, the gourmand always blessed with a *bon appetit*. Since Elaine had once regaled me with tales of their food in Haiti, these descriptions meant to lure me to the isle a year before, I looked forward to the day's work and the fitting reward of a good dinner.

Elaine was on excellent behavior this particular day —or, at least tried to be. When she wanted, she could— with all her brightness and energy—dredge up a lot of marvelous stuff. And that she did on rare occasions. She had a fine sense of drama, a sprightly way of evoking the past, and a now-realistic view of John Barrymore. Like Leda recalling her night with the webfooted Zeus, Elaine's memories were spectacular and often wry. Certainly this woman had the best and worst of it all and she saw both sides. Knowing my own lifelong idolatry of Barrymore, she felt free to give me the warts on either side of the profile, knowing that as a final portrait my picture of her John would still be heroic.

Though there was business as usual, I knew that without the usual limitations on our time, I would get enough work done this day. Then there was dinner to look forward to, followed by more work—better than before—mellowed as she would be from a hot bird and a cold bottle. I took advantage of the day, knowing it might never come again. I asked about the great moments and I asked about the worst. I asked what she remembered with pleasure and with pain. I asked what she could feel guilty about.

I spoke of the dead man the way a mortician speaks with his helper while preparing him for public exhibition. I was detached and aroused in Elaine the necessary clinical observations that cooled passion could presently allow. We spoke of John the man, not just Barrymore the actor. Were they indivisible? I had the giant's dimensions. Now I wanted to examine the cartilage, the hair, the nails, always aware that they—along with sentimental fancies—could grow after death.

Elaine got caught up in the work that day. She was carried away and marvelously articulate. I recognized the telltale signs of truth: the racing breath, the shining eyes, the words that tumbled.

It was two o'clock and then four and then six as I still sat listening to her hair-raising stories of Barrymore's jealousy and drinking. Some, most of the horror was of his own making. Some was fed by Elaine's youth and need for excitement. Whatever, when he was in his cups, this god could become a demon. From princely courtship and Byronic sonnets, he would sink to smut and violence, brutalizing those who loved him and mortifying those he loved.

John Barrymore could be the elegant gentleman actor one moment and pee in a crowded theater lobby the next. He gave the nineteen-year-old Elaine a birthday party and had as guests Irving Thalberg and his wife Norma Shearer—then the king and queen of MGM and most important to his career *and* Elaine's—and after one glass of wine glared at Elaine and noted, "In my day, tarts were not allowed at a gentleman's table except to be served as a sweet," and then after one more tipple and losing all semblance of wit or sanity said, "Norma, what do you think of these whores who are never seen publicly without their lady mothers?" after which he squeezed the neck of the decanter to breaking—using it as a substitute for Elaine's throat.

These excesses were flattering compared to the neglect from which his own children suffered. This fascinating artist could turn both devil and bore just like that. It was always the booze and that afternoon, Elaine was serving it straight. It had at last happened. The Bloomingdale's gift-wrapping, the manicured recollections that would preserve the legend, the self-deception that justified her life, were all gone. Up to now there had always been a tolerant smile about the drinking, a smugly raised eyebrow concerning the jealousy. But this session was different.

With chilling eloquence, Elaine came through for me. It was like our first day. This was the meat and potatoes she had promised and I ate greedily, demanding more and more, knowing rightfully that it might be the last of such feasts.

"Then there was the night, Sandy—that terrible nightmare of a night—in New York when John really tried to kill me."

"Pardon me?"

"And almost did. He had just come out of a coma. For forty-eight hours he lay waxen, rigid. We were twenty stories up in our apartment on Seventy-ninth Street. John, resurrected, announced coldly that he was going to throw me off the terrace."

"Just like that?"

"Just like that."

"What had you done?" I asked.

"I'd just called the doctor, and through him hired a nurse—a male nurse. When John came to, I fear, he thought him too male. John was certain that I'd been sleeping with him, that he was a lover in disguise. But who wasn't? Any young man anywhere near us was suspect. And when John went into one of his jealousy scenes there was nothing one could do. I can hear him now. 'Those bastards have a million disguises. Window cleaners, elevator boys, radio repairmen, bellhops with those tight pants. Don't think I don't know what goes on in the world of petty services? Do you think you can trick me—a veteran?' John was convinced that poor Dr. Essel, his physician, was a pimp who ran a male brothel and serviced the likes of me.

"Now it is true that when John woke up, came out of his coma, the nurse was giving him a colonic—an olive-oil colonic—you may well raise your eyebrows, dear, but it does the trick. It brought him back. I'm quite an expert in these matters. It brought him back, all right, but John was outraged. The posture didn't suit him. And with rage he always had the strength of ten. That 'big, blond stud,' which John kept calling him, flew like a timid girl the moment his patient got violent. *Flew*—this dedicated man in white—leaving *me* with a homicidal maniac."

My empty notebook was, at last, filling up as she went on.

"John kept circling me on tippy-toe. It was the most terrible sight, and he was smirking like a gargoyle and hissing invective. I remember thinking he looked like Ethel and Lionel and Satan as well. Even his eyes had turned color. Then he stopped circling and closed in. Twisting my arm, he dragged me out to the terrace through the French doors. The hedges, the privet hedges we had planted together, tore at me as I found myself half through

100

them. He was now screaming about the parade of boys he saw me with after his death."

Elaine's voice was dead now—like an actress giving a perfunctory reading of a scene she'd played a thousand times.

"He was holding me over the edge and the street below rushed toward me and I felt sick.

"'I will not allow you to make my grave a mattress!' he said. 'Only if you die first can I have peace, slut. You've come as high as you could.'"

"Didn't you scream or anything?" I asked.

"One didn't interrupt Barrymore doing a scene. He would have been doubly enraged.

"'Well, child of the asphalt,' he now intoned, 'you are going home at last. Back to the gutter!'

"His face was right over mine and I felt he wasn't acting. I felt this was the McCoy and I felt something in my terror that was so like love that I thought I must be as demented as he. I must have lost my sense of survival along with a lot of other things. How did I ever survive that night? How did I ever survive all those years?"

"How *did* you survive that night, Elaine? You've left me hanging by my toes."

"He asked me to beg him to live and instead—I asked him to kill me—to give *me* peace. In a moment we were crying together. It usually ended that way."

Of course, I thought, she must have enjoyed it to a point. I always remembered that schoolgirl pinup of John as Svengali on her dresser back on West End Avenue. It was a giveaway.

Elaine revived us both with a drink. She needed one now. I had never thought of what she did or had to do when he was in a coma or intractable or in a hospital. I asked about this. Elaine now sighed deeply.

"It was just before we married, dear, when I visited John in one of those places. It was run by a man named Kelly—in California—and it was pure Hogarth. Creatures who used to be men and women—remnants of human beings—wandered through the corridors as I was led to John's room. They opened and closed their doors, slipping in and out, ogling me as I raced through this madhouse. There was one old woman I'll never forget. She was in a straitjacket, and with her ecstatic eyes and her arms around herself, she was a horrible picture of self-love. That embrace! Oh, God!" Elaine shuddered, and so did I.

The pages of my notebook were flying as she continued.

"John emerged from the corner of this little dark room he was confined in. There was a tiny window and the light was diffused. Everything was blurred around him. All I saw was John, his eyes staring, his fingers raking his hair. His face was Death. Oh, my dear—if there was anything worse than John arrogant and aggressive and after my scalp, it was John contrite, helpless, begging for love and pity. There he was—*my* idol, and *he* was on his knees in supplication—begging, whining, sniveling. I couldn't stand it. I tried to help him to his feet, and instead he pulled me down to the floor. I heard a terrible cackle of laughter in the next cell as he tried to make love to me. I was sure that we were being watched. John saw my terror and he fell back. His face was like a child's.

" 'Oh God in heaven,' he wailed, 'what have I done to my little girl? Forgive me. Forgive me. *Please!* Even God forgives sinners, so why won't you? Please, please, please!'

"It was unbearable and I fled, I had to flee—that smell of paraldehyde. I started driving home but I had to pull the car over to the side of the road, still hearing that voice, that *'please!'* And I couldn't stop sobbing. I felt something

102

crack inside of me. It was that day, at that moment in the car, that I knew—"

"Knew what?"

"That I was in love, really in love. But it was only after my heart had broken."

"Elaine?"

"Yes."

"Is it all right if I say that up to that point you—you weren't sure that you had one?"

I waited for the thunder. Elaine looked at me a long time.

"Yes, Sandy. Yes. O.K. You can say that."

It was quite a day's work.

I pitied both Mr. and Mrs. John Barrymore. The great star whose glow had attracted Elaine and died light-years before she'd ever come on the scene. She and her mother were late arrivals at the tragedy but they still got into the act.

Blinding themselves to the facts, they kept drying Barrymore out, dressing him up, giving him avocado facials, shining his shoes and his star, and kept trying to pin him back to the sky. But he always came undone.

Did starry-eyed Elaine ever really believe that she would become Ophelia to his Hamlet, Cordelia to his Lear? And is it possible that to her horror, she did become both?

That long day gave me the bulk of my material. I knew Elaine much better and I now knew Barrymore too well. As keeper of the flame, Elaine played with fire and couldn't complain about her burns. But as awed as I was by the enormous gifts of Barrymore, his descent into the bathetic and his wallowing self-indulgent disregard of others—especially his daughter, Diana, with whom I had once worked in Hollywood—were unattractive in the extreme.

Behind the classical portico was the classic slum of

the alcoholic—a place of alleyways and drool and stumbling souls with outstretched hands—a terrible place to live in but worse to visit when one cares. I'd been there. I didn't know how Elaine—for whatever reasons—could have set up housekeeping on the curb. I pitied the great actor, but I found it difficult to adore him, and this was creating a problem since Elaine still did despite her stories. I was Elaine's ghost and my necessary empathy was slipping away as I heard more and more terrible tales and read enough of his notes to document them. This was going to be a tough book.

It was now ten o'clock. The work had been good but I needed fuel. I was starved and increasingly aware that nobody was cooking anything, although Edna had been in the kitchen unit, barely able to be contained in it with the door closed. *Perhaps the food has been cooked and simply needs heating.* We had had those drinks and I was reeling, since there was nothing inside of me to absorb the alcohol. *How do these dames do it?* I thought. *They never eat.* It was ten-thirty and I was evidently not to be served dinner, but wouldn't they starve too? And then I realized that their trips to the john must have been the answer. They must have been eating in there—gulping down sandwiches or even hot meals for all I knew—and with my bread, of course.

Though weak with hunger, I rose. I would bring the whole outrageous siege, this war of attrition, out into the open.

"Where are you going?" Elaine asked, as I started for the door, my notebook in my pocket.

"I thought I'd get a hamburger. I'm starved."

That would do the trick. She would be shamed into the kitchen.

"Oh. All right," Mrs. Barrymore said. "I guess we've really worked enough. I thought we might go upstairs later to a party at some neighbor's but I'm exhausted. Good night, dear."

"Don't you want anything to eat?" I asked.

"I'm not hungry," she answered, apparently having stuffed herself in the john with food delivered by her mother and partially supplied by me. Edna, who always looked as if she were listing slightly dexter, smiled crookedly, her fingers doubtless sticky with contraband food, and hoarsely bid me good night.

My coffee, milk, and bread were never seen, much less eaten nor drunk by me, and I left the house unfed and never to be invited again to stay on to dinner. That was my one invitation. I worked from ten in the morning until ten-thirty at night without once being offered a vitamin tablet. Perhaps John Barrymore died not of liquor but malnutrition. This occurred to me while I was wolfing a hamburger on the corner—and they, I am certain, were tackling the rest of my provisions supplied on their demand. Or perhaps they were upstairs, and having outwitted me, were up to their ears in chicken tetrazzini.

They were not to be believed. I recall that one morning, when Hurricane Alice or Bessie or whatever was raging, I was literally swept across Fifty-seventh Street to their house. I arrived soaking wet, freezing. I removed my shoes and jacket and sat shivering on the couch.

"I don't know how you even got here," Elaine said in annoyed amazement. She probably thought that the rain would keep me home and she could once again cavort with all the Bloomingdales.

"I am freezing," I said.

Edna shook her head and sucked in one cheek in hardboiled acceptance of Mother Nature's heartlessness.

"Look at him. He's drenched," she observed.

"For Christ's sake. Give me a drink or a cup of coffee. I'm going to catch my death."

"Oh!" these great hostesses said in unison, and I got a cup of instant.

I wonder if they still have my pound of Maxwell House and if they might get botulism if they use it.

Elaine was not, in my opinion, a very giving woman and I knew that she had now exhausted her material and patience. If the book was going to have to be written, not out of whole cloth, it certainly was going to take some doing. This was not to be an article but a book. It seemed to me that writing it as a play—with the use of much dialogue, quick changes of sets and costumes, plenty of bravura acting and the genuine characterizations of the leads might be the best approach. And that is what I did.

Elaine was good about all of this. I recall a line of dialogue I concocted for the ailing actor on that first meeting between him and young Miss Jacobs. As young collectors of trivia or elder students of our folklore may remember, she did pursue the aging actor until she landed him, but the chase started with her arrival at New York Hospital, where the alcoholic profile was being dried out. The teenage girl was a reporter on the Hunter College paper and genuinely enthralled with the Barrymores in general and the great and handsome John in particular. There was nothing this schoolgirl didn't know about the family. She had really done her homework. In an effort to impress the actor on that first interview, Elaine had paraded all this familial intelligence and then started on his career, about which she knew even more. In an excess of acquired facts, she now displayed one she would have done better to forget. She quoted a panning his famous Hamlet received in London from Clayton Hamilton.

Engaging as the child must have been to the declining prince of the royal family, it occurred to me while writing this scene of their first meeting that their roles must have been defined and even established by the still assertive and

Olympian actor. His relationships were all too tempestuous to be—at their most romantic moments—utterly devoid of divine right. Also, I felt that Elaine's charm was getting a bit thick and some self-imposed comeuppance would endear her to the reader. Her previous aggressions were inviting a slap on her bottom.

Elaine in the narrative now admits that she had been insufferable. "I talked on and on in that hospital until my gentle host looked down his divine nose at me." Now I needed a line of dialogue to give the breath of life to the narrative. A line typical of the Olympian Barrymore who was both literary and colloquial. I needed something witty, condescending—even a little cruel. I watered my plants and stretched my legs. And then it came.

"And where did you get all this information, my dear Miss Jacobs? Has your mother been playing Mah-Jongg with Mrs. Rosencrantz and Mrs. Guildenstern?"

Elaine was not only a good sport but roared with laughter, insisting that if John had thought of it at the time, he would have said it.

Since in this world of manipulated readers, one printed word can alter a thousandfold the true picture, there isn't the slightest doubt in my mind that fact and fiction have now dovetailed and Elaine, herself, now believes he did say it. And damn it—this is what has made so much of my work fascinating—in essence it is true.

Yes. Despite all the troubles the book miraculously got written and Elaine miraculously approved it. Most of the press judged the book on its own merits, although that one critic who spoke of Elaine's exacting that last pound of flesh from the Great Profile, by his Shylockian allusion, proved positively that poor Mrs. Barrymore would go to her grave as Elaine Jacobs.

We sold to paperback and there was a slight flurry of recall when Elaine was interviewed, but the book died aborning. The public no longer cared about Ariel and Caliban and their dusty shenanigans.

When *Saturday Review* called and asked to do a piece, Elaine and I met with the reporter at the Stork Club, and for over an hour and a half Elaine honestly and charmingly deferred to me as I tried to answer all of the man's questions concerning our work. When the article was published, I was neither mentioned as coauthor nor codrinker. It was precisely as if I hadn't been there at all. It had been a rather chic séance and evidently the journalist, like most people, just didn't believe in ghosts.

Elaine didn't fare much better and soon left for Haiti. If we had depended on our wages from those *Sins Remembered,* we both would have starved to death.

Bette
Davis

It was when Elaine Barrymore left me writing at the church before our renegotiation that a mutual friend told me that she had just had a long talk about me with Bette Davis. "I told her all about you, Leggins," the brilliant Kaye Ballard said, "and she wants to meet you."

The actress was desperately looking for a writer with whom she could work on her autobiography, and Kaye didn't have the slightest doubt that I was the perfect choice. It was, I said, most astute of her and when could we get together and was she joking because if she were it would be—all things considered—the grisliest of jests. Bette Davis! Kaye simply batted her gorgeous green eyes and asked if I were free on Tuesday night to come to the Blue Angel where she was appearing and she'd reserve a table for us. Was I free on Tuesday? I could think of nothing that could deter me but death—and so it was arranged.

I always judge artists by their best work; it is the only way. Everyone can be terrible, few can be great. When Bette Davis is good, she's magnificent. And I have seen her magnificent often. With Garbo off the screen since 1941, there was no question that, as the first actress of the screen, Davis, though she had begun to imitate herself, could not only buck any wind but pull herself out of any doldrums as well, and through her own impetus. By the time she was "through" in pictures in 1950, she returned as the last-minute replacement for an ailing Claudette Colbert to do her best work yet in *All About Eve,* giving a bravura performance of remarkable subtlety. Having always found her brilliant, fascinating, and sexy, I could barely contain my enthusiasm and anxiety. What would the great Miss Davis think of me? I went off to the night-club without the vaguest notion of how I'd fare, but in full knowledge that at least Kaye would have given me advance publicity unequaled in zeal by anyone since Saul of Tarsus.

Bette Davis arrived at the club on the arm of Fred Ebb, who—in those pre-*Cabaret* days—was writing special material for Kaye. Miss Davis was appropriately in leopard skins, though the spiked club was not in evidence. She was very fetching that night in her leopard culottes and jacket, her blonde hair bobbing, her immense blue eyes ogling, her nervous, veined hands fluttering like agitated birds. She was not a disappointment. She arrived as Bette Davis.

A group of us sat at a tiny table in the semidarkness typical of such clubs, the only light on the matter supplied by me as I kept lighting Miss Davis's eternal cigarette, a pre-women's liberation convention now relinquished but then still extant, and which she accepted with one blanket "thank you" early in the game. This was a queen, and that was that. We all of us discussed Kaye's immense talent, which, along with the rest of us, she greatly admired, and the theater in general. It was fun hearing her candid views on everything and everybody; and though she never looked me in the eye once all evening and though I was simply a human cigarette lighter, I felt, with stargazing sentimentality, that I was now part of theater lore.

It is amazing how powerful is the myth of these famous players, how residually effective the years of glamorous exposure and legend building. If one adds to these an honest respect for accomplishment one comes up with idolatry, which Miss Davis has greatly enjoyed from many. She has, of course, become a cult. Passionate, intelligent, dedicated and strong, it is not Tom Strongheart I am describing, but Bette Davis.

In the public's eye she is a termagant. In Spain she has always been called *La Lupa*, the she-wolf, but to me she is certainly a cat lady, a feline familiar posing as a woman so she can get her work on earth done undisturbed. Only her laugh, her claws, and her extravagant gift for survival reveal her origin. Bette Davis is a primeval force, and I don't believe now that she or anyone else could have halted her triumphant stalk through the Hollywood jungle or the ravages that lay in her wake. We are just lucky that Bette chose the theater as her milieu. Her produce has been well worth the dust she raised. If I think of her as a head of state or general of the Wacs, my blood curdles. The world would be a different place today, which might not be—on reflection—such a terrible prospect. It is the glory of the creative process that those powerful needs and aggressions that so often attend the artist enrich us all when properly harnessed.

Sitting there in the Blue Angel, knowing her only through her characterizations and my own instincts, I am aware that I was observing her in a social situation which demanded containment. She seemed to like Fred Ebb and deferred to him in a very feminine manner. She seemed not to like me and only laughed silently at my frequent attempts to be uproariously witty. I knew that this first meeting was important and despite all sorts of campaign tactics previously planned, I found, as always in my life, I could not check my nervous, spontaneous flow of chatter.

It was not until we all repaired in the wee hours to the comedienne's little dressing room and I felt time running out and Miss Davis running down, that I interrupted the general babble and whispered hoarsely, "I hear that you might be interested in working with me, Miss Davis."

"Why don't you call me after Christmas when I'll have time to think," she aswered softly. "Right after the first, perhaps."

"I will wish away the time, Miss Davis," I replied with the zeal of an Elizabethan courtier. But like the sovereign with whom she has always so identified, her pronunciamento had ended this subject and she had turned to say her farewells to our hostess.

Early in January when I called Miss Davis, she invited me to her house on East Seventy-eighth Street. She had rented it for the year, and it was charming. She answered the front door herself and she looked wonderful in daylight—very soignée in a beautifully tailored pants suit with a fine diamond pin. Her hair was beautifully groomed, her makeup judicious. It was all in the finest taste, her lovely house filled with her own New England furniture. Bette Davis that January day was the great lady and the proper daughter of her sometime screen mother, Gladys Cooper. The old lady would have been proud of her. This was not a film star, but a woman of quality.

She led me into a formal drawing room, its only hint of Hollywood the two Oscars that balanced her mantelpiece, over which I seem to remember a not very good portrait of her.

Though she was considered past her peak, over the hill, in a deep valley of her career, Bette Davis was not one to be pitied or patronized. That has, I imagine, been an impossibility since her childhood. If she were never to work again, her star would be fixed. She has been too great for too long ever to be obscured in any way. I was impressed by her that afternoon. She was alert, intelligent and well versed.

She also listened as well as spoke that first day. She was quite obviously taking my measure; the lady was interviewing me for a job, after all. Still, as many a good housekeeper before her, she and her household were also on trial and being seen by the applicant at their best. There are women who shine their houses up before a new cleaning woman arrives, and this is not vanity but good sense. This is the standard to which she expects the employee to repair.

Bette Davis was scrubbed, waxed, and polished to an inch of her life at our first interview. But she was not a hothouse flower. She might have been on her best behavior but it was Bette Davis all the way—simply at her best. She was direct and honest.

She now asked if she could read my book on Dagmar. She was, of course, interested in seeing how I wrote. I explained that I had written the memoir in a manner I thought appropriate for the lady whose words they were supposed to be, and that I would adjust my style to approximate hers were I to be entrusted with her book.

"I understand. Of course. My God, is that a ladybug?" she cried as she leaned forward to look in my lapel.

"Yes. I've always loved them and a friend gave me this in Paris. It's brought me luck so far. I was rather hoping that—"

"I'll be right back, Mr. Dody."

She fled from the room only to return a moment later with a felt hat. The brim was pinned up Aussie style with a ladybug.

"Do you think they're relatives?" she asked with a smile and I knew that it had, indeed, brought me luck.

I sent Dagmar's book on, and Bette called me immediately. The women were so dissimliar that I again was sure that Davis would brush the entire concoction away as a dedicated weight-watcher might an apple strudel.

"I love Daggie!" she announced, using Dagmar's nickname. "She's honest and warm and witty and I loved the way you handled Mutzie. You know, I have a mother, too, and she's great *but!* Anyway, Daggie is a fascinating dame. I want you," she concluded.

"And I want you, Miss Davis."

"Bette!" she corrected me.

"Bette."

"Now there's only one fly in the ointment," she continued. "You're too good to want to do this one without credit and Putnam is insistent that no one but me has it. It's stupid, but they feel the public will more quickly buy the book if it thinks I've written it. I'm an actress, not a writer. It's so unreasonable; and why in God's name would you want to do this without credit?"

How dear she was.

"They made this very definite with their writer," she went on and my heart sank.

I wanted Bette Davis obviously. I knew her book would give me prestige and sales. I knew that her book could be a best seller if I did a fairly decent job, something I never even in my dreams imagined the Godowsky book could be. But the indignity of the ghost status was such that I was now in a dilemma. I had hoped that Davis, a New Englander of candor and secure ego, already world famous, would allow me collaborative credit. Obviously she wanted to. There was always something in this world to take the edge off of happiness, always the dark cloud that ruined the silver lining. Like getting a windfall and immediately needing your teeth fixed. It was a sad situation. A day before I would have been ecstatic that the Davis book was mine for the accepting. And now, though it was— thanks to the great, big, fat Italian heart of Kaye Ballard —I would get no credit.

This was only our second meeting, and Bette had made me a lovely lunch in a far more informal setting. We sat in her library looking over her garden, now frosted and bare, *like the hearts of the gods,* I thought. *This is where we probably would work. My God, this is Bette Davis and the job is mine.* But I dreaded a repetition of the bitterness I was made to feel with Dagmar. *But, of course, we didn't even sell any books. In this case I'll be compensated with a fortune.*

"It's going to be tough enough to have them accept you at all, but as far as *I'm* concerned—and I'm who counts—you're in."

My invisible agent, who was also Elaine Barrymore's, was a nice *Mittel*-European gentleman. He was thrilled when I informed him of the flirtation I was having with Davis. Elaine's infidelity had driven me to this and I had every intention of pressing my suit. He agreed. When the time came, I had told him, he could do the negotiating, but we were still in the first stages of the courtship. I wondered if he could help me to get the credit I wanted so badly, and from his past unassertive performance with Elaine and me, plus Putnam's preferences, I thought I might do better myself.

"Tell me, Bette. Would you be willing to give me an acknowledgment, inside the book itself, not on the cover but inside, if they're so adamant about the other and I can't get it? I want you very much, but I really just couldn't sell myself this short. It isn't fair."

"Of course I will," Bette replied. "I'll not only give you a glowing acknowledgment if it all works out but

I swear I'll fight to get you the real credit you deserve as the writer. I promise."

We looked at each other for a whole minute.

"Then it's a deal as far as I'm concerned. Of course," I suddenly remembered, "there's the question, the vulgar question of money. Dagmar and I split fifty-fifty."

"That," Bette responded wisely, "is something that you and I must never discuss—business—if we are to be as close as you tell me and I know that this work demands. Our lawyers can solve it all."

She was all smiles now.

"I assure you it will be all right. I always know these things and I want you. You're right for me. I can tell. You won't be unhappy. I'd be a fool if you were. The work wouldn't, couldn't be as good. That's something the Warners never learned and Sam Goldwyn always knew. He always got the best and paid for it."

I called the agent with the good news and gave him the telephone number of Miss Davis's lawyer, who was momentarily somewhere in Maryland. Bette and I couldn't have been more delighted. She would be in New York for a year, only visiting her mother back in California, but not even that until the children were finished with school. She made a sacred oath, after hearing about Dagmar, that she would give me an eight-hour, five-day week until I had sufficient material. Certainly for two months, since it was still January, and perhaps more if necessary. I might add that she never wavered from fulfilling this promise, and was even more professional and dependable than her reputation had already suggested.

My saintly agent called the next day.

"I'll find something else for you," was the first sentence out of his mouth. "You'll never work with Bette Davis. Forget her!" was the second.

"Forget her?" I fear I screamed. "I barely know her. Are you mad?"

"It's bad news, Sandy. Her lawyer won't come near what you want. Not even a quarter of it."

This financial wizard, whose function was to take care of business far beyond the grasp of artists, I discovered, had offered to accept an absurdly low percentage, which was still refused.

"It's too bad. Please forget Bette Davis. You'll never work with her," he repeated.

"Oh yes I will," I said, knowing that Miss Davis wanted me and knowing that Miss Davis got what she wanted no matter what. In this case it would be somewhat on my terms.

I was dining at the home of a friend, Sidmore Parnes, who refilled my glass and sat in amazement as he listened to me call Bette on his telephone. I had been unable to get her all day. I was distressed and let her know it. I didn't understand how her lawyer delivered such ultimata as I'd heard about a negotiation; and I couldn't understand how such a marvelous project could be destroyed by his rigidity. I must have become emotional and words like "injustice" and "indignity" abounded.

Bette at that time adored Tom Hammond, her lawyer, and suggested that something must have gone wrong with my agent. She now suggested that I deal with Hammond myself, which I did the following day, negotiating a fairly satisfactory deal after seven hours of friendly argument. I can only imagine that in the breaks in our conversation, the lawyer was relaying my sensible demands to the actress. All in all I fared very well in percentages, although a limit was put on my earnings. At that time, though, I found the ceiling high enough to accommodate my big head. I was now going to do the life of Bette Davis. What did money matter? Wasn't it more important that my stock as a writer and biographer rise with such an exalted association?

I was to receive from Bette the first installment of my share of her advance when I signed the contract with her, which also allowed her an out if she wasn't satisfied with my work after three or four chapters. My arrogance was so great at this point that it never occurred to me to demur at such a request. I was that sure that Davis would be pleased. Nonetheless when she now—since money was involved—asked sweetly if I would perhaps give her a sample chapter to make her even more secure, I decided against it. For my own edification, I had done about ten pages in a manner I thought perfect for Bette Davis; it sounded like Bette Davis and had, I believed, style. It was a pastiche of proclamations, about herself and everyone else, that set the tone of the book—frank, unsentimental and driving. I rather liked it as a test but I had given in enough.

"I really think, Bette, that it's a little unseemly for me to audition at this point in my life."

"Good for you," she replied. "You're quite right and I respect you for it. Good for you," she repeated happily. "I'll see you Monday morning at ten on the nose."

It seemed wise at this juncture to speak to the publishers and inform them that the ball would start rolling; Bette gave me the name of our editor, who was then vice-president of Putnam—Howard Cady. I called him and received, for different reasons, the kind of reception with which Viking had first greeted me. Mr. Cady informed me that Miss Davis had refused the company's help and was not being cooperative, and had received a generous advance. He wasn't in the slightest bit interested in hearing my ideas or even speaking with me. The actress was acting unilaterally and without their sanction, and the whole business was an outrage.

I seemed doomed to these strange relationships with publishers. He really wasn't very kind to me, and Bette, when she heard about it, was furious that her writer was treated rudely. But she was also typically resolved.

"Sandy, my dear, there's one way to end all of this nonsense with Putnam. We are going to give them one hell of a book! Remember, ten sharp, Monday."

And we happily signed our contract.

I was sitting with Bette amidst the happy clutter of her library, a blue notebook on my lap, my hand twirling a pencil. My legs dangled over the arm of the fresh chintz-covered chair near the fire which raged at my back. A glowing Bette Davis in jeans faced me across the room, her feet very much on the ground, her head in a cloud of home-made smoke. Pottery hens stuffed with cigarettes were strewn around the room, along with slop bowls filled with kitchen matches. When she wants a smoke, she means business. She doesn't have to reach, no matter where she happens to be. In those days, I was still smoking, and between the two of us the room looked like an opium den at Walden Pond.

At my prodding, Bette was remembering, reliving, never regretting. We had just touched an old wound and I thought I'd give her a breather.

She had told me of her father's abandonment of his little family, his abandonment of her, her mother's faith, and her father's absolute indifference to her, but her face flushed with anger as she recalled a rejection that still—and more apparently—rankled.

Bette had just admitted an early defeat, had confessed that if ever she could have had a total mental breakdown, this would have been the time. It was not a romantic entanglement, an unrequited passion, a family crisis. It was her rejection as a student at the Civic Repertory Company on Fourteenth Street, and by Eva Le Gallienne herself. It was then the only dramatic school she could afford and her failure to pass muster was a catastrophe—or so she had thought. Bette's work, her career, would always come first, and its success or lack would effect her more than anything.

She would never get over that unsuccessful audition, conducted when she was nineteen and obliging her to play a Dutch woman of sixty-five. She had flared in rebellion at what she felt was an unfair test of her talent, and Miss Le Gallienne had not reacted favorably to her reaction, which might have been the problem. She was all ice as she dampened the hellion's spirit. If she hadn't recognized the spark, she certainly didn't extinguish the flame. Nothing could stop Bette Davis.

This professional rejection stuck in her craw. Perhaps, she was as angry with herself.

"I was so awful. I heard myself drone on and on and I couldn't stop. I had started and couldn't stop and I felt the disapproval. I felt the chill; but that's why I wanted to enroll with her, to *learn,* to *cope* with just this sort of challenge. And I told her so!" she added, eyes popping.

She couldn't get over this failure. It was astonishing. In the face of her subsequent accomplishments and celebrity, the scene becomes ironic, satisfying—feeding, as it does, the myth. But Bette would always smart from defeat, though her fame has eclipsed the splendid Miss Le Gallienne and her talents have long been unquestioned by anyone.

I watched her nervously stack magazines, carefully lining them up. She now rearranged some objects on the coffee table. Her quick gestures helped to dissipate the energy the old anger had generated. Pretending to write

120

busily, I drew a caricature of her, and the light from the fire played upon it seeming to make the face mobile. The expression changed. Even a likeness of her fought repose.

The actress had kept her promise. At ten o'clock on the nose each weekday she would descend the stairs ("My directors always had me suffering on staircases.") and we would work straight through to cocktail time.

She was fifty-three years old at this point and although time had altered what I believe was once beauty, she was still an attractive woman radiating health and energy. In contradiction to Dagmar, every ounce of her was used productively. Unlike Elaine, here was a woman whose talents, attention span, and sense of direction matched her dreams. There she was, divorced from Gary Merrill, her fourth husband, and superbly running her house, down the stairs of which—just before her appearance—would tumble her attractive children, B.D. and Michael, on their way to school.

"If anyone should ever ask me about the winter of nineteen sixty-one," she loved to say, "I shall tell them it was totally Sandy Dody and the dentist!"

Lucky for both of us, the dentist and me. He got her mouth in perfect order and I got her to open it. Her cooperation was exemplary. Not before or since have I been given the dedicated cooperation I received from Bette Davis. As a collaborator and as a hostess, she was indefatigable, gracious, and disciplined.

Although she was at all times responsive, she was still, those first couple of weeks, reserved. We were still feeling each other out, she was still "on," her makeup and clothes casual but exacting, her strong views revealing her work rather than her emotions, her tastes rather than her commitments. Every day she opened up a little more. She was a fascinating subject, Bette, frankly made up of two selves. Ruth Elizabeth Davis, a neat, bright, affectionate New

England girl who longed for husband, children, and a home with samplers, and Bette, a raging force hell-bent to perfect and present her own gifts to the world and willing to sacrifice Ruth Elizabeth's dreams to do it. The women were always in battle. Ruth Elizabeth was virtually defenseless against such power as Bette had. The former was down if not out and the latter strutting still, but scarred by the conflict.

One only had to look at Bette's face to know that she was ravaged by her own passions, that she was possessed—driven, and far beyond the strictures that Ruth Elizabeth and her species could impose on themselves, Bette could do this as an artist, however, and therein lay her brilliance. When she wasn't working she was a cyclone locked in a linen closet.

Davis had done nothing professionally important since *All About Eve* ten years before. After her successful tour in *The World of Carl Sandburg* and her Broadway revue *Two's Company,* sickness and divorce had filled her life. Another Academy nomination for *Baby Jane* was in the near future—there would always be something but it didn't matter, I mused. Her star is fixed.

In barely two weeks, although we were to become infinitely closer, we had already arrived at such rapport that I really wasn't surprised when she interrupted my reverie. Father-confessor and sinner were already becoming one. It was remarkable how attuned we were to become.

"You know," she said softly as she lighted her thousandth cigarette, "every star that lasts is known for one or two roles, roles the public identifies them with. Garbo will always be Camille and Anna Karenina, Gable is Rhett, Laughton Ruggles of Red Gap and Henry the Eighth. I have been lucky—very lucky. I must have a dozen. And that's why," she added with no vanity whatsoever, "my star will never fade—no matter what."

We stared at each other and I didn't even bother—
nor need I have—to record that I was thinking the same
thing. It was becoming a commonplace. Of course, what
she said that day was true. There are few actresses who
have created more memorable parts—some of them in pot-
boilers which she dignified simply by her presence. Some
were the kind of Sardoodledom that kept Bernhardt such
a busy woman in the *Belle Époque*. Anyone of a dozen or
more performances would justify Davis's fame. Most screen
favorites when sentimentally recalled seem to smile through
a vague progression of pictures each melting one into
the other. A Davis devotee can—at the drop of her name
—recall in sequence a stunning series of characterizations
which she managed to create, almost always, without the
best scripts. With few exceptions—*Of Human Bondage,
Jezebel, The Little Foxes, Dark Victory,* and *All About
Eve* (all extraordinary performances)—most of her pictures were sow's ears she not only transformed but filled
with cash, despite her greatly shared conviction to the
contrary.

Bette was legend. I had first seen her in *Seed* when
I was a kid and I went on to contribute almost single-
handedly to Warner Brothers' coffers for the next twenty-
five years. I rarely saw a Davis film only twice. I thought
I knew, through years of closeups and angle shots, every
nuance of her. Now I was in her home and catching
glimpses I never dreamed of.

She had thrown herself wholeheartedly (as she does
everything) into the mother-and-housekeeper role. When
I had arrived a couple of weeks before, a couple—butler
and maid—had just left for some forgotten reason, and
Bette was quite typically going to replace them both—one
for two—and the house would sparkle and function as
never before.

I used to call her Bette Dervish. The end of one job

simply heralded the start of the next. If she wasn't polishing the silver or brass, she was darning socks and knees of breeches or waxing furniture. Life to this passionate pilgrim is work. I almost believe that she gets a sensual pleasure out of labor. It is some erotic compulsion, this need not only to govern the affairs of man but to alter matter as well. There is no part of the terrain that escapes her eye or is not meant to be improved by her interference.

Though Bette is undeniably God's sister-in-law, her advice was ignored at the Beginning and the Good Lord knows *that* was the original sin—the entire mess in Eden being the result. A barbed wire 'round the apple tree, a more stringent screening of the tenants' applications, a little fumigation—in short, a bit more attention to detail—and the story would have been different.

I will give this to Bette Davis. She never wastes time in self-pity or in ancient bitterness. The fact remains that God didn't listen to her; hence things are not perfect, ergo she must work twenty-five hours a day to make them so. Bette learns fast. She has never again volunteered her advice, simply her service. *Cut out the middleman* is her motto, and an intimidated Lord has allowed her her way more often than not.

She certainly tidied things up somewhat, definitely improving and cultivating not only Warners' but her own lot, of which, along with Voltaire, we should all approve. What is good for Bette has been pretty good for the general public. Bette Davis is the greatest of stars. And we all know what that means. Well—one does not complain when a giant of a man stoops to enter a low-ceilinged room. One doesn't say, "Look at that terrible posture. Look at the ugly line of the neck and the hunch of the back." Unlike the rest of us, he has had to accommodate his outsized body to the mean dimensions of his environment. He may have to deform himself momentarily in order to traffic with his fellows, but outside of their milieu and in the world at large he is able to reach heights unapproachable to them. We understand his social predicament because it is a physical phenomenon and easily observed.

But what of the outsized emotion, the grand passion, the genius of some individuals? These heroic endowments, when not employed in field or studio, are equally unadaptable in a society scaled to lesser men. The need for adjustment demands of a giant a like contortion. He is not like other people, and when attempting to have tea in a dollhouse, he is reviled for breaking the china.

We must pay for everything in this world—especially for greatness—and no matter the talent, there really are no gifts. It was one of the many things that Bette Davis and I agreed on. She was much too wise to have expected to steal the whole show and also get off scot-free, so she was pleased when we said in *The Lonely Life,* "There are no gifts. The gods are Yankee traders." It is one of Miss Davis's many strengths that she has always been ready to pay her way. What she demands and exacts from others with pressure she herself gives naturally. As an artist she is highly respectable. As a worker she is indefatigable.

I think, after all our talk on the subject, that she understands as well as accepts the price for her career. One cannot achieve such stature without dwarfing the men around one and consequently earning their eternal resentment. She has come to live with all of this too. She has learned to live with everything except a husband, and this, (as *The Lonely Life* explains) has also been inevitable. Surely it hasn't been because the lady is not a homemaker. It is because she, herself, is such a powerhouse. As Bette herself, along with her mother and other New Englanders, might say, she is a caution.

The vibrations between us were at their best, my

work going along smoothly, when Bette—after about two weeks—innocently asked me if I had seen the recent interview that David Susskind had done with Nikita Khrushchev. We had been speaking of men, and Bette—pretty hard to please in that department—gave Mr. Susskind as an example of an attractive one. One doesn't argue that kind of thing, and so I simply took note of her taste. I always found that a genuine colloquy rather than interrogation brought about the best results in my work. Easy conversation monitored to a slight degree by me, usually only in choice of daily topic (childhood, career, family, philosophy), allowed spontaneity and unpressured revelation. Bette and I liked each other, both had lots to say and talked eight hours a day and could have extended it. Great things happened. But today Mr. Susskind dominated the dialogue.

"Don't you think it was a brilliant interview?" Bette now asked, allowing, I believed, her libido to blind her.

"I'm afraid not, Bette. In fact, I found it embarrassing."

Her blue eyes flashed.

"An embarrassment? To *whom?*" she now asked, using that strange technique she had developed late in her career of catching her breath and audience attention between syllables. Em-bar-rass-ment! She could even, when pressed, manage to split a syllable and did now.

"To who-um!"

"Well, to me, for one, and I think to the country."

"I-would-like-to-know-why?"

This latter question in the staccato rhythm of a death sentence imposed by the last Manchu empress.

Before I could answer, she allowed me a little room to maneuver or at least reconsider. This was obviously not arguable opinion, but dictum.

"I think he's great, and I think it was a brilliant interview."

She was serious, I realized.

"Well, Bette—he certainly managed to land a plum. It was quite a feat to get the head of all the Russias on his little program—a miracle—and for that I give him high marks as a go-getter; but that's it for the credit side."

"Whhhhhh-y?"

"Because after landing Khrushchev, whom everybody else wanted as a guest, he proved too mean-spirited to be a gracious host."

"What?"

"Because with one eye on Nixon and the red-baiters, he was so petrified that he'd be considered soft on communism that he spent the entire program being insolent, accomplishing the reverse of his plan."

"What plan?"

"The plan to discredit him—Khrushchev—and single-handedly show America what a good little American he—Susskind—is. Gad! What a performance. Do you know what he accomplished, Bette?"

"I'm eager to hear!"

I was, and had to be, calm.

"By having anti-Soviet commercials between the breaks, which was unthinkably tasteless, and by his impudent behavior to an elderly head of state, this snotnose managed—all by himself—to change Nikita's blustering Tartar image into that of a lovable old moujik. When Khrushchev asked your friend how old he was and then simply remarked that he had a son his age and didn't he think he should be treated with a little more respect, the television public was unexpectedly treated to a circus featuring a power-drunk showoff and an intimidated but patient bear. Not only was Susskind *un*kind, but witless

127

as well. If you don't mind my saying it, Bette, it was—
on the contrary—an outrageous performance!"

"But I *do* mind!" Bette now shouted, as she rose from
the couch and stalked to the fireplace. She popped a cigarette into her mouth, grabbed a long kitchen match and
struck it on the seat of her pants in a grand gesture. She
now kicked a log for good measure. There was a lot of
heat in that room that February day.

"Now hear this!" she puffed, and I closed my notebook over my pencil as she went into an eloquent rage
before my unbelieving eyes.

She was enraged with me and now sang the praises of
Mr. Susskind, while she reviled me for my lack of judgment, my arrogance, and my own grandstanding on the
subject. It was quite a scene and as it went on, I became,
for the first time, a bit concerned. Bette and I had had
discussions before and we both liked to hold forth, so I had
felt no compunction about delivering my little speech on
the television show in question. But Bette was being Bette
Davis in one of her own films. She was having one of her
famous "let him have it" outbursts. She was seething,
contemputous, lethal.

The argument she was making was indefensible to me,
her flag-waving not worthy of her. Most disturbing, however, was her overreaction to my opposing view and this,
my first encounter with the temperament which was as
legendary as her talent. The tongue-lashing was suddenly
over and Miss Davis looked at me steadily, her nostrils
flaring, the back of her wrist beating her hip in cheap
imitation of herself. She made another try.

"And *now* what do you think?" The tone was omi-
nous.

"Exactly what I felt before. Nothing has changed,
Bette. Susskind didn't have the courage of his convictions
and made a hero out of someone he wanted to prove a

128

villain. From any point of view he botched it up. I really don't think we are getting anywhere, dear, and our book is more important."

One does not brush Bette Davis aside. Nor write her scenes. The follow-up was awful. I do not exaggerate when I say that she now pulled out all stops. Smoke and flame were escaping from her every orifice. Eyes were rolling, hands were flying, cigarettes waving. She crouched before me as if to spring. I was terrified. Expletive followed expletive. Her range of invective was endless, her fury coloratura. This was an aria, the kind she handled so brilliantly in *Of Human Bondage* (nomination number one) and *Dangerous* (Oscar number one). I half-expected her to call me "gimpy-legged monster, a cripple, a cripple, a cripple!" as she had Leslie Howard.

While fascinated that we were making history of a kind and that I was a twenty-year-late replacement for the silken actor, as a writer I watched us with omnivorous eyes, treasuring every decibel, though my heart was thumping and I felt sick to my stomach. Not even my father—in his prime and my nonage—had been so terrible to behold. This was a sorceress, and if at the end of her maledictions I was not dead or turned to stone, I was surely going to be out of a job. This was not a scene one survived, much less forgot.

I just couldn't sit like a mesmerized spectator at my own death, so I put my pencil in my pocket, and closed my notebook, my eyebrows raised in self-consciously patient acceptance of her fit. It was meant—the expression— to save face. Her rage was something to study. It had form. It peaked, it rested, it replenished itself and rose higher, it plateaued, it became textured. It was horizontal and then again vertical, climbing, climbing—and then came the climax.

Bette now stood directly in front of me, her feet

planted far apart. She threw her cigarette into the hearth, her fists were now placed on her hips. She lowered her gaze and bared her teeth. The voice was steady with the heat of dry ice.

"And *now* what do you think of Mr. Susskind?"

It was obviously the end of our relationship if I didn't agree with her. She would have it no other way. This marvelous book I knew I could write was going down the drain, and with it the chance to pay off my debts not only to others but to myself. This book I felt would be a success. Wasn't there some *good* compromise I could make at this point? Wouldn't I be stupid to throw away a chance like this because of David Susskind? Hadn't good men always been forced to compromise in order to arrive or consolidate themselves once there? *If Franklin Roosevelt could in 1936 refuse to lift the embargo to Spain in order to insure the Catholic vote, why can't I be expedient? Because it was a mistake,* I answered myself. *Because he would have won the election anyway and the world might have been a better place. Anyway, my mouth is too big to make the presidency.*

Bette had a bead on me. She wouldn't even blink those eyes.

"Well, *Mr.* Dody?" she demanded.

I didn't have long to decide, and it was really a simple decision. Who in hell cared about David Susskind? It wasn't that. It was the whole idea that made my stomach turn. It would also herald an impossible future with her. Better good-bye, now. Fast.

"Bette," I said slowly, "volume has never lent credence to an argument. We will never agree if we argue this the rest of our lives. I'm sorry, but that's the way I feel. Now please let's not waste any more of our session. It's been too good so far."

This last remark was a tacit refusal to accept our

obvious fallout as the finish. Bette now did something amazing. She stamped her foot and turned to the mantel, from which she grabbed another cigarette, lighting it in her favorite way, by striking her bottom—an excellent idea, I thought at the time. She then marched to the couch and sat down, opening a scrapbook so she could pretend to busy herself. I, in turn, waited for the ax to fall and pretended to study my notes. *The longer the silence,* I remember thinking, *the healthier for me.*

We did not look at each other for a few minutes and the air slowly to be sure—started to clear a little. My mouth was dry, but I didn't dare clear my throat. There could be no sound of any kind until the right moment. The fever hadn't broken yet. It seemed much longer, of course, but about ten minutes later I asked Miss Davis a not too personal but necessary question whose answer would break the ice without creating an avalanche. Others followed and within a half hour our work was continuing effectively. The storm had passed, and I didn't know how I had survived it. I soon found out.

Bette answered the phone at one point and after a brief conversation she ambled over to the fireplace to stoke the fire on her way back to the couch. She turned to me with a smile.

"You're not in awe of me are you, Sandy?"

Her tone was neither threatening nor unpleasant.

"As an actress, as an artist, yes. Perhaps I am. As a woman and a subject, *no.* If I were we would have a lousy book."

She now extended her hand which I took.

"We will never have another argument, my dear," she said. And we never did.

I realized then that the whole scene was a screening, a test which I passed by not buckling under. I was to learn that Bette Davis did this to directors, writers, husbands—

men. If one buckled she became insecure. She wasn't interested in bucklers or yes-men. She wanted to trust someone and she set standards which few passed. All her professional and personal life, Bette sought the strength she suspected that she alone had. This she readily admitted. What she only later allowed was that she sought the struggle to the death as well—when she found it. Bette is a warrior by nature. She loves the sparking of flint against flint. Who could have dreamed that that was a performance? She's that good, ladies and gentlemen.

If I had agreed with her after those mad scenes, I would really have been out. Bette now trusted me completely and from that afternoon on, she not only remained wonderfully cooperative, but in her deep trust, allowed me to dig deep. Bette opened her heart to me. There was little, if anything, she withheld as time went on, and my work went swimmingly as we developed, I believe, a great mutual regard.

Our workdays more and more extended beyond drink time through dinner, where I would join her guests like a visiting psychiatrist or doctor in residence. She would more often than not introduce me not only as a friend, but as "the man who is working on my book," and insist that rather than the work she had expected that it was marvelous fun. I heartily agreed. It was. In the first place, her opinions concerning her work and her colleagues interested me. The slow awakening to her own motivations and their employment in her art intrigued me. That she was an excellent cook didn't hurt and that she danced like an angel made the evenings lovely. The kids would put on records and Bette and I would occasionally give them an exhibition. She was really wonderful—all in all an enviable partner. When I thought of the cluttered days with Dagmar and the empty ones with Elaine, I knocked wood. My work on *The Lonely Life* was certainly made painless by Bette's social grace and love of work.

"What do you usually eat for lunch, dear?" she had asked at the beginning.

"Anything simple," I had answered.

And Bette would make me simple filet mignons or chops or perfect omelettes, when there wasn't a superb encore from the night before.

"Bring up your sweaters. I'll Woolite them with the kids' stuff," Regina Hubbard would suggest. "God, how dirty clean little boys can get."

Yes, I was fond of Bette Davis. Now that we were *en rapport,* she revealed great insight about herself, or at least a willingness to acknowledge—once I introduced them—the demons that possessed her. She was, as most of us, simply helpless to change. There were many mornings when Bette would look at me balefully as she made her first entrance down the stairs.

"You," she would say, accusingly as she pointed at me. "You! I dreamed last night about something we were talking about and I realized—much to my distress—that you were perfectly right. Father's departure *was* and *is* to be reckoned with, something I'll never get over. Isn't it something how those wounds never really heal no matter? Do you mean that with all men—?"

Bette was strong. She was unwilling to blame her parents even when they were blamable. I remember her saying one day, "If you're born cockeyed, have them fixed or become a comic. Only shut up about it." Good for her. But in an autobiography, as in life, it may be to one's advantage to know what propels one even if one is powerless to control it. Words can not only express what one feels, but often by their very employment shed light on shadowy, unformed thoughts, so that by the very process of tracing them, one for the first time draws a conclusion. I suspect that our book gave Bette Davis more insight than she formerly possessed. After all, she was busy living her life and achieving her goals. She had no time to look inward. Bette was a doer, and though Helen Hayes's great career is as legendary and took as much discipline and work and drive, she has had spiritual ambitions and an occasional serenity, both of which allow for true reflection.

Although Bette is intelligent, she is essentially emotional, instinctive—reacting immediately with either a yelp of pleasure or a groan of pain to the latest that life has to offer. Her children did not live in a dull household.

The children were attractive, Bette's daughter B.D. (Barbara Davis) Merrill an extension of herself and therefore the apple of her eye. She was barely fourteen at the time, tall and pretty and physically precocious. Like many young girls she adored horses and unlike most, she was, through her mother's devotion, the owner of one. She used to ride in Central Park every day and showed promise of becoming a fine horsewoman. (Judy Traherne in *Dark Victory?*) Bette's son, Michael Merrill, was a remarkably handsome boy of seven. If B.D. had her mother's confidence and outgoing personality, manly little Michael kept his own counsel. Though amiable, he seemed a rather grave little boy and perhaps a trifle tentative. I felt a depth in him, a self-containment unusual in one so young. He lived in a household with two strong women and perhaps had to steer a course between Scylla and Charybdis, both of whom he evidently loved. Bette, in turn, adored both kids and enjoyed roughhousing with Michael, partially to give him the kind of tough, physical affection a father who was not absent might supply, and also, I'm certain, because she enjoyed it.

Mother and son would sometimes roll all over the floor, wrestling and laughing gaily, though I always felt that the boy was conscious that he was romping with a leopardess simply in the mood for play, a leopardess who might in a change of mood devour him. Still, Bette had all the earmarks of a conscientious mother. She and Gary Merrill had adopted Michael and also Margot, a third child, when both were five days old. B.D. was her own blood child, born to her and her third husband, William Sherry.

Tragically, it was discovered after almost two years that the curious lethargy and temper tantrums that little Margot displayed were nothing less than symptoms of a brain injury undetectable at birth. The Merrills bravely kept her at home until her involuntary aggressions so threatened the other two children that they were forced to send the child to Geneva, New York, to the Lochland School where she still—I would imagine—resides, happily if vaguely taking Christmas, Easter, and summer holidays with her loyal family. Bette certainly has never shirked a family obligation. I met the unfortunate child a few times during a couple of these visits, and both Michael and B.D. were easy and considerate with their sister, who seemed in her erratic and muffled way to be delighted that she was with all of them. I was particularly touched by Bette's sense of responsibility and the unsentimental manner in which she exercised it.

I was made, in all ways, a member of the family, and was not unmoved at one point when Bette gave me a photograph of herself with all three children and inscribed it, *Such as we are, your gang.* Though Bette was a charming playmate as well as coworker and, since our "scene," almost yielding in her cordiality and desire for my approval, I still couldn't settle for less than illumination of her character, which demanded the ticklish probing that could again threaten our working relationship.

Bette used to describe certain films of hers as productions in which everyone got on famously and all was sweetness and light—"the ice cream factory"—and the picture emerged from all this goo as a stinker. I knew what she meant. One very often has to create waves in order to land anywhere. She has never balked at doing this—nor could I, if I wanted a serious book. I had to avoid the temptation to let well enough alone and be grateful for the lovely atmosphere that now prevailed. And so I poked and delved around and touched nerve ends with some trepidation, and not once did Bette seriously object as she honestly attempted—for the first time in her life—to examine her life and give it form. I wasn't looking for a fight, God knows, but I was willing to risk it.

I was fascinated that Bette Davis—all of her life and on her own admission—respected and sought strong, intelligent men. She had admired her brilliant father and was still looking for his approval, although she would spend the rest of her life punishing him by proxy for abandoning her. No matter how she mourned her father's removal from her young life, she also reveled in not only her survival without him but her eventual displacement of him as breadwinner and father to a family of women and children, including her own mother.

In our work and, indeed, through her honesty and permission in our book, it is made very clear that Bette's ambivalence toward men, her need plus her anger, would inevitably destroy, despite its depth, any relationship with them—including my own. This I had learned through Dagmar: that among my discoveries concerning a subject were the lurking dangers to myself. It is as if I were to do a book on a man who confessed to me, during a particularly gut-spilling session, that he was an unregenerate kleptomaniac. While I was writing the fact down and admiring him for his candor and cooperation, it would simultaneously occur to me not to leave my ring on the bathroom sink. I might not be judgmental, but surely cautious.

Listening to Bette's progressively franker evaluation of men, I did not forget—though she might have—that I, too, belonged to this vulnerable category. In the intimacy of our confessional, like priest or doctor I had supposedly transcended gender, becoming not only her writing hand but alter ego as well. We now got on so famously that one day Bette announced that we were so alike, so independent, so healthy in our own sense of identity— so strong, so fun loving, so talented, and so adorable— that we could probably make it as a couple. It was only fitting that the ceremony follow our honeymoon, which I knew could not last forever. Like her son, I knew that I was cavorting with a jungle creature and I could be clawed to death at a moment's notice.

"Do you know why we get on so well, Bette?"

At this point, my every observation was being treated like the latest bulletin from Delphi, and Bette lighted another cigarette and hugged her knees in happy expectation.

"Because we *are* independent, because we are not involved emotionally. Because we are friends—neighbor sovereigns who respect each other."

Bette Davis is often a gentleman as well as a lady, and she agreed. Anyway, I was still to do no wrong. Bette was feeling safe with a male. She was being approved of by a man she respected, who, she had properly intuited, was going to be a positive force in her life. In much the same manner as a patient first resists and then falls in love with his analyst, Bette became most randomly impressed by my opinions, touchingly dependent upon my ability to unravel her tangled emotions and grateful for my reassuring first-told tale.

Papa was leading her out of the wilderness and not even scolding her for running away and getting lost there.

She was being uncritically loved—something, unlike Dagmar, she would never have dreamed of demanding but which by the nature of our work she was receiving. She could unburden herself of anything and know for certain that I would understand.

One afternoon after a particularly good session in which she had probed deeply and offered up an extraordinarily human if self-damning revelation common to all of us, she (and this is in a sense the high point of our relationship) regarded me with real innocence. I never remember any grown person speaking with such ingenuousness.

"How can you like me, Sandy, now that you know how wicked I am?"

She was plaintive and touching.

"But Bette, everyone has thought these things. Some, not even villains, have even acted on them. You have simply—in that typically thorough search into the depths of a characterization—verbalized a humanness lesser, more timid souls would dissemble. How can I *like* you? I adore you for it."

I was shaken by Bette's sweet and childlike terror that she had fallen from grace. It was a facet she rarely has shown in her public and private role as Avenging Angel.

My subjects—despite the impression I seem to be giving—do not always become children in what more and more sounds like my godlike presence. However, it is not entirely untrue that these frantic doers, these people of affairs, who as interpretive artists, for the first time walk through a mirror with me, *do* get lost in a wonderland and don't stray far from their guide. It is a rare experience that is never to be forgotten by either guest or host, but it reaps a strange harvest later.

As writer I always knew that I must profit from our

"oneness" before it shattered—as it always had to. In Bette's case, I didn't know how as yet, but I had seen the notches on the lady's gun belt and I learn from other's experiences if not my own.

"I can't wait until you meet Gary," Bette announced one bright morning. And before she could go on, I noticed that for the first time in weeks she was carefully made up, determined to look her best. Bette loved to rub some rouge on her lower lip and then transfer it to her upper by smacking her lips noisily—with one big pop. It was a wild, uncaring gesture that I saw had not been employed today. A hint of eye shadow, a general freshening and refurbishing were evident. Bette was particularly pretty that day. I mentioned it mischievously. Her eyes sparkled as she pooh-poohed my romantic notion.

"Merrill?" she screamed. "He's coming to visit the kids and I'm putting him up for a few days. I mean why not? He's always living on a friend's couch like he's still in from college, and he might as well be near B.D. and Michael. They adore him. But *dear*, get *that* out of your head."

But her eyes now danced and looked bluer than usual—like the Danube to lovers.

It had always seemed to me that Gary Merrill's name and all facts relating to him—despite the fact that he had suffered the same fate as all the other men in her life— were always considerably softened. I was convinced that as marriages went, this had been a fairly good one. Unlike her other mates, Gary Merrill had his own career, his own celebrity. He has always been a good actor and Bette knew it. If she hadn't, I doubt whether their relationship would ever have ripened enough to go to seed. She never would have bothered. Operative lack of talent is most unattractive in a lover. To be removed from the arts is one thing; to help destroy them is another.

They had met, Davis and Merrill, on the set of *All About Eve*, had doubtless melted into the wonderful characters of Margo Channing and Bill Sampson. They were certainly attracted to each other to begin with, but the magical admixture of art and biology carried them into an extension of the screenplay—a ten-year serial whose residuals outlasted the tenure of their drama. There was the marriage, the work together on stage and screen, there were the children and the memories and the embers in the ashes. I wanted to use the shining brass bellows near me and rekindle the romance.

It was useless, although it was clear that this relationship would always echo with its own sound and fury. Bette's invitation to stay was a sign of goodwill as well as affection of a sort, and Gary Merrill's acceptance and affection revealed that even their antagonisms were comfortable and born of passion and begrudging respect.

"I have a feeling that you and Merrill are going to hit it off. You're both crazy and wear those little tweed hats and old jackets, and Gary is the only man in New York who walks down Fifth Avenue in walking shorts when it's hot. He doesn't give a hoot in hell about anybody but he does have style, Merrill. And he's bright as hell. Do you know Merrill's one fault—as far as I'm concerned —the one *great* error in his life? He should never have gotten married—to *any*one."

I distorted my face in exaggerated shock and she let out a horse laugh.

"And neither should I—I know!" she now added.

"Well. You had a great old time for a while, Bette. Some people never have it all—for five minutes."

"True! And I wouldn't have the kids—and they're *so* great. Really. You and he will hit it off. Merrill!" she concluded, the word taking on the virtue of an improper noun.

"I'm eager to see you together."

"We were together for ten years," she remembered with a smile.

When I met Gary Merrill I was sorry they still weren't married. I liked him immediately and understood why the relationship had lasted as long as it had. He is a highly intelligent man with a strong personality of his own. He knew Bette every which way and had, obviously, the capacity for love. His sense of values was keen, and one felt that though he was a free soul, his loyalties would be deep and, with half a chance, his devotion unwavering. Yes, it was sad that they were not still married—unless I, too, was taken in by the Channing-Sampson fiction. They seemed very right together.

Gary Merrill had a light touch and Bette always insisted that she was humorless—an opinion with which I unreservedly concur. It isn't that she couldn't be amusing or easily amused or even lighthearted on occasion. It is that she is burdened with her gifts—always preoccupied, as most stars, with the business of and fear of no longer twinkling. Gary Merrill laughed at the human comedy in which he was cast. Bette was always doing a rewrite.

Still, they were right together. You smelled and tasted the rightness. There was much more than the intimacy of a divorced couple who had also shared a great professional moment, fated to be lovers to future generations of movie buffs long after their careers and romance and very lives were ended. There was a comfortable enmity. There was an undeniable affection that lurked behind their sardonic acceptance of their separation. It eased a lot of tensions, and was not unpleasant to behold.

Merrill was an expansive man. His acceptance of my presence in the house, knowing that I was going to chronicle his ex-wife's life in "her words" and that his role in the book couldn't possibly—under the present auspices—be a flattering one, was almost saintly. He was amused by the situation. I don't believe he cared a damn what I might say about him, and it was this quality I found so attractive. I had only to watch the children bubble with excitement and Bette primping before his arrival to know he couldn't be much less than met the eye. It was true what Bette had said. We *did* like each other.

Though he was out of the house the first couple of days, either on business around the theater or on junkets with the kids, we would all get together at the end of the day for a drink. He was a delightful fellow and Bette, I must say, seemed to enjoy our enjoying each other.

It must have been the third or fourth day when Gary arrived home just as our workday was ending and Bette asked that I stay for dinner.

"Merrill, make Sandy and yourself a drink and have one ready for me. I'm just going to change."

And she left us. Mikey had gone upstairs to do his homework and B.D. was riding in the park. Gary fixed us a drink and I relaxed, although I left the notebook open. After all, I might get some damned good material by just lifting a couple with him. Bette laughingly suggested that I was always trying, at five o'clock, to get her loaded so she'd spill the Boston beans. And I would laughingly agree that it was so, but her one drink wouldn't do the trick.

Gary and I could manage more than one or two, and we were having a grand old time while Bette was upstairs. He was a great dialectician and told some hilarious stories that spared no one. He also, with some prodding, gave me some interesting stuff on their marriage, though not one word of it couldn't have been said in front of her. Gary had style in all things. He knew I found Bette stimulating and I had watched him when first we'd met. He would sometimes allow an expression to cross his eyes that almost looked like sympathy, and I thought that he probably believed I was having a rough time with the lady. I could be just as loyal as Mr. Merrill and Bette fared damned well when she wasn't present.

I can see him now, sitting at the desk where he had answered the phone at Bette's shouted request. He was leaning toward me, finishing a mad tale, and we were roaring with laughter when Bette made a beautiful entrance in a hostess gown, her hair exquisitely groomed, her whole appearance comely and smart. She was apparently pleased with the vibrations in the room and our flattering observation that she was looking lovely. She also looked extremely young that evening, and her eyes met mine for a second and then moved on conspiratorily. She knew what I was thinking and the extra beat meant that I was insane but it would be fun talking about it later.

But I was sure that I wasn't wrong. I was going to accuse her of still being in love with Gary and tell her that it was obvious it was hardly unrequited, and why didn't they both relax and enjoy it? I had already informed her that she was cheating herself by feeling about men the way she did. Bette was vastly amused and not in the least disturbed by my attempts to rekindle the old flame.

Bette stoked the fire and put some nuts out while Gary fixed her a drink, placing it on the coffee table. He then returned to the desk and his own glass.

"Sandy, did you ever hear about the—?"

"Merrill!" Bette interrupted as she smoothed her hair and lighted a cigarette.

"Your drink is on the table, Bette."

"I know."

She picked it up, took a sip and walked over to him. I will never forget it.

"Let me sit down," she now not as much asked as directed.

She was smiling a bit thinly but the breathy delivery meant she was on.

"I thought you were sitting on the couch," Gary said charmingly.

"I-was-but-I-want-to-sit-here."

"Don't be ridiculous, Bette. What the hell is the difference? Why don't you just sit down? I was just telling Sandy about—"

"It's my [breath] seat, Merrill!"

"They're all your seats, Bette. Look around you. You have quite a choice."

And it was true. There must have been nine or ten comfortable places in that library to sit but Bette Davis wanted to sit at the desk because Gary Merrill was sitting there. They were both still smiling, Bette towering over him, blowing smoke rings leisurely, her fingers rubbing against each other like crickets, and Gary with squatter's rights—firmly ensconced—sipping his drink in the happy knowledge that possession is nine points of the law.

"I'm not [breath] joking, Merrill. I [breath] mean business."

"I'm not either and I do too." He answered and his smile was a little less congealed than hers.

And then I knew what was happening. It had taken me a moment. This was typically Bette, but it was also beyond that. I was Bette's biographer and knew only too well that she starred in her relations with husbands as well as her films. I knew it by hearsay. She was now going to supply me with proof positive. By the same token, Gary knew that I was seeing them together at a moment that would surely reflect their years of marriage, and under no condition was he going to be caught and be recorded surrendering. The audience was the catalyst. Neither could back down, and certainly Gary would have been an idiot if he had. Bette should never have brought the whole silly thing to the point of real confrontation.

These two intelligent people continued this scene with diminishing good humor and, at last, Bette had the nerve to turn to me, a fascinated but unwilling witness to this nonsense, and say.

"I leave it to you, Sandy. You have the same passion for justice that I have. What do *you* think?"

This was obviously the Merrill tango and it takes only two. I wanted no part of it. In Scotch there is truly veritas.

"I think—between you—you make a reasonably sensible four-year-old."

That's what I said, and they both laughed weakly but would not yield. They would, nineteen years later, still be there, neither giving an inch, if B.D., five minutes later, looking stylish in her riding breeches, hadn't rushed up the stairs and entered the room. It must have been like walking into the middle of a movie one has already seen.

"I want [breath] to sit there."

"Would you please light someplace and get off my back?"

"I want [breath] *my chair.*"

"You've got eight others."

"Merrill! I'm really getting [breath] angry now . . . I've [breath] had it."

B.D. listened impatiently for a couple of seconds, became bored with what had once been the familiar, and did what no other living creature could dare do and still live. She put the tips of her fingers on her mother's chest and unbalanced Bette who toppled over onto the couch.

"Oh, mother!" was the girl's only comment.

Oh, brother! was what occurred to me. I never again toyed with the idea of encouraging a possible rapprochement.

Things were always humming at the queen bee's, and one day, Bette asked me—since we were both Jeffersonian and Rooseveltian Democrats and had both voted for Mr. Kennedy—whether I wanted to attend the inauguration ball with her in Washington a couple of weeks hence.

"I got an invitation from Frank Sinatra, who is arranging the evening, and if you drive me to Washington, you'll be my escort, my fine feller. We'll take B.D., who will *flip*. Kennedy is her *dreamboat*. If you have tuxedo you'll travel!"

I have rarely even remotely contemplated suicide. I do not drive. I can barely change a light bulb. The entire world of technology has bewildered me since birth. I not only do not drive, but hate flying. Walking is my favorite mode of transportation, which makes it difficult to get to Europe.

"Well? I thought with your enthusiasm, you'd be up the wall. Will you [breath] drive me to the [breath] ball, Sandy?"

"If you're going in a coach and six, I will."

"And what does all of that mean?"

"Please, Bette, I could die. I don't drive!"

"You don't drive? But everybody drives."

"Not me. I can just about use the telephone. If I had the time to learn, take a test and get a license, which I don't, I'd fail anyway."

"It's tough. I just can't take a guest, Sandy—only an escort."

"I understand and I could die."

And that's how I missed, by being a nineteenth-century moron, an historic twentieth-century evening and the apogee of the Kennedy myth. Bette and B.D., of course, regaled me with stories about the marvelous night, from the blizzard through which they had to drive with such difficulty, to their glowing meeting with the shiny new president, for whom the future so cruelly promised to be even brighter.

Bette was only too pleased to share good times, as well as work, with me and not only with the kids and Gary but later, with her sister Barbara who came East to visit. Bobbie contributed to the household greatly, and to my ever-growing notes on Bette. Also to the lifelong sibling tensions which in no family are ever dissipated, even by sobering middle or old age. I have seen octogenarian sisters and brothers scrap with each other in reflexive repetition of some dimly remembered battle for Mama or Papa. It is, of course, not enough to know why you resent your sister if the original and totally remembered reason has wounded deeply enough.

Bette, after all, became the star, with Mother backing her all the way, sacrificing herself and anyone else in her dedication. Bobbie, a serious music student and a sensitive girl, was evidently expendable, since the sisters weren't an act, and Bette started moving up. No matter Bette's continued affection and devotion throughout her struggle and eventual ascension, Bobbie doubtless wished that it were she instead who could be so magnanimous—bestowing gifts, advice, and sympthy from such an enviable height, not only on herself but on her daughter and grandchild as well. Bette has become the paterfamilias.

I liked Bobbie. She was a good gal and always ready to pitch in—no matter what. The women remained close despite their separations which, never that I know of, became estrangement. They had suffered too much together in their childhood.

It was their mother, the remarkable Ruthie, who interested me. She lived in California—in a house far grander than Bette ever had or even wanted. Ruthie was the dowager empress, and Bette, ever grateful for her years of sacrifice, begrudged her nothing. She was eager that I meet her and I looked forward to it. I was fascinated by Bette's ambivalence toward her mother. Fascinated that Bette had so displaced her father with her entire family. As Harlow Morrel Davis once did with his wife, Bette now continued, with far more constancy as well as generosity, to listen with disbelief to Ruthie's extravagant demands, and to meet them at any cost.

Her mother, who knew only too well what Bette's success cost since she paid as great a price for it, relaxed into a kind of empty-headed mistressdom once the job was neatly done. She didn't seem to have the slightest conception of the work that Bette and every other hardworking star in Hollywood does. It all seemed, once success came, that Bette was just wandering around the studio being adored. It was an intriguing switch and one that I had never thought of though I had seen Bette, in *The Star,* give a brilliant performance in a most realistic picture of an exploitative family. But Bette, after complaining about her mother, would always add most genuinely, "But how can I refuse this great woman anything after all she went through for me? She had such *guts,* she was so *un*complaining when things were rough for us and she was supporting Bobbie and me with her photography."

Bette was troubled about her mother, and after a session in which she would shake her head in impatience, she would then talk of sending her some extravagant gift which she knew Ruthie wanted. Well, we all have these relationships and not many of us, after really taking, can give as much as she, Bette, liked to give. From generosity I am sure. But also from the catbird seat.

She did a lot of entertaining from there, and she entertained well. Bette was an unpretentious but lavish hostess. Unlike many of the other stars, Bette loved reliving her early New England years, and preferred clambakes and chicken fries to formal dinners. In the dining room

148

was a round, lazy Susan table she had found somewhere way Down East years ago, which traveled everywhere with her. It was a marvelous table, constantly replete with relishes and cruets and pepper mills. When Bette was having people in she would get out her huge pewter dinner plates and her friends would sit in happy profusion around her—the swiveling centerpiece a charming but unnecessary conversation piece. With Bette and now me at table, there was little danger of silence.

One evening, with other guests that included her adored dental surgeon Stanley Behrman and his wife, delightful Gig Young and his then wife, the charming Elizabeth Montgomery, the conversation and dinner were progressing admirably. I was managing to talk and eat more than anyone else and while in the midst of this dual marathon, it occurred to me that I would love some more butter on my corn. I did not see it on the table anywhere. I was about to make a concerted effort to find it, when the table went swirling. It was like Monte Carlo with the house frankly controlling things. Bette had spun the wheel, stopping it so that the lost butter dish was directly at my fingertips.

I was astonished not only by her coordination but by her keen observation—indeed her clairvoyance—since I had really only thought about the butter, barely scanning the Susan as I chatted with Miss Montgomery about unicorns, concerning which we both had incredibly much to say. I now looked across the table with a grateful smile and Bette winked, neither of us missing a syllable in our separate conversations. She could be quite a gal, Bette, with a keen eye and genuine interest in people, two qualities that have enriched her art.

When she played Fannie Skeffington years ago and conveyed the terror of a great beauty losing the battle against decay, she was only thirty-five. The Countess di

149

Frasso, after seeing the film, asked Bette how in the hell she could possibly know at her age what it was like to lose youth and beauty, and Bette didn't know. She assumed that it was instinct, one of the mysteries of the creative process; and this is true. Inspiration is often miraculous but often instinct is simply the sum total of observations subliminally recorded. *What is it about that guy that makes me squirm?* One sometimes "instinctively" dislikes a man on first sight because his ready smile has the promptness of another smile, belonging—one may have forgotten—to another congenial man who once did the observer in. Obviously the more one absorbs consciously or subconsciously, the more one can be squeezed out of. An artist is a sponge.

"Why aren't you married?" Bette asked me one day while I was making note of something she had just told me. "You're frightfully eligible."

"I suppose because I haven't met the woman I want to marry."

"Why would you want to when you can have all the advantages without marriage?"

She now warmed to her favorite subject.

"Artists should never marry. It's a big mistake. And, my God, with frozen foods and dishwashers, men don't need us. And if we can have a child without men—and it will come to that—then there'll never be another marriage ceremony."

I took note of this, thinking it was a typically Bettean conceit. She now looked at me impishly.

"You interest [breath] me. I'm sick of talking about myself—believe it or not. Tell me about *you*. What really makes you tick?"

I threw my notebook across the room and she caught it on the fly. I followed it with my pencil, after which I lay back in mock reverie as she smirked, having every intention of pursuing her quest.

Bette Davis and I—and all of my collaborators—often exchanged confidences. As I've said, only by volunteering information have I been able to elicit it. But Bette, today, showed great curiosity about my family, my friends, my dreams. She did have a genuine interest in people, a real desire to exchange views on art and politics and literature. Of course, through these pleasant colloquies I gleaned much.

It was always gratifying when we agreed, not in the least because I prefer peace in a relationship, but because I was able to commit to print a point of view I had long wished to advertise. Bette Davis could be my platform. My feelings about a special actor or politico, a minority group or majority misconception, the tempus, the mores—though uttered in words that would approximate Miss Davis—could possibly influence others. As my collaborator-cum-patient always came to identify with the writer-cum-analyst, so in turn did I fuse with the subject, leading her by suggestion and/or attractive presentation to agree on a topic which I could then pontificate on with impunity, since it was proper for her image that she concur.

This is not to say that a stated opinion was not Bette Davis—simply that it was voiced by her only after encouragement. God knows, Bette wouldn't have agreed with something she didn't feel.

"Don't you agree, Bette," during a particularly congenial session in which we were discussing acting, "that John Gielgud—especially remembering his Hamlet—my God! what a pure performance—is a most immaculate performer, in a sense the greatest?"

"Brilliant! There's no question about it. There's intellect there and a religious devotion."

Always eager to add another pearl to Garbo's crown, I would ask, "Who, in all Hollywood, as an actress—and knowing your standards, I bet I know—do you admire more than any other? How much it's Garbo?"

"But who else?" Bette replied. "She mastered the medium. *No* one has ever worked so effectively before a camera."

If I had said, "I'll bet it's Sonja Henie," of course Bette would have disagreed. She felt this about Garbo but might not have volunteered it for any number of reasons. I wasn't being contrary to her instincts or inconsistent, nor would Bette have allowed it had I been. I was never untrue to her dicta—simply gently manipulative (though, perhaps I didn't have to be and just enjoyed using my gifts of persuasion). I wanted Bette Davis at all times to be revealed as an artist who knew her peers and appreciated greatness. I wanted her, at all times, to be seen in the best possible light. Acting was her religion, and the dark side of her star could be described by "herself" in more profound, self-deprecating, and secular terms.

Bette Davis happens to be sure of her gifts, and therefore generous to fellow actors. When she was the "fourth Warner brother" and—as an immense draw—powerful enough to control things, she always had the best actors she could get as her supporting cast. The record is there. She didn't have to look tall by appearing with pygmies.

Now, *had* Miss Davis been an actress ungenerous to others, I—in an effort to reflect her truth (but still with care)—might, by omission, save her from such an accusation of meanness or jealousy, but I never would have attempted to convey the opposite. Never!

Bette did obviously esteem Garbo, but actresses really do not sit around extolling other actresses' virtues. It just isn't generic. For her sake and mine, I had to incite her to such testimonials. Once I heard her—and truth be told,

Bette could expostulate on anything or anybody with very little need of help—establish a viewpoint, I could write it up in a manner which would please her and, I hoped, the reader.

Often, after she had voiced an opinion on a subject, I would enthusiastically concur and then add a sardonic touch at which she might laugh, thereby giving me tacit permission to set a mood stronger than she had originally suggested. This because it was to our mutual advantage at this point and on this subject—say, acting methods—that Bette Davis arrogantly and candidly pontificate with all her bluff impatience. This was her cachet. At another time—and in a gentler mood—she might approach the subject blandly and be too bored to return to the subject again, thinking it had been exhausted, and thereby cheating me and the reader of her typical astringency. In order to involve her passion, I had to raise the temperature, to put on the heat, as it were.

These views on acting are genuinely Bette's—as well as my own—but brought to the boiling point, so that when I was ready to write the little treatise on acting in the book that I felt must be part of a biography of such a serious actress, I would be allowed the leeway to attack and caress, to sting and bludgeon. In short, to be Bette Davis defending her craft.

There were times when Bette would regard me shrewdly, and I knew that she knew what I was up to and went along knowing that I could be trusted. While acting, she doubtless did the same thing with a coplayer with whom more tension could create a finer scene. She once told me that in her first and brilliant *Elizabeth* she had a difficult time with the "dashing but limited" Errol Flynn, who played Essex, though she had requested Laurence Olivier. She said that Flynn "didn't or couldn't return the serve," and that it was impossible—though the scenes were so written—to volley with him. Knowing Bette, I'm certain that she tried to incite him as any creative actor would. I also thought she underestimated him.

With her favorite, Claude Rains, her scenes were a different story. She herself was so impressed with his Napoleon III in *Juarez* that she told me she forgot she was the star of the film and, playing the Empress Carlotta, so awed was she by her pal's sovereignty that she became what she should have been, an itinerant petitioner in one of the most powerful courts of Europe. Bette loved working only with fine actors who stimulated her.

Of course she discussed all of her great roles with me, and I was astonished by both her insight and blindness. Like most actors, Bette is at her greatest when not thinking too much. It is a mistake intelligent actors make—especially when they have become a legend and very grand. I was much more impressed by her instinctual approach to Mildred in *Of Human Bondage*. Rather touchingly, Bette could not understand her preknowledge of such as Mildred, and was, in her puritanical youth, quite scandalized by her empathy with a young woman absolutely her opposite. With none of the experience that might even obliquely have suggested an approach to the character, Miss Davis awesomely became her. There was no experiential material from which she could draw with that nonexistent past. She was still an innocent, if this can be said of any artist whose connection to the Source is never broken.

Years later, as Leslie in Maugham's *The Letter*, Miss Davis now became a typically English colonial seething on a rubber plantation. I heard, years ago, from Geraldine Fitzgerald, while I was working on one of her pictures, that Miss Davis quite incredibly spoke with exactly the accent and inflections of a Briton who had lived for years in the Far East. Quite an accomplishment for our New England pilgrim. Miss Fitzgerald, a beautiful actress herself, was astonished by this phenomenon, and so was I! The Davis always researched her roles, reconstructing a character to the smallest detail.

I was thunderstruck when while working with me Miss Davis discussed one particular scene—by far the most memorable in the film.

Having been tried and acquitted for killing her welcome lover and having at last confessed all to her husband, Herbert Marshall, he decides (with what must be English sportsmanship at its keenest) to forgive her. Leslie has now won complete amnesty, but bereft of her lover, no longer caring, filled with revulsion for such slavish adoration, she refuses deliverance. Instead, in a dazzling moment, she shocks him and the audience with the famous line, "I still love the man I killed!"

According to Miss Davis it was at this juncture that she and her director, William Wyler, had a set-to. He wanted her to look directly at Mr. Marshall and Miss Davis insisted that no woman could say such a thing to a man's face, that the confession would rise unconsciously and not be directed *at* him. She persisted in looking away from him. It seems a battle royal ensued, with our queen marching off the set. Mr. Wyler, of course, knew exactly what he was doing and Miss Davis was beyond her depth.

Despite the nonsense and the happy defeat she suffered at her favorite director's hands (though on frame it looked like a draw to me) Miss Davis on her unchastened return conveyed emotionally, though her feverish brain led her elsewhere, precisely the right disdain for such contemptuous idolatry. Without knowing why—an evaluation which I am certain would enrage her—and allowing (if she must discuss the subconscious) Ruth Elizabeth Davis and the popular star to block her road, with the chips down her creative genius still took over and she sailed right over the hurdle.

I will never forget the electrifying manner in which she read that line, and the accompanying look of dementia on her very special face. It added up to a human equation so subtly realized, so primitive, both so destructive and self-damaging in its guilt-laden aggression, so eager to hurt and so hurt by thus hurting, that Miss Davis managed to lay bare the core of such a woman—and all of this in a melodrama and despite herself. It can only be inspiration.

How did Joan of Lorraine acquire her military knowledge? Bette Davis is all actress. She needn't—in fact cannot, as you will later see—be writer and director as well. I know only that those eyes in that scene, filled as they were with both terror and gratification, revealed exactly what Maugham and Wyler wanted. The container and the contained again. The vessel and the wine. Well, Bette Davis *is* a crystal glass.

In *All This and Heaven Too,* Bette, this time a most passive nineteenth-century governess—genteel, refined, resourceful, and loving of her children—her character so exalted, her relationship with Monsieur Le Duc, her employer (Charles Boyer) so antiseptic that it drove the actress wild, still managed to convey all of this wholesome passivity though she informed me that she didn't for one moment believe that they were not lovers. Though in fairness to Bette, who preferred using the Marquis de Sade as an historical source and not the governess' niece, Rachel Field, who was only the author, there *was* precedent for such a conceit. I still suspect that it was really a thorn in her side that Monsieur Le Duc, being so French and everything, didn't complete his elegant pass. How could he live in that household all those years, with a neurotic wife with whom he had no relationship, and not have succumbed to Bette's more sensual charms that lay underneath all that sweetness and light?

Again, I felt the intrusion of the star and the projection

of her own ego; but, say it I must and will, this was never for an instant indicated, no matter how much she may have toyed with the idea. With all her wiles and willfulness, her superpride in her femaleness, and her strong sense of identity, Bette Davis at her best was always too good an actress for such foolishness. Always at the moment of truth, her instinct would deny such aberrations. Ideally the artist triumphed over both the actress and star. When acting, Bette never lost the inner truth, though she did a lot of talking around it. All the signposts led not to a hell of a mess but instead to Paradise. Actors are magnificent. Their work is witchcraft.

There is very little that Bette Davis doesn't intuit about acting, and for that matter, about her own projection as a star, hence her exemplary behavior with me, which transcended her affection and friendship. She knew that my machinations—if such they were—were good for her. She knew that I not only admired her but also had a soft spot in my heart for her. It is also true that she knew that she could eventually veto anything she found offensive or not to her liking. It was her autobiography, only she was signed with the publishers, and every word was going to be approved by her lawyers and herself. This made what we were doing fun. All these high-flying, daredevil confessions were exciting—even *with* a net.

Only once did I have to remind Bette that some of the text would sound deprecating, but she had always to remember that the moment she was off to Hollywood to make *Lady for a Day* for Capra, and I started work on the book, to all intents and purposes it was the East Coast Bette Davis who would be writing the book and self-deprecation was something else again. She was used to candor to begin with, and was shrewdly aware that admitting, for instance, that she was a bitch was the surest way of convincing the reader that she was not.

Once Bette had decided to open the floodgates, there was no stopping her. This, of course, was almost rule of thumb. Her confidences concerning her family, her husbands, and her agonized ambivalence toward men became on occasion reckless. My pencil would stop, and I allowed the lady to purge herself, never having the slightest intention of using the material.

It was one of the most fascinating aspects of my work that in every solitary case, the initial reticence to open up became a refusal to shut up. The flood of confidences was often fed by inventions as well. Some subjects would gladly admit to murder—in order to see the adoring and now adored ghost's eyes light up with excitement.

Because the writer, once a threat, is now worshiped, his needs must be satisfied. He is handed bombshells as if they were bonbons, and he must be wary of this eagerness to please and examine these "confessions," which in the first place might hurt rather than help the book, and finally would enrage the very subject who has offered them once she has been released from the spell and recovered from her infatuation.

A patient being successfully—or at least pleasantly —analyzed, who has found relief, safety, and a willing, eager ear, is hard put to relinquish it. *What can I do to extend these visits? Where am I ever going to find anybody to listen so uncritically and interminably again?*

Of course there were revelations of which I didn't have to make note. They were colorful enough to retain without reminder. And that, really, was all my notes were, reminders; a key verbless sentence, designed—usually illegibly—to recall an anecdote, a theme or salient fact; odd spellings of names or places; important dates without which I could not build a work chronologically. All of these minutiae have great accumulative value, adding authenticity to what could just be a random recitation of facts. All of these data, plus future elaborations or descriptions, can and do fill countless notebooks. The commencement of any book brought a chill of horror when I saw the quantity of notes that had to be organized. However, it was often the material I could not record that was the most important. The partners now not only share the same future but the same past. During the sessions prior to the start of my real writing, the relationship between subject and writer was uniquely close. Few relationships are closer. One human being has bared and shared her life, and then, in a final act of questionable generosity, as a dividend, bestows all guilts and doubt upon the other. The confesser has been absolved and the confessor, like Sartre's Orestes rather than Isabella's Torquemada, is now tormented by the demons—*les mouches.*

"My life is in your hands!" is an expression I was used to hearing.

Almost two months after we had begun work, Bette looked at me helplessly.

"There just isn't anything more I can tell you. It's a wonder you have an ear left. Is there *anything* you don't know about me?"

She was right. I was filled to brimming and had been reduced to asking what her favorite colors were, a not in the least frivolous line of questioning, but terminal nonetheless. We enjoyed each other so much, however, that we kept up our sessions, I—more and more—blending into the household, like a family friend.

One day toward the end of this period, Tennessee Williams called to ask Bette to appear in *The Night of the Iguana,* a new play. There had been talk about her being in this work some time before and now it was ready to go. Bette gave me the script to read—hardly for my approval—but because she was eager to know what I thought. I begged her to play not the flamboyant landlady but, instead, the antiseptic spinster—a part which, as I remember, Mr. Williams had written for her. But Bette wanted to return to Broadway as a virago, as Bette Davis, and Mr. Williams encouraged her most mistakenly, I believe, to do this. I seem to remember that Katharine Hepburn was wanted for the other role, but she was unavailable for personal reasons, and Margaret Leighton was signed for what I told Bette was the "Williams woman," who would represent his eternal theme of shimmering sensibility trying to survive in the crass world. But Bette—who has always preferred, despite her brilliance in other parts, the aggressive roles—insisted that this was the part for her, the part her public would expect her to play.

She left for California, a new movie, and a reunion with Ruthie a few days before her birthday, and in euphoria. I remember buying her her favorite scent and her mild chastisement that such extravagance had better be followed by a good book that would reimburse me. Gary and I took her and the children to Grand Central and put them on a train. Bette looked adorable with Alice and Tinker, the dachshund and poodle, in her arms. Wendy, the Siamese cat and, doubtless Bette's familiar, probably willed herself to Laguna.

Bette kissed me good-bye and assured me that she was absolutely certain that I would do a "great job." She couldn't wait until I sent her some chapters.

"Please don't worry!" Bette whispered. "I don't know how in hell you're going to decipher those notes, but you'll do it. See you in the fall!"

And she was gone.

For four weeks—until May—I walked around in a stupor unable to start work. I had tried to organize the notes and just couldn't start the damned book and then one day I sat down and didn't get up until four chapters were done. These were the chapters that had to be approved in order for the contract to go into effect. I had a typist do them up neatly and sent one copy to Mr. Hammond, Bette's lawyer, and one to California. And I held my breath.

Tom Hammond called me the following day with pleasure. He was certain that Bette would be pleased. He had spoken to her on the phone and was authorized to make the next payment. With this reassurance, I tied myself to the typewriter. In one more month I was finished with half the book and proudly sent it on to Tom.

Friends had invited me to spend the summer at Cornelius Estates on Fire Island, where I planned to complete the book. It was now the end of June and in a fever of excitement I was eating and sleeping Bette Davis. I didn't budge from my typewriter. This was a labor of love. I sat in the sun on that grayed, bleached-out wood balcony on stilts facing the Atlantic, and happily sweated it out. I don't believe I ever wanted so much to please anyone, and my occasional forays into the ocean or walking that glorious beach did not divert but replenish.

I still do not know how Bette got me on the phone because we didn't have one. Hard pressed to recall the particulars, I would imagine that I had left some neighbor's number with Tom Hammond, in case of any emergency, and Bette managed to track me down. When she wants something she is stopped by nothing. How wonderful, I thought, when I heard her voice from California. *She adores the book so much she had to call.*

"Sandy?"

"Yes."

"Bette!"

"Bette! How are you, darling? How did you ever—"

"Sandy, Ruthie—Ruthie just died. That marvelous woman whom we've destroyed! Ruthie—gone! We can't, just can't go on with the book. Ohhhhhhhh!"

And with this final, jungle cry she hung up.

In one moment she had shattered the whole dream. I was destroyed, and not at all appropriately dressed for tragedy. Bathing trunks and a sailing hat do not lend themselves to such a moment. I was a grotesque, oiled up, and in the middle of typing a sentence I now need never finish. I sat staring at the ocean in shock, and then I asked permission to make a call and telephoned Tom Hammond's office. I was sorry that Ruthie had died, but what had this to do with our book? Was Bette serious about canceling the whole project?

Tom—an extremely kind and put-upon fellow—did not know what to say to me. Bette was distraught and wanted to abandon the whole project. She might certainly change her mind in time; he was quite certain she *would* eventually, but right now—

"But what the hell am I supposed to do—just forget the book? I've been going full steam—"

"I know, Sandy. I think you should continue."

But the happy rhythm had been broken. I returned to the porch. The typewriter, the open scrapbook, the pile of papers kept from flying by two great shells, a half-devoured peach, the salt-sweet air that so mingled with baby oil, and new, black, inky ribbon created a scene from the past. I was observing it from outside.

I took a long walk—up to Water Island many miles away, and swam and walked my way back, expending energy. I remember running part of the way. I then sat down at the typewriter, pulled out the page I was working on and replaced it with another. *Dear Bette*, it began. I wrote a condolence letter. After all, I knew what it was like to lose a parent. I had lost both. I spoke of Ruthie Davis's character, her stamina, her gift for living, and I also genuinely but not without peripheral guile spoke of Bette's devotion and her mother's good life once success had been achieved. I had never minced words with Bette, and there was little reason to start now.

Wasn't the most fitting memorial to such a woman, a life story in which she, as the catalyst, emerged not as a one-dimensional, sentimentalized pie-baking Mum, but a rounded, heroic woman replete with the ego needs that made all the miracles possible? Wasn't Bette aware that the greatest compliment she would pay her mother was to do exactly as we had planned, trace Ruthie's ascending graph from beginning to end? How could she possibly emerge as anything less than marvelous? I hoped that Bette would remember my feelings about Ruthie, and how on balance she would certainly fare superbly. She, being a full-blooded, strong dame, would be as appalled by any synthetic evaluation just as Bette herself would. I walked to the little post office and mailed it.

It had come to me while I was walking to and from Water Island, that Bette in our oneness was forcing me to suffer her guilts. It was perfectly fine to discuss Ruthie's lesser qualities with me, but now that she was dead, Bette was devastated by her seeming act of disloyalty. She had sent out bad vibrations, probably even felt—as children often do—responsible for her mother's death. To whom had she said these things? Sandy held in his mind and his writing hand information she had handed him. He, therefore, was guilty too. And he must suffer as she was suffering. Weren't we Miniken and Maniken? Why in God's name should I be spared? I knew—because I knew Bette so well—what she must be thinking, and I knew that she would come around. I had only to wait it out and give Ruthie her due, give Bette the words with which she could once again gain her perspective about her mother.

About a week later, Tom Hammond told me definitely to go on with my work, which I was doing. Bette had told him she had received my letter. She was back at work making the Capra film. I resolved to finish the book by September, which I did. By the time it was proofread, edited, typed up and ready for presentation, it was October and Bette was back in town to start rehearsals for the Williams play. She was thrilled that Tom felt so strongly about the manuscript, and though she hadn't read it ("I'm scared [breath] stiff."), she thought the publishers should see what we had wrought. Tom now sent the completed manuscript to Putnam and I received a phone call from the same gentleman who had told me at the outset that he would have nothing to do with me.

Mr. Cady loved the book. He was going to leave Putnam for another position, but he had promised Bette, and now he promised me, that he would not depart until our book was launched "as our important title of the season." He asked to meet me and I went to Putnam and pleasantly listened to his flattery. He had only the most negligible editorial changes to suggest. I was gratified. Within a couple of weeks, *Ladies' Home Journal* had offered what was once a bloody fortune to do a condensation, and a paperback house had offered to buy the book. Bette and I hadn't found a title as yet and I, at last, came up with *Through a Glass Darkly*, which she loved. Ingmar Bergman was to announce a new film with that name and that was that. "Two great minds [breath] run in the same [breath] direction," Bette decided lovingly. As a joke I had suggested *Bette Davis—Ah Men!*, and we had laughed, and then she came up with *The Lonely Life*, which I never liked but which was decided upon.

Bette had still to read *The Lonely Life*, but so much money was now involved that Tom Hammond was treating the publication as a fait accompli as negotiations went forward. Bette had me to dinner and told me how happy she was for me. Everyone—her lawyer, his brother, the publishers—simply loved the book, and she couldn't wait until she could really start it. I was not unconcerned with this cavalier attitude toward not only my work but our project, but I put it down to nerves. She was returning to Broadway in a Tennessee Williams play and she hadn't been "legitimate" in many years.

Mr. Cady now talked with me seriously. He apologized for his initial coldness and now offered me warming compensation.

"It is true, Sandy, that we insisted that Davis not give credit to a writer. We have always felt that a book sells better if the public feels the immediacy of the celebrity. However, we are so pleased that we are willing to give you jacket credit."

All the labor had been worth it. Not only would Bette be pleased but I would now be listed as coauthor. There was no end to my good luck. But something told me to be cautious.

"Howard, I am most gratified, believe me. Of course, it means a great deal to me and for my future. But do me a favor, will you?"

"Anything. I'd like to make things up to you."

"Just don't say anything to Bette about this unless I'm present. I have a feeling about this. I know that Bette is fond of me and will be delighted. She has promised that she would ask you to give me such credit but, well, if I'm there when you suggest it, I can say, 'Bette, isn't it wonderful?' and she'll definitely agree. If I'm not there—I don't know. I'm not quite sure."

"I promise. We'll probably have cocktails there next week together. I'll arrange it. You want to do the captions with her? She'll probably want a hand in it."

"Of course."

Two days later, Howard Cady called me.

"Sandy! I've done something terrible to you and I don't know quite what to say."

My heart fell.

"I was over at Davis's last evening talking some business over and I just couldn't help it. It just slipped out about you and the great job you've done and my eagerness to have you get what you deserve. I told Davis that Putnam would be willing to reverse itself in this case and give you full credit as a collaborator."

"Yes?"

"She was delighted. She's mad about you, you know."

"Go on."

"Davis agreed wholeheartedly. She said that she was an actress and not a writer, and you'd worked so hard and it was great with her."

"What was the terrible thing you did to me, Howard?"

"Well, about fifteen minutes later, Tom Hammond told her he thought it was a big mistake and she had to agree with him."

"I knew this could happen."

"I know and I'm really sorry."

I was too.

Bette Davis now, according to the letter of our contract, wrote out a few lines "so everyone will know how wonderful you are," and I should like to reprint her acknowledgment, which appears on a page all by itself in the hardback and was forgotten, along with her dedication to Ruthie, in most of the paperbacks.

> *I attribute the enormous research, this persistence of putting together the pieces of this very "crossed"-word puzzle which comprises my life to Sandford Dody.*

> *Without him this book could never have been! His understanding of my reluctance to face the past*

was his most valuable contribution. We were col-
laborators in every sense of the word.

March 8, 1962   *—Bette Davis*

Bette had salved her conscience. She had still to read
the manuscript when she invited me to the first rehearsal
of *Iguana*—and suggested that I hide in the theater just
in case I could conceivably add anything to the end of
the book. Of course I jumped at the chance.

There on the empty stage, the naked light bulb and
a few wooden chairs its only appointments, stood Bette,
Margaret Leighton, and Patrick O'Neal—who was really
in a tight spot between them. Other members of the cast
were hovering about, but the three principals were down-
stage waiting for Frank Corsaro, the director, to continue
the rehearsal. Bette had script in hand, her horn-rimmed
glasses, slacks and Capezios denoting work time. She
was for all the world Margo Channing starting a new play
—with a little Genghis Khan thrown in. Miss Leighton,
a lovely, diaphanous actress, was taut, bone-thin, also
bespectacled and in slacks. Opposites but utterly professional—both. I could feel the tension between them. The
yielding, feminine Bette Davis who cooked for me and
opened her heart was gone. She was now onstage—in
the arena—and her very nose was twitching, seeking out
the first sniff of blood. Because Bette in the arena is not
Christian, but lioness.

The theater was dark and I could not see anyone else
or at least make anyone out. Bette had told me that she
also had her friend Mrs. Claude Rains hiding somewhere,
and I knew that the playwright would certainly be lurking
about.

When I came in the three principals were moving

around the stage, feeling their way. Then Miss Leighton made her entrance, carrying a valise, with Mr. O'Neal; and Bette, after some dialogue, took the valise, starting upstage. She suddenly stopped and turned to the auditorium. She removed her glasses.

"Ten [breath]nessee!" she called into the darkness.

"Yehs, Beddy," the playwright drawled.

"Tennessee, I don't think this bitch for one moment would pick up her bag and carry it. I just don't think she would. What do you think?"

It was obvious what Mr. Williams thought. He had written this in as a stage direction and Bette was already rewriting the play—rewriting Tennessee Williams. She happened, I think, to be right. Maxine Faulk, the character she was playing, might, as landlady, find it difficult at best to be menial with her betters but certainly so with this ascetic woman—especially in front of her lover. Bette waited for an answer now, her left hand nervously twitching, her mouth pursed in assured expectancy.

"You're quat raght, Beddy—quat raght. Fohget the valise and start up without it."

He had already told her to be Bette Davis and he was going to have to live with that. Mr. Williams, who had slowly descended from the divine heights of *Streetcar*, wanted very much to reverse the trend and have a success this time. He felt that Bette's presence could assure it.

"You're quat raght, Beddy," was doubtless the first of many retreats. Bette was back. She was flexing her muscles again, and all the sweet humility she can display in sickness or defeat was gone. Bette is her most charming in foul weather.

She should have played Hannah instead of Maxine. It was by far the better part, and its quivering, filigreed character structure would have contained her and still allowed her gifts a showcase. I suspect that Bette could have been a great Hannah. She was not a great Maxine because no one had the strength and/or the inclination to discipline her. She therefore pleased the screaming mob whose opening-night greeting was so boisterous and prolonged that she was forced to step forward and acknowledge it, albeit with touching grace. This welcome could have made any actor mad with power. Along with a permissive management it helped make her performance something less than triumphant.

As easily foreseen, Margaret Leighton's tense, seething spinster won the the hearts of the audience and critics. The final curtain brought her the accolade and Bette a restrained ovation, which is not to say that her public did not continue its love affair with her—blocking traffic, howling and chanting, and proving her the great and loved star that she is. In time-honored fashion I do believe that that mob would love to have drawn her carriage through the streets—unaware that she would have made it impossible since she certainly would have insisted on driving herself.

In any event, the adulation she received was earned throughout the years and not that night. Bette would have her way; that has been both her blessing and curse.

The opening was a few days after Christmas and we went back to her house—a few of us—to await the critics. The inner circle—her lawyer, her biographer, her agent. There was no one from the play, since they were all celebrating at another party. Bette was unwinding and, though happy with her reception, she was doubtless aware that it was not going to be her night. Bette has never tolerated second place and once laughingly told me that she walked off a miniature golf course in a rage because she missed the putt that would have made her the winner. I was concerned not only for her but for myself. She still claimed that she hadn't read *The Lonely Life* but was approving its sale to the magazines with the proviso that she could make a few changes if necessary. I certainly wanted her in the best possible mood when she did make them.

Bette was not having the best of relations with the rest of the cast and I don't believe the less than ecstatic reviews that we waited up for that night, and the general feeling that the whole affair hadn't turned out as she'd planned, helped any. She was not feeling too well and I got the impression that she would not be with the production for the run of the play. I also felt, more and more, that this general deterioration of goodwill could affect everyone with whom she was in contact. The Christmas spirit was somewhat dampened though Bette was a holiday girl. She loved holidays and the house would reflect—from Halloween to Guy Fawkes Day—some of the season's joy. Christmas was a loved season in the Davis house.

I love Christmas also and remember shopping for gifts for all the Merrill children, and for Bette, of course. Nothing too expensive, since my latest payment was being held up by Bette's delay in accepting the final script, but I chose the gifts with care, struggling over a suitable one for little Margot.

"You've got to pick up *your* Christmas gift, Sandy," Bette announced one afternoon. "I've got everyone I love the same thing and they just arrived. I hope you'll be pleased."

I hoped so too. It would be, I trusted, not too costly, but something I could treasure from Bette Davis. "For everyone I love!" I feared that she had done too much.

On Bette's insistence I dropped by late one afternoon to collect the present. There was a huge carton in the living room. It came from Boston, I believe, and Bette repeated her admission that pressures (the tour, the opening) had forced her to buy the same gift for all her favorite people. She then proudly removed from the carton one of many.

It was a twelve-inch styrofoam Jack Frost with a top hat, a bell round his neck and a red Christmas ball for a nose. There was a little wire arrangement on its back in case one ever wished to hang him.

Furious now that everyone was rushing her for decisions, Bette developed a virus, settling in bed with medicines, *The Lonely Life,* and a butcher knife. She was reading and making corrections for the *Ladies' Home Journal* condensation now. I didn't have a hint that I would never again see my manuscript. When I called to inquire about her health Bette announced with faint bravado that she was going to go through the book with a fine-tooth comb.

Now Bette Davis, in what I can only imagine to be delirium, further salved her conscience concerning my billing. She was in the process of collaborating.

Stories that she had told me with great feeling either dissappeared or were changed radically, revealing second thoughts about their authenticity or simple resentment that they had been used at all. Chunks—pages long— were removed, only a line or two replacing them with a rickety bridge between the remaining thoughts. On occasion—after a shocking amputation—she indulged herself in a few disjointed paragraphs.

I realized what was happening only when the magazine printed its prepublication first installment. What had been the *Journal's* splendid condensation was now an illiterate botch. It was a wanton attack on a work. It was vandalism! And it was Bette Davis. Obviously, *Ladies' Home Journal* was stuck with their O.K. of her O.K.

I spoke with Bette and she testily repeated that after all it *was* a collaboration and certainly I expected her to do *some* work on the book, and I recall that I felt we would work together on corrections—an evident misconception on my part. By contract, she was boss lady.

There were sections that could easily have been removed with skill by any writer—as tonsils are by a surgeon. But Bette took over. It was like entrusting a child's enflamed throat to an actress wielding a knife. I begged to see the script as it was coming in. But now that Bette had taken charge, I no longer existed. It was pure Kafka.

My trips to the publisher's office to beg them to save the book, if not from Bette's excesses, then at least from her limitations, fell on deaf ears.

I was appalled. My gentle brother Jerry, incapable of such machinations himself, sat at table as I ate with him and his wife, Gaile, at their house. "Don't be ridiculous," he said. "You don't think a publisher is going to cut off his nose to spite Davis. Sandy, you're imagining things." But the publisher did and Sandy wasn't. With the expert assistance of Bette Davis our book was abandoned.

Bette did her job, left the show, and returned to California to make another film. Summer was upon us. Each succeeding installment was worse and I remember throwing one across the floor and tearing another up. When the actual book came out I think I got a couple of copies through Tom Hammond—I was ready for Creedmore. Misspellings, illiteracies, inaccuracies, and typos, all created by her meddling, slipped into the book and were frozen for all time. No one was inclined to change them. I doubt if there have ever been so many in one volume. I haunted Putnam. I can only surmise that someone said, "Let her stew in her own juice." Unfortunately I was in the kettle with her. A demand for more books was not answered with another printing. Unbelievable. I was caught in the crossfire.

Could it have been, I wondered, that Bette also was

caught in a conflict—between that good egg named Ruth Elizabeth Davis whose Emersonian piety was battling with Bette's ego needs that demanded sole credit and jurisdiction over the work? I believe she was being pulled apart. Miss Davis was far too decent a person to allow such goings on without suffering over it. She wanted to be sole author and she also wanted God on her side. What better way but to do a little writing so she could accomplish both ends?

Then, added to this, there was the usual syndrome. Bette had unburdened herself and now I knew too much. I'm sure that in her confusion she believed—since she had told me everything—that she had now written it as well. All my subjects have felt this way. To live a life and to write it are of course two entirely different things. In any case, Bette, an actress, returned to Hollywood to act. She had the good taste to remove herself from the scene and me from her life.

This "wonderful man who has done such a great job" became, or so Bette later said on television (*only* in answer to an indiscreet question about me), a man who was excellent "with dates." I could have been an Italian gardener.

Bette was now the writer and she was putting some finishing touches on our book. They were as arbitrary as they were outrageous.

Not once but many, many times Bette reminded— cautioned me: "Just don't ever confuse my darling Ruthie with Gypsy Rose Lee's mother! Ruthie might have pushed but she was nothing like Rose and never interfered with my work and her whole New England background was different. Mother was a lady."

I had never thought to compare the two women in any way at all—though all stage mothers share as nursing mothers some similar characteristics. But the remarkable Rose Hovick and the astonishing Ruth Davis were still so dissimilar that it would have been unthinkable to compare them in print.

I was therefore stunned to find at the end of the book a celebration of Stephen Sondheim's remarkable lyrics for Rose—the very character she asked me to avoid.

"Curtain up. Light the lights. We've got nothing to reach but the heights." She even added for good measure as the last line, ". . . and everything did come up roses." It didn't at all, Bette.

Because of her unsupervised meddling, the autobiography of a great actress now records her opinion as to the brilliance of the Lunts in O'Neill's *Strange Interlude,* the play she and Ruthie had just seen at the end of Chapter Five—a small section she rewrote. This appraisal, no doubt, would have been accurate but for one small matter. Mr. Lunt did not appear in *Strange Interlude.*

On page 161, Miss Davis made her most grisly contribution. We now have her mother, Ruthie—even after Bette's first marriage—refuse to relinquish, not the *reins* that life and I had given her, but the *remains.* I quote.

Still mother found it hard to relinquish the remains.

One would think the poor woman an overzealous mortician. This brand of nonsense prevails, but my very favorite of Bette's changes proves that God is in his heaven. It is her uncharacteristic illiteracy on page 297 and I quote exactly.

He (Marlon Brando) like I, had made enemies.
He is a perfectionist also.

You both certainly is, Miss Davis. The state rests.

The fact that all this was inevitable did not make it easier for me to accept. It is my gift that I see the end at the inception. It is my stupidity that I try to change it.

It is often not noble to fight the fates—simply arrogant. I was doomed from the beginning to be Bette Davis's victim and I should have relaxed and enjoyed it. When one is cast with such a co-star one should play it to the hilt, especially if the pay is good and one's career is enhanced by it.

An artist such as Miss Davis must be treasured, and it is true that I have lost none of my regard for her. There are great waves of affection as well. It is only my sentimentality that made me once believe that such a multifaceted star could be embraced without laceration. That which made her at all times exciting also made her sometimes insufferable.

One day during our sessions she asked me how I was able to take my disillusionment concerning her. She sincerely regretted that the intimacy of our talks would have to, by their nature, disenchant me. She imagined that the revelation of the real Bette Davis standing there on those feet of clay would throw me. It was very dear of her. Did she think, I asked, that I believed that the girl who played Mildred and Leslie and Jezebel could possibly have been made of spun sugar?

Nothing that Bette ever revealed could disillusion or even surprise me. What I had still to learn was that another human being could not always be expected to accept such revelations with grace. It is my failure. Without Bette's ego needs and satisfactions, she couldn't be what she is. She must never be underestimated as an actress, Bette Davis.

"You are not in awe of me, are you, Sandy?" she had once asked in another crisis.

"As an artist—yes, madam, but no, not as a woman. Or we would never have had a book you could call your own."

Robert
Merrill

Nice guys don't become stars but Momma wasn't a nice guy so he made it. If ever there was the quintessential Mr. Nice Guy it is Bob Merrill. Almost touchingly happy with his lot in life and still surprised by his renown, Robert Merrill was the least likely candidate for the opera. He was barely theatrical enough for musical comedy.

Robert is a breezy man, but without his mother's drive he would have been a minor-league baseball player who was voted best-liked on the team, and the only guy who never even frowned at the ump. The press would have found him the most cooperative player of the century, and the kids could probably have traded seven Robert Merrill cards for one Hank Greenberg.

An easygoing and self-styled comic, Bob takes only one thing seriously. He's a rare bird. Singing is his one concern, and it comes naturally. His is the classic story of the child's gift that fulfills the mother's dream, of another artist who resents the tyrannies and tithe that go with them. Another star who sits on top of the tree because Momma put him there. No one can be as amiable and unassuming as Bob Merrill and have achieved his station without someone else doing the driving.

Bette took over the wheel from Ruthie and Elaine worked side by side with Edna; but Bob, as many men I've known, warms and lights a room while someone else clears the forest and cuts down the trees for firewood. Marion Merrill, the little woman made of circles like a Renaissance drawing of a cherub, and an excellent musician herself, has dedicated herself to the preservation of that light. Bob went from mother to wife, from one strong woman to another, with only one false move—his five-minute marriage to the pretty soprano Roberta Peters.

It was a mistake soon recognized and rectified by both parties, and Robert was safely ensconced with the perfect wife for an opera singer. They have a son and a daughter, but Marion really has three children. That evidently is how they like it and that's the way it is. Certainly the Merrills are a contented couple—a most sensible combination of star and director. They naturally gravitated toward each other and though I may have found that Mrs. Merrill always had to be captain, I also found that Bob Merrill today still looks and sings just fine. I can hear Marion now. "What can I tell you?" she would ask rhetorically, her eyes narrowed, her brows furrowed in painful admission of her infallibility. She could be irritatingly right—and often. I attribute Bob's well-being and long career at the Met to this devoted woman's relentless pursuit of his happiness, her excellent table, and the well-organized life this organizer has instituted for the family. He's a lucky man to have found Marion.

If there is a price for the heroic in life and art, there is inversely a price for niceness. Boiled chicken will never give you ulcers but it's never going to win a kitchen a star rating either. I have always wanted my opera singers to be formidable, to have princely airs and ivory-handled walking sticks and the sepia-photographable glamour that goes with such station. I would prefer that they lived exclusively on champagne and caviar and quantities of unheard-of sex while they hemidemisemiquaver with passion and break into song at the very mention of the Grand Corniche.

This of course is my insanity. Caruso—the ultimate of tenors—was a Neapolitan groundling and not the Principe di Savoia. Pinza, *the* Don Giovanni, was anything but a grand seignior offstage. Still I found it sad that life cast Robert Merrill in a role he could only sing.

Bob Merrill's voice is beautiful, his musicianship exemplary, his stage deportment impeccable. Unlike all the bastards and bitches that have infested the Metropolitan and made its stage glow, transforming it, Robert simply appears, sings, delights the ear, and exits. The generals in his life led him to victories, but kept him from charging himself.

Born into poverty in Brooklyn's Williamsburg to a sweet little tailor and his bitter wife, Bob (once Moishe) knew well the value of the security he achieved. The most sweet tempered of my subjects, Bob never once evoked by design or inconsideration my ill will. Our relationship, echoing his personality, was unruffled. There was never any haggling over money or billing or percentages, since everything was decided and agreed upon at the first meeting.

I had my doubts about the book but Macmillan was excited by the possibilities. Bob was a popular guest on Johnny Carson's television show, which everyone knew sold books along with everything else so generously displayed. Bob was also an extremely well-liked member of the Metropolitan roster of stars.

Our editor was an opera buff and a Sunday singer himself, and he felt that we could have an extremely successful book. With Robert Merrill's opera and show-business audience and his ethnic charms, one imagined his also getting—like a politician—the entire Jewish vote, the musical Italians, and then the galleries and standing room at the opera house. A regular guy, Bob bridged the cultural barrier; and Joe the hard hat, knowing about Bob's baseball background and his short-haired cronies, would just as likely be interested in this guy who "could sing so fast during that Figaro bit" from *The Barber of Seville*. O.K. I was sold. If I did a good job on Mr. Merrill, we could sell books all over the house from the Diamond Horseshoe to the Family Circle, and it would be a change in pace for me. It was a man, it was the opera, it was a different milieu than I had ever known. There was going to be, in the early part of the book, a colloquial Jewish cast of characters and an opportunity throughout to style the narrative to fit Bob's Brooklyn-Broadway personality and really go all out on the dialogue. Shades of Odets, Singer or Miller—I didn't know as yet. I had defeated myself by writing Bette's book just as she talked, and had managed to write Dagmar's in the subtlest of accents. Elaine was no challenge in that department, coming from pretty much the same Manhattan background as I.

This was going to be a rags-to-riches tale and I wanted it to be touching and funny and like him. Once more, it was enlightening to enter another person's world. This one a most pleasant world. The Merrill children were delightful: little David, a skinny imp of seven with whom I could play when things got rough, and little Lizanne who should have been called *Bis,* she was so much an encore of her mother—a round doll-like little girl born with all the sound instincts of a concierge.

Bob and I worked out a schedule and he was good about it. His house was in New Rochelle and I commuted, rain or shine. When the weather was fine we lay talking on the lawn, and on wet days we worked in the library or spacious living room. Marion was what she would call a *bala-busta,* and not only was the bar always open but her light lunches could keep me filled for weeks, and when I stayed on for dinner they were feasts. They had an excellent cook, but Marion didn't need anyone. She gave me a lot of good recipes; and Bob gave me a lot of good material. I was pleased with his work. When he had to be in town, I would meet him at his tailor's, his singing coach, the opera, the recording studio—or the Russian Tea Room, where, as were most of the dining musicians, he was treated like the czar.

During this period, I met both Merrills in town, went along as they hunted for paintings, and actually dined on Canal Street with them, after which I was taken along with the family to Coney Island. It was at all times a good relationship and Robert couldn't have been more cooperative. They were generous hosts as well as dependable partners. I liked them very much. I spent many evenings at the opera, of course, with Marion in their seats or backstage with Bob or—when the house was filled—simply let loose from the stage entrance to make my own way. I loved it. This was still the beautiful old house on Thirty-ninth Street, and I pity anyone too young to have known its red-and-gilt beauty and its echoing walls. Through Bob, and my need to sop up the atmosphere, I was allowed easy access and I really got to know that house inside and out. I even have a few pieces of it decorating my own apartment, bought from the wreckers and treasured especially after my trips to the new building in the Lincoln Center complex.

Bob responded well to the literary therapy I had become used to employing. He was Pavlov's baritone. A key word would set off marvelous reflexes, and in the most atypical of confessions, something I never expected from this typical Jewish boy, Robert gave me the sweet and lowdown on his mother, who made Napoleon's Madame La Mère, Herodias, Clytemnestra, and Gypsy's Rose look like Mother Machree. He was astonishingly honest about her and not one whit less grateful than he should have been. He was aware of her contribution but painfully sensitive to the harm she had done. Though Bob was quite cognizant of the facts, being the victim, I attributed this insight to his smart wife. This was one of the dividends earned through his merger with Marion. How could these two women—the mother and the wife—ever have got on?

It is one of the dramatic truths that these mothers, doubtless unaware that their sacrifices are always selfish, claim an unrealistic rebate at the end of the line. For doing what they are helpless to avoid, they demand undivided love, priority over the mate, lover and child, and what amounts to alimony on your unapproved "remarriage." The use of illness and age as blackmail is too common to belabor. But Bob allowed me to build this memorial to her as long as it was made clear—and it was—that he would have been nothing but a *nebbish* without her and her gallantry. Lillian (Lotza) Miller, his mother, was a natural phenomenon and he understood and bemoaned the shadow she cast over her whole family.

I think that *Once More from the Beginning* is the most satisfying job I've done. I have Bob to thank—first because of the hilarious material, and second for straightening me out. He accomplished this by just being himself and sharing his life with me.

In need of a job again, I still felt superior to the project when my *Mittel*-European agent, who had told me to forget Bette Davis, first tried to sell me on Robert

181

Merrill. Although an admirer of the singer's work, I wasn't enthusiastic. A meeting was arranged at the Gotham Hotel bar.

If my agent was *Mittel*-European, Bob's was the living end. Eventually she was bequeathed to me when she generously took over my own melancholy agent's duties. But for her faith, she should have been a self-flagellating nun. She listened to complicated negotiations with curiosity, sympathy, and a true appreciation of drama. Her head would nod in a devotional rhythm that spoke of an ancient grief. This gesture of classic tragedy, I was soon to learn, was a blanket ritual that would cover all of the catastrophes her passivity might create. It was a case of weeping before the fact. When things got really tough there was always what I used to call her hasty retreat.

She had a formidable coiffure, unpolished onyx eyes, and a very sweet smile. She was the kind of motherly Jewish woman who—knowing nothing about you on introduction—still greets you like a mourner making a condolence call.

While Mr. Merrill, editor Bob Markel, and I chatted about the opera—the singer amusing us with anecdotes—I felt the lady's eyes searching mine. She was looking for something. *How marvelous!* I thought. *She really cares about Merrill. She's examining my character—rather obviously but it's touching—for sympathy. She's trying to protect this vulnerable fellow.*

This was not so, though she certainly loved her client. No. She was simply trying to determine my background. Mr. Merrill and I, though we got on immediately, seemed to come from different worlds. She was looking for a *landsman*. She wasn't sure.

"Are you English?" the lady asked.

"No. Just affected." I answered.

She had to try again. She hadn't got what she wanted.

I had come by my snobbery naturally—from my father. Theater people are usually unrooted, brought up as they are in stages, their *mise en scène* created especially for their individual drama. There were times when my father's accent made mine sound like Casey Stengel's. Theater was our religion, the Lunts, Shakespeare, and Bobby Clark my gods. Bob's and my backgrounds were poles apart, mine lost somewhere between Our Crowd and Our Gang.

I was suddenly amused and as usual on this subject, insufferable. I decided to be the liberal gentile. I used my loftiest two-seconds-over-Heathrow accent.

"Who could have imagined that the *forbissiner* Germont, the *momser* Scarpia, could be such a warm and open guy?"

"Forbissiner! Mahmza! the agent screamed, hope springing in her breast. "How he knows Yiddish." Her eyebrows rose to collide with her hairdo.

"Why not?" I asked.

Her eyebrows now quickly lowered, wrinkling her brow as she scrutinized me with delight.

"What New Yorker doesn't?" I added. "It's such a colorful tongue."

Her heart fell again as I sipped my daiquiri and smiled my most nonsectarian smile.

Merrill and I liked each other more than I had expected or thought possible, and Macmillan liked us together. As I remember it, my agent and the editor dashed off to their respective affairs and we three lingered over our drinks, now that another meeting, along with contracts, had been planned. We were having some laughs when Bob ever so tentatively asked how I spelled my name, a subject the reader will remember that does not bore me. However, this time the question was pointed. I decided to help matters somewhat.

I confided that my grandmother was Jewish—neglecting to mention that my grandfather was also—along, quite logically, with their progeny.

"My grandmother, you know, was a Jewess!" I announced.

I knew the image would evoke a handsome doña with an El Greco head, a large nose and an even larger fortune, with lands extending from the Pyrenees to the Mediterranean. She would create greater awe than all of Christendom. To confuse them further, instead of discoursing in Latin, a sometime diversion of the Sephardim, I gently dropped a few more Yiddish expressions I had picked up from an Italian dancer and a dead uncle who had been in vaudeville. A man who loved a good joke and repartee, Bob laughed comfortably after I made a note of one of his mother's homilies and said, "Quoth the *maven.*"

"You're *Jewish?*" the agent lady now asked, bug-eyed. "Not that it matters—it matters?—but Bob would feel more *hamisher.*"

"I'm very fond of Jews," I admitted.

"Oh?"

"What are you making such a *megilleh* about?"

"*Megilleh. Oi!* How he knows words, Bob." A dimple appeared in her cheek, a glint in her eye. "With that *punim,* you couldn't be Jewish."

"What word?" I parried. "Isn't McGiller Irish?"

On again, off again, Finnegan. His whiskers and his *payis* blew up his chinnegan. I'm not always very nice, but Bob Merrill was, and for all my fooling around, I was seriously evading the issue.

It was the astonishing fact that unlike all my other books in which I felt I might be helping my subjects, it was Robert Merrill's simple and mostly joyous account of his vivid past that made me laugh at myself and my lingering insecurities. I almost envied his roots, burrowing deep from the dirt of Williamsburg back to the soil of Sholem Aleichem's Poland. I started living his book, feeding on, instead of just feeding. The assimiliated have been created. I felt less so by writing *Once More from the Beginning*.

Bob's story really started with his parents' marriage, which was not made in heaven but in what used to be called the old country. Abe Millstein (Miller) a quiet little pale-faced boy—legs akimbo, fingers bleeding as he learned his trade—was promised to his master's daughter, a pretty child with a soprano voice she inherited from her cantor father, but an awesome gift for dissatisfaction that was all her own.

Emigrating to Brooklyn, they left one ghetto for another. Papa was lucky enough to get a job in a sweatshop and never rose above it. His serenity earned him no money but all of his wife's contempt. Mama, who changed her name from Lotza to Lillian, would come to change many things. She would will things better. When she heard, for the first time, Moishe (Bob) yell "Mama" from the courtyard of their tenement, what she heard was the call. She and her son would never be allowed a moment's rest again until he sang at the Metropolitan Opera.

These early years of poverty and parental bickering, of wretchedness and tyranny, were evoked by Bob with a vivacity and humor I trust I got into the book. Only the Jews along with the Italians can suffer so joyously. I fell in love with his whole *mishpocheh*.

What a cast of characters he offered up for the drama.

GRANDMA MILLER—who hated her daughter-in-law, Lotza, almost as much as she hated her husband, whom she kept locked in his room, letting him out only for important occasions and high holidays. Not a warm woman, she always called our protagonist "that woman's kid."

UNCLE LOOEY—a sweet little tailor who was America's doorman. He brought the whole family over one by one, getting them all jobs. His seniority, and only this, earned him the role of peacemaker and judge for the family. Sipping hot tea through a cube of sugar, Looey would invariably make the wrong decision, but he looked like a patriarch, which was half the battle, and Mama knew how to con him into winning her wars.

THE PROPHET—the last resort in any crisis Uncle Looey couldn't solve to Mama's satisfaction. He lived in Manhattan under the Williamsburg Bridge, and in a torture of wisdom which might have been an epileptic fit, this ancient, waxen, nicotine-stained sage would exact from the air what Mama wanted to hear—for a fee.

TANTE LESSER—a large woman who was built like the Bridge Plaza bus and was even more dependable. She was a cook in a hospital but spent all her spare time helping family and friends. At one point, with all credit gone and no money left, she arranged a robbery so Lotza and Abe could collect insurance. She even made enormous footprints to the firescape and Bob was frightened of the giant *goniff*. Papa was stunned that anyone would bother for such spoils—an old *tallith,* moth-eaten mink tails from a muff, and a brass candlestick. He was kept innocent of the facts. Mama and Tante Lesser, in cahoots, kept their dark secret, morality coming in a poor second to survival in those Depression years.

TANTE ESTHER—a dear hypocondriac who could belch at will, especially if told that she looked well.

UNCLE SAM—her husband and only real illness. A carpenter and muck-a-muck with the union, he loved to ridicule Moishe about his early stutter and baby fat.

UNCLE ABE—the rich relative, a dress manufacturer who had a radio only he could listen to, a Persian rug only he could walk on, and an automobile he and his top-heavy wife, Molly, would park economically on Second Avenue so he could lord it over the hoi polloi while they posed eating hot rolls.

COUSIN MEYER COHEN—the country cousin in the Catskills, through whose kindness Bob was to see his first tree, which he hugged in wonder.

THE PULITSKER PROGRESSIVE SOCIETY—FRIENDS AND TOWNSPEOPLE—who banded together to assure themselves if not a prosperous life, then at least a decent burial. Only the lucky members had a reservation on eternity. The society had affairs where Mama sang and everyone danced the *hora,* but it was their dues which guaranteed them a burial plot that would save them from potter's field.

CHAIM SHAPIRO—pauper and economist, who starved to pay these dues but shrewdly determined that if he lived to be eighty and a member in good standing for those fifty years, it wasn't such a bargain. Conversely, if he were to drop dead soon, preferably immediately, he might not have such a bad deal. He set himself a course of happy self-destruction so he could get real value for his money.

What a cast! And how I admired them all for surviving the rats and the roaches, the cold, the prejudice and, most of all, each other.

Towering above all of them:

MAMA—Lotza Millstein Miller, singing her Polish folk-songs and then Jeanette MacDonald's complete repertoire at bar mitzvahs and weddings in order to scrape up enough pennies to fight the fates and Poppa—training her Moishe for the destiny she herself had planned. Best friend and worst enemy, she was obviously everything to Bob. Certainly his passage across the bridge, to fame, to fulfillment, to his first bravos.

While Marion ran her house, took care of her children and saw to it that Bob and I were comfortable and well fed, Bob talked and I listened. We did this at ping-pong with the kids, at a golf range off the highway, listening to music, or lying in the sun, covered with oil. We worked all through the spring and I felt that after four weeks or so, I would be able to start the book while Bob went out West for a tour and then on to Rome and a recording session.

He now spoke easily of everything except his singing and his mother—both subjects far too serious to be lightly treated. I realized that this was going to be the book. Mama and her "singer mine."

At first Bob treated everything flippantly. At first! The poverty, the Jews, even Mama. That was soon changed with some prodding. The pain is less if one rewrites one's life. It is one of the remarkable things about autobiography that the writer can live his life over again with a bit more grace and ease—if he's allowed to. The function of the ghost is to earn first the irritation, then the love, and then the hatred of the subject by demanding no less than a perfect pearl.

The only topic Bob wouldn't touch eventually was his marriage to Roberta Peters. In a sense I almost felt that it had been a superimposition on an otherwise dramatically consistent life; but I had to pursue this. Certainly the publishers had asked about that marriage at our first meeting. Everyone wanted to know why the musical romance of the decade, frowned upon but staged by Papa Hurok, who was loath to give the bride away, lasted something like five minutes. Everyone from Krafft-Ebing to Walter Winchell was solicited in hopes of finding the answer. The opera and radio world buzzed with dark gossip and when I broached the subject, Bob shrugged his narrow shoulders. It was the only thing in his life he didn't seem able to level with me about. There wasn't an approach I didn't try—to no avail. He dried up on the subject. I talked turkey with him.

If he ignored the incident in his life story, the reader would surely substitute his own Gothic tale. A series of them were already echoing in the Met's dressing rooms. Why not come clean with me and tell me the secret of the alcove? I would protect him *and* Miss Peters. Both —to everyone's surprise—had eventually remarried and had children, which quieted the more clinical rumors, but it didn't silence them. When next I went to New Rochelle I again thought—interrupting another train of thought—I could startle him into opening up. Nothing. He simply repeated—with little credibility, since the villains attended the ceremony—that his mother-in-law and the disapproving Hurok were behind Miss Peters's decision to leave him. The story was so flimsy that it barely covered his embarrassment. It was impossible to write and I seriously considered skipping over the entire incident, which was, of course, impossible. I would have to find a way.

I went to Marion. How foolish of me to have been so discreet. She wouldn't mind. Didn't she know *everything?* And all in all she was a good egg. Usually a willing talker, she was, like everyone else, silenced by the question.

"But you've got to help me, Marion. I've got to write *something* about that marriage, and Bob just isn't giving me anything."

"What can I tell you, Sandy? I wasn't around then. It was before my time."

"So was Henry the Eighth and you know what happened to his wives. Bob must have told you something. Knowing you, you must have found out."

"What can I tell you, Sandy?"

"A great deal, I suspect."

"You'll have to ask Bob."

And I was right back where I started. Into my notes went a big question mark. I would have to find a way to tackle this. I would have to satisfy both publisher and reader with some kind of explanation, and I would have to satisfy myself. And with all of these satisfied people I would have to have the Merrills' O.K. on my solution. After all, I always kept forgetting, it was *his* life.

It was impossible not to like Bob, and I never even tried. I watched with interest the gentleness with which the not always gentle Mr. Bing treated him. The patrician director of the Met had once fired Bob for breaking his contract and rushing off to Hollywood in a futile attempt to become a combination of Bing Crosby and Nelson Eddy.

Bob brought out the father in me, and I wouldn't have hurt him for anything in the world. He is a strangely vulnerable man, the quick smile and the fast wisecrack a method of appeasement as well as need for approbation. They were first employed, I would guess, against his mother and then the toughs at school. His jokes may not be hilarious but they are disarming. His humor is good natured. Beneath his bravado there is a shyness, and at the end of the day I was sorely tempted to give him a star for his notebook. I watched such men as Jean-Louis Barrault, who directed him in *Faust,* do just that. He brings the father out in everybody. Robert aims to please and he does. He applies himself, get "A" for effort and is eminently dependable, no small thing in my book.

Liked by all, the little boy from the other side of the bridge, through his natural talent and unusual dedication to it, has sung for and broken bread with senators, presidents, cardinals, and movie stars. Robert Merrill arrived and I hope he stays a long time. It is certainly thirty-five years since his Met debut as Germont in *La Traviata.*

In this world of cold, Nordic sopranos and hot-tempered Italian tenors, with everyone who isn't singing, screaming, and upstaging everyone else, Bob is a maverick. His early success brought conceit instead of ego, and he had been so impressed with his brilliant notices and the excitement of his own claque that he had faltered in his disciplines. He was flying high and aimed West, where he bombed in Hollywood with the film *Aaron Slick from Punkin Crick*. It was his luckiest break. He had flirted successfully with disaster and now he was up Punkin Crick without a paddle. With real humility, he prevailed upon Rudolf Bing to pardon him—no mean trick—allowing his return to the Met. It took time, but Bob grew up in the waiting. On his return he was never again to falter, applying himself as never before and, after his marriage to Marion, gaining the confidence to build a repertoire worthy of that voice. Though he never stopped having fun, it was in reward for his work and not a substitution for it. Instead of becoming part of the ephemeral decor, Bob Merrill became for longer than most a Metropolitan fixture.

His Escamillo ceased to attract screaming bobby soxers and I doubt he's sung it for years, but his Germont in *Traviata* and Ashton in *Lucia di Lammermoor* kept the real opera buffs in their seats as long as he remained in the company. I remember with delight his rehearsals for Lucia with Joan Sutherland. Those gorgeous voices, the impeccable musicianship of those recitatives, the beauty of that second-act duet.

That was a glorious opening, and after the performance, which marked the start of Robert's twentieth year at the house, Johnny Carson hosted a party in his honor at Voisin. It was quite a night, with Walter Cronkite Viennese-waltzing like the Student Prince and Judith Anderson and several security guards making the place safe for Hubert Humphrey and his very nice wife. Humphrey was the feather in Bob's cap on that celebrity-filled evening. He was campaigning for the 1964 election but found time enough to join us in Bob's honor. The vice-presidential nominee was in high spirits, not blessed with the second sight that would have foreseen the self-destruction in accepting second place on that particular ticket. Like everyone else he liked Bob Merrill, and with that much I cannot quarrel.

Bob introduced me to Miss Sutherland that night and she was to be reckoned with. Talk about larger than life! Knowing how I adored her voice, Bob dragged me over to her. I took her hand for kissing, but the great soprano demurred.

"One moment, my dear," she sang sweetly. "If you are going to be courtly we're going to do it right."

She then slowly and with comic deliberation pulled

off her opera-length white kid glove. One expected it to be as endless as Beatrice Lillie's—and it almost was. She then extended her hand once more, grandly—very grandly—and I started at the fingertips and worked my way up to her lovely shoulder. She was delicious and gay and altogether a lovely woman that night. Truly she is—especially when she sings—as Bob says, like a giant running swiftly.

I met many fascinating people through Bob Merrill. But one night I got the surprise of my life.

Robert was opening the Metropolitan as *Rigoletto* and it was the last season at the old house. The gorgeous old Met was on its last legs but dressed to kill that night, and I sat luxuriating in the lovely spectacle, the Merrill box being the perfect vantage point for such a treat. It was a gala night and the audience was as distinguished and burnished as the glittering auditorium itself. I was always thrilled with Bob's voice and amused that his one-time wife of five minutes was still his Gilda. Such is the repertory of the opera, I fear that I kept peeking at Mrs. Merrill, to detect a hint of pleasure at what was obviously an off night for Miss Peters. I could not.

Two boxes from us sat Mr. and Mrs. Richard Milhous Nixon, in evening dress of course but quite informal since the future president was then between engagements and simply in private practice with Mudge Rose et al. on Wall Street. It was a quiet period in his life but I was never in any of his periods an admirer of Mr. Nixon and so busied myself during the intermissions, knowing that Marion, as an acquaintance and wife of the star, would doubtless spend some time with them.

During one of the intervals, returning from Sherry's, I caught sight of Mr. Nixon lumbering along near the stairway with a couple of young people who I imagine, not then recognizing them, must have been one of his daughters and her escort. Mr. Nixon looked glum and hell-bent to get back to his seat. There was at that moment no one about; and then I came into view along with two or three others and he became galvanized. "And what do you plan when your studies are over this year?" he asked the youth suddenly, his expressionless face now smiling, interested, avuncular. It was obviously a rhetorical question and no answer was expected. We all continued our race with the second-act curtain.

Robert was in marvelous voice that night. One cannot help but paraphrase what his father must have said on Passover, "Why should this night be different from any other?" and at the final curtain I rushed back to see him before the mob could take over. I explained to Marion and Robert's brother and sister-in-law, with whom we were supping later, that I wanted to take notes backstage for the book.

I used the shortcut near the orchestra pit and arrived at what, I must confess, no one has ever missed since the great move to Lincoln Center—those slums of dressing rooms. Unbelievably Bob was sharing an impossible little john with Jan Peerce and the whole place was ramshackle, thereby heightening the contrast between both the illusion and reality, backstage and performance.

I heard the shower and waited outside in the hall, looking out the window onto Seventh Avenue. A trickle of people opened and slammed doors while shouting congratulations to cold-creamed happy faces, gratefully done with their chores, and then I took my notebook from my dinner jacket and leaned against the wall while I tried to record the growing excitement. When my head raised at a noise, I saw an incredible sight. Richard Nixon was rushing toward me, his arms outstretched, his face beaming with excessive pleasure. He was coming at me with such speed that I couldn't even jump aside in time. My instinct was such that I wanted to turn to see at whom he was aiming but there was just a window there and a blank wall. It was me, all right.

And then I was there, in Richard Milhous Nixon's arms, being bear-hugged. I am not unappealing but quite honestly rarely evoke such magnetic attraction.

"What an evening! What a performance," he cried. "Bob was great—the whole night was great."

He tightened his grip and I observed that his tuxedo was the worse for wear, due no doubt to the heat of his excitement and the series of banquets that must have preceded this evening. I had heard that he was an opera buff and must confess that he was displaying a little-boy pleasure that seemed the McCoy. My mind worked more quickly than my tongue, which was unusual for me. Of course. He thought I was Bing. Sir Rudolf and I really do not look alike but we are both tall, thin, graying and balding. The evening dress and the notebook outside the star's dressing room. *Robert, Lieb Freund, nur eine Sache fehlt. Perhaps if you do not make that cross until the middle A zu Ende ist!* Certainly I'm younger but my work has been aging, and from a distance, perhaps . . .

In any case, before I could do more than recoil from his embrace and reserve the pleasure of pondering the austere Sir Rudolf's reaction to such a demonstration of appreciation, Mr. Merrill opened his door crying, "Dick!"

"Bob," was Mr. Nixon's answer and now they were bear-hugging.

"You know Sandy Dody?" Bob now said, and Mr. Nixon, with his genius for landing on his feet, accepted this new intelligence without missing a beat or bothering to explain our emotional meeting to me or to Bob or himself. Of course, in fairness, it occurs to me that he may be *such* an opera buff that after a brilliant performance, he may attack the first person who comes into sight.

In a few seconds the dressing room was overflowing, resembling, indeed, the Marx Brothers' stateroom in *A Night at the Opera.*

Mr. Merrill, like all stars, knows everyone and was equally at home with Truman, Kennedy, Eisenhower, and Johnson. Unlike most, Bob has never lost his surprise at having arrived at the top, at being up late with the grown-ups; and this is a most appealing quality.

Being a ghost, as one can see, opens doors and cans of worms beyond the grasp of mere mortals. There have been moments of fun and frolic, and by the time Bob and I had talked ourselves out I had had many an enjoyable time with him and his family. I knew backstage at the Met the way I had known the five tiers and every inch of standing space ever since my first *Hansel und Gretel* in another time.

I was content with the several notebooks filled with Jewish relatives and Italian opera singers. I had every subject covered and documented except one. The one with the huge question mark.

The Merrills went off on tour and I to London to sop up the theater and the countryside with Kaye Ballard and some other friends. When I got back I settled down to write *Once More from the Beginning.* The only obstacle in my way, except my own initial fears which exist with every book, was still the Peters business. It seemed unhandleable. Other than that I was having fun with the early childhood and that marvelous family.

I wanted two things now. To solve the Peters problem and not to make Lotza Miller, Bob's mother, into a Jewish joke but the real, live, marvelous gorgon she was. I was fascinated with the woman and wondered whether Stephen Sondheim in the ultimate "Rose's Turn" in *Gypsy* didn't reveal prototypically the inevitable hatred of the driving mother for the child that has arrived to

196

replace her. All of these women have got to the top of the heap on the backs of their children, only to realize when all the dust has cleared that fulfillment is really not transferable. The victory is really not theirs. They are managers, not artists, and contempt and jealousy—though they would never admit it as Rose did in her explosive hysterical revelation—replace the devotion and joy born of that second chance around. "When is it *my* turn?"—that shrill and desperate cry of the stripper's mother whose sacrifices have brought her nothing but someone else's success—was Rose's verbalization of all the sloppily veiled and amorphous anger these monsters feel for their beloved children.

Why else do they all turn into "mistresses," demanding a largesse that could break their donors both financially and emotionally? Why else did Bob's mother (always original) not object to his marriage to Marion, which might somehow justify his scandalous apartment away from her, but in a private meeting with the girl, suggest that she pick out a big engagement diamond. "Mine girl, carats like from the grocery in a bunch. He's got plenty, mine son the singer —plenty." Was she now identifying, no longer with Bob but with his future wife? Was she never going to be herself?

Who was Lotza Miller? The mother of a famous singer. A star by proxy.

Though everyone of my subjects was vaguely aware of this, only Bob (the only man, mind you) was willing to let me say it all. Could it be that for all the horrors the ladies went through, they could more sympathetically empathize with Mama, first rebelling and then identifying? Of course, until the first section of my work had been written and approved by Bob, I couldn't be sure that he *would* really accept her portrait. There is always the danger that the first view of their life will stun. If there is disapproval, the whole flow of work, as you have seen, can stop, making any continuation doubtful.

When I finished the first fifty pages, I made an appointment to go up to New Rochelle. Macmillan approved the manuscript. Now I had to get Bob used to seeing his ideas and family in print for the world to see. I like to read the first pages aloud to my subjects whenever it is possible. My enthusiasm for my own work, a sympathetic reading that doesn't miss a nuance, a little personality thrown in, doesn't hurt. At any rate, the first draft of *Once More from the Beginning* was so illegible that it demanded this kind of personal performance. I dined sumptuously and then started reading. Fortunately it worked. Both Merrills liked it—Bob nodding his head happily throughout and Marion's expressive face giving and removing stars like Wanda Hale of the *Daily News*.

The agent *kvelled*. She absolutely adored the work. And from a *shaygitz!* How in the devil *did* I know so much Yiddish? She now announced that the Merrills were ecstatic and that was all I wanted to know. I could now, with this green light, forge ahead with fresh vigor. The encouragement given by the subject at this point is of utmost importance: What subliminally seems a presumption becomes completely natural. I had now become Bob Merrill and I didn't have a care in the world—except for damned Roberta Peters.

I now was given access to the archives of the Met and studied the press reports of the romance and the wedding, which was handled by Hurok, the principals, and the press like a Jewish coronation. Bob had leveled with me about everything else but I just couldn't buy the innocence with which I was always greeted when this subject came up. I was literally stopped in my tracks when I arrived at this juncture. There was no one I could go to since the Merrills had pleaded the Fifth. Anything Roberta Peters might say —assumming she would even talk to me—would be worthless in Bob's autobiography. Nobody's conjectures or inside information could be of any avail. I simply had to generate the answer myself, making it reasonable to audience and Merrills alike. This seemed impossible.

A fugitive thought led me to the answer. A remembered remark of Bob's. He had more than once said that tenors were impossible but once laughingly added, "the baritone never gets the girl." We had laughed together at the time and I had made a note of it.

Always feeling that the marriage was something less than the culmination of a great passion, that there was something more synthetic than mysterious, I now threw myself into the charade. It was a tightrope to be sure. A high wire. But I believed that I could keep the delicate balance.

I returned to my notes and the press reports. Both Robert and Roberta (my God, even *that* was precious) were young, attractive, and talented. It was fairly recently that the mastodon diva had been replaced by Lily Pons and Grace Moore and Gladys Swarthout. They were all predecessors of the lovely Miss Peters. Mr. Merrill was not only a favorite with the critics but with the young. The bobby soxers who were making Frank Sinatra a superstar on Forty-third Street—no doubt with some help from Mr. Sinatra's managers—were invading the Family Circle and standing room to swoon over Bob Merrill—no doubt with some help from *his* manager. This was a time-honored practice in the theater and once the flame caught it could and—in Sinatra's case *did*—spread like wildfire throughout the country. Robert Merrill's manager, Moe Gale, as all good managers, knew how to promote his client. Though this was never even suggested to me by Bob, and may have been untrue, it seemed likely to me now that a boost to both young Bob's and pretty Roberta Peter's career was in order.

What better way of making them household words

than to have them become what Broadway called an "item"? *They met at the Met.* By the time the press got through with them they were in love.

I could certainly buy the flirtation and the romance. Why not? Bob was definitely on his way up, young Roberta possibly a flash in the pan, having at the last moment, replaced (in the best Hollywood tradition) Nadine Conner as Zerlina in *Don Giovanni,* garnering great reviews. Discovering that she was really named Peterman, Bob thought they had more in common than singing and, according to him, they started seeing each other though she was a most dedicated singer with her own mother guarding her all the way. Neither mother, it seems, was delighted with the match, though Lotza would at least be able to justify Bob's treacherous move away from home. Sol Hurok, Roberta's mentor, did not like the idea, thinking it would be bad for the girl's career, which seemed odd, considering that both singers intended to continue at the Met. Presumably a pregnancy would be utter betrayal, Bob the only possible traitor. The Montagues and Capulets again! *Romeo e Gulietta.* I couldn't very well report, with either tact or accuracy, that nothing made much sense, but I could imply it.

By showing little or no emotion and through a simple funny recital of the ceremony and my choice of observations, I could say plenty though.

The ceremony was at Temple Emanu-El and Robert —with his brother Gil, who was best man, and another pal —got stuck in the Greek Independence Day parade and was a half hour late. Everything seemed designed to whet the appetite of the public—even the late curtain. *Could he be standing her up?*

They became a romantic entity because of the pressures surrounding them. Robert and Roberta were "convinced" they were good copy, and illusion and reality became hopelessly confused while the two kids reveled in the publicity and all the fun and fanfare. The minute they decided to get married, RCA Victor summoned them to record some love duets. It's lucky they were recorded immediately.

Temple Emanu-El was packed to the doors, indeed, to the curb outside, with waiting fans and folding chairs, and the performance would soon be over so that they could applaud the stars and the attending celebrities who ran the gamut from Mrs. August Belmont to the Williamsburg Feldmans.

While the rabbi was talking of God's blessing, Robert Merrill glanced at his bride. He had told me that she looked as if she were about to break into a duet with the holy man and that's what gave me *my* cue. This was a *real* collaboration. Bob now cast the wedding, starting with Jan Peerce as the cantor, Chaliapin the rabbi, Giuseppe di Luca the unhappy Hurok, Ernestine Schumann-Heink as his redoubtable Tante Lesser, Lotte Lehmann as Mama, and Maria Jeritza as Mrs. Peterman.

Nothing was real about the marriage now. This was a scene from an ever so light opera. When the rabbi completed his aria and hitched the two songbirds, Robert and Roberta dashed up the aisle and into the crowded streets where their fans went wild. The show was over and some old celebrity-chaser was heard to say, "Look at them, Sadie, the perfect couple. It's a fairy tale!"

And that's exactly what it was. And everyone now went home for coffee and cake, including the actors. As Robert said, "Roberta was a kid; that was her excuse. I was an idiot; that's mine."

The opera goes on forever, however, and it is literally true that for richer and poorer, until death, laryngitis, or retirement them might part, the Metropolitan continued to schedule Roberta as Gilda and Robert as Rigoletto. And that is the truth of it.

Bob and Marion gratefully bought the treatment of the marriage and laughed, with Bob's insisting that it really was no deeper than that. I don't think it's impossible. The hurdle was cleared and the rest of the book went smoothly until some of the Merrill family—successful in their own right—decided their background was too vividly presented. I could hardly have made them Van Rensselaers or Stuyvesants, which they might have loved. Bob and Marion, who have absolutely no pretenses, fought these demands to rewrite history and we got on with it.

All in all, when I consider what can and has happened to my work, I came off wonderfully until I got momentarily loused up with Vera Vandal, the scourge of Publisher's Row.

At the finish of the book, I was exhausted and ran off to London to do a job for NBC, a rewrite on a narrative to be read by Mary Martin over the Japanese and Vietnamese footage of her *Dolly* tour. Her contractually irrevocable and saccharine rewrites made Bette Davis sound like Emily Brontë. Obviously it was my fate to have the ladies give me a going over. But on my return this one at Macmillan was something.

After a good editing job all was now marevlous, and the Merrill book before printing was to go to a special editor who excelled in Yiddish, Italian, and opera. With this final polish, all spellings would be made perfect and uniform. The manuscript, after Bob Markel and I had gone over it, already needed a typist named Rosetta Stone, but I was grateful after former neglect to have such coddling. *This* book would have a sheen. Ah life! There seems to be no end to the variations on the theme.

The young woman whose identity to this moment has

been carefully kept from me was a frustrated novelist. When after three weeks I kept calling Macmillan for the finally polished manuscript so that I could give it one last check before the printers took over, it was finally sent on. I was jolted by the first sentence. I did not recognize it. From first to last, this maniac had rewritten the book—changing images, facts, dialogue, and insights, altogether changing the book's viewpoint as well as its style. Obviously this student of Yiddish, Italian, and opera was suffering a major breakdown—not, I pray, entirely due to my prose style. This woman decided to sacrifice herself to her idol, the velvet-voiced Robert Merrill. My editor, who had not yet read her corrections, loyally stated that she was the "best dame in the business." "But what business?" I demanded. "Murder?" Of course, when he saw the evidence he restored our original manuscript to the lowliest comma —every hint of her existence removed along with her identity.

Obviously fearing that, in my hysteria, I might do the woman in if I could find her, she was, so I heard, fired, imprisoned, and then deported, all of which I never believed. She survives! My keen eye recognizes her style on the doors and walls of our subways.

When *Once More from the Beginning* was published, Bob did his best to sell it. He appeared in department stores, on television, and radio to no avail. He saw to it that the book was mentioned everywhere but in the libretto of *Il Trovatore*. But the public, happy to pay fifteen dollars to hear him sing, wouldn't pay six to read about him. It was sad; and my heart was heavy.

The only leavener was provided by Robert Landry in *Variety* who in his review of the book was excessive in his praise of the "lower case collaborator, Sanford Boddy." I couldn't win.

Still, I profited in other ways, Thank God I have

only done the books I knew I'd enjoy writing. At this time I wanted to work with Leontyne Price, who loved Bob's book but was too self-effacing to consider an autobiography. The great soprano, always gracious, refused my blandishments. Instead, Jan Peerce asked me to work with him, and it was I who refused, knowing from his background that I would be writing the identical book in a higher key. I could have called it *Once More from the Top*. He also admitted that he was shocked that a nice boy like Bob Merrill could talk about his mother that way.

I needed the advance, but I didn't believe that this would be a step forward.

The Three Misses

Miss Elsa Lanchester

Lest it be believed that my charm—considerable though it may be—has never faltered, it has and quite dramatically. I too have been rejected—by experts. The widow Laughton, Miss Elsa Lanchester, loathed me on sight. We were so chemically unsuited to each other, her vials smoking and fuming to such a degree at my mere introduction into the space around her, that I believed she might go berserk. It is true that the casual spectator and even her physician might not have known the difference but, being the victim, or as she might see it, the catalyst, I would have known. She surely would have done me in.

This extraordinary player, whose gifts are equaled only by the strings attached to them, was interested some years ago in doing a book about herself and her late husband—or so I was told. An agent—whom I'd known through a Baha'i neighbor who painted her four walls black and had a tiny, silver-framed portrait of Hussain Ali as her only decor and recreation—called and asked if I were free and at all interested in writing of the acting couple.

Both Laughton and his mad consort were favorites of mine. Both of them gorgeous artists, he at his finest a great actor, she at her least a foursquare English eccentric. There wasn't the slightest question that I could interest a major publishing company once the lady and I fell in love with one another.

I believe that she was staying at the Essex House on Central Park South and the young agent—filled with the high hopes of any agent about to arrange a match that would set the literary world afire—walked me briskly through the park, extolling the lady's virtues, her brilliance, her eagerness to work, and most of all her warmth. "She'll *adore* you," he declared with an insistence I found almost insolent. I needed no such assurance.

When the door of her suite opened at our summons, I almost sprung back in terror. Standing before us, in an orange tent that covered an immense body from throat to toe, her hair a bright red afro, her dimpled face a mass of aggressions and retreats, superimpositions and recesses, all of it framing great crazy eyes, was the bride of Franken- stein. After greeting my companion, she pointed at me madly and I half expected to be turned into a gingerbread man. She backed up a trifle to allow us to negotiate the entrance and then placed herself in the room, arranging us around her. She was marvelous.

"I hear you're interested in doing a book on *Charles*." She screeched his name.

"Well, yes, because I heard that you were interested in doing such a book."

She narrowed her eyes and pursed her lips as she glared at the agent in mute reprimand for some act of indis- cretion. Then, like a dollying camera, her eyes swept across the room and landed on me.

"How can I do an honest book on Charles? *Charles!* How could I tell the *truth?* He has a brother who owns a hotel in the north of Britain!"

"May I tell you, Miss Lanchester, before we go on, how very much I have admired your work—in films and at the Turnabout Theater in Hollywood."

Being incurably starstruck I recalled some of her best roles. Both she and her husband, aside from being remarkable actors, were enviably the kind of characters that remain permanently in the public's mind.

"You and Mr. Laughton, as a working couple, as artists, and as husband and wife would make a fascinating book. For two originals to be—"

"My God!" she fumed, her flames licking my toes. "I can't bear him. His enthusiasm. I would go stark raving mad being near him. He'd exhaust me. Stop it. Stop it, I say! I couldn't possibly work with you."

"Well," I laughed gallantly, though burnt to a cinder, "there's evidently little danger of that."

If she weren't the leading character in a Punch and Judy show, I might have been hurt, but she was possessed. The agent sat across the room, frozen. Obviously geared to snatch victory from catastrophe, he sat smiling like someone at a foreign play, reveling in the gestures and sounds of the performance, and not having the dimmest notion of what was going on. There is something to be said for this technique.

Miss Lanchester, left to her own devices, rattled on about *Charles*—a word she always screeched—and her private life, stunning me with her candor. She was spitting and sputtering—all hot sparks and no one was safe now, especially poor, brilliant, dead, probably charred Mr. Laughton. She seemed to be battling with herself since there were no more comers.

"I can't tell about *Charles!* How can we write—how

do you write by the way? I think you can send me one of your books. Davis will do. Bette Davis will do."

I was bewitched by this raging conflagration, and I found myself still interested in the approach the book could take though at the same time I knew that I could never work with her. I spoke of their collaborative work on the screen and the fascination their relationship, their unusual partnership, would have for the public. She suddenly crackled.

"You're such an admirer of *Charles,* what do you think his best role was?"

There were so many I could have chosen. The man's career was built on tens of cornerstones. *Ruggles of Red Gap,* Captain Bligh, Henry VIII, Rembrandt. It was an endless list and I thought an obvious one. It seemed also poor judgment to concentrate on his early life when as a mature artist he was so impressive. There was one part late in his career I thought a model of great acting.

"I saw *Hobson's Choice* three times!" I confessed.

"I knew it! His *worst* acting. *Charles hated* it, *detested it.* It was the *worst* thing he ever did and *you* saw it *three* times."

Could this be her ballet? I thought. *A mad rigadoon whose jumps and flourishes will end with her demand that I drop everything and do her book?*

In any case, I rose to leave, deciding to take no more —while the agent stared at me. He had obviously escaped into a lighthearted catatonia and was still smiling vacantly.

Miss Lanchester also rose, all that orange and red flaring, and she swept across the room, almost setting the draperies afire on her way to the telephone. *My God! I'm being bodily removed. The burning bush is calling the house dick.*

"How about Scotch?" she demanded of me. "Do you drink Scotch? *Scotch!*" she now hissed.

The apparent attempt at civility faltered in mid-sentence as the gesture of reconciliation exploded into still another aggression. Only fire contained can warm one. It is the nature of the element to burn wildly, spreading devastation as it pursues its course. And I was very definitely in Miss Lanchester's way.

The bottle arrived, but its dwindling presence wasn't much help. The holocaust was ended with a farewell toast. I was glad to get out of there alive.

You can't win them all. But some are mortifying defeats.

Miss Katharine Hepburn

She is a woman whose fine bones, Bryn Mawr accent, and a list of distinguished roles all combine to give the impression of a shining intelligence. Her life-style has been at once unconventional and respectable, rebellious and exemplary. Like Beatrice Lillie, who could chant the naughtiest of Sir Noel's lyrics as correctly as if she were singing "God Save the Queen," she is always beyond reproach. Her hauteur is such that a commandment broken by her would be made to seem a prissy and needless restriction quite deserving of her impatience.

Certainly Katharine Hepburn is her own religion and one must therefore accept her on pure faith. As if to prove her transcendence over earthly matters, the lady—regardless of part—has, it is apparent, not combed her hair in over fifteen years.

After an abortive attempt to work with Rose Kennedy —a most exciting prospect and project that ended, while

I was in Paris, as much by Chappaquiddick as the lady's apparent reluctance at that time—it occurred to an editor, a publisher, and myself simultaneously that Katharine Hepburn would make a splendid subject—outspoken, singular superstar that she is.

Moving easily from lovely maiden to handsome matron, Katharine Hepburn has escaped the awkward age. She has never been less than marvelous to look at, and that will never change. I remember the first time I saw her—as John Barrymore's daughter in *A Bill of Divorcement*. She was a laser beam. Her intensity, her linear elegance stunned the viewer. Her very mannerisms and affectations were wondrous because of the courage with which she displayed them. One wondered if, indeed, they *were* affectations or simply the generic peculiarities of a new species. This, of course, is what a star is.

Barbra Streisand has accomplished such a revolution, breaking *all* the esthetic rules and in her case turning the concept of beauty upside down. Hepburn did not have to do this. In any epoch, she would have been considered beautiful—especially when she was young. Her features were delicate, her countenance agreeable to an extreme. It was only in the matter of her aberrant style and comportment that, like Streisand, she reeducated the viewer.

I always admired Hepburn's refusal to be altered in any way by the powers. She and Garbo towered over the terrain. Together with Bette Davis, these three actresses—for different reasons—scaled the heights, achieving such prominence that whether or not they work again, they will remain the distinguishing features of a now-dead city.

Katharine Hepburn will always be a star with, it would seem, a never-decreasing following that thrills to her flat New England speech though she be Clytemnestra, Eleanor of Aquitaine, or Clara Schumann. The lady makes not the slightest attempt to accommodate herself to a character, but simply makes it her own. Like George Arliss once did for himself long before her, she has managed to convince the world that an incredible variety of historic figures resemble, to the last freckle, Miss Katharine Hepburn.

But what she loses in depth of characterization, she makes up in winning performances that—in their familiarity—never cease to please her admirers and even divert her detractors. In *Philadelphia Story, Summertime, Alice Adams, Little Women, The African Queen,* and her perfectly tailored pictures with Spencer Tracy, the marriage of part and personality work perfectly. Then there is the added stamp of her personal integrity. Personal integrity in actors—as with most people—is simply the insistence that one's demands, no matter how unreasonable, be met at all costs.

Katharine Hepburn, for all these reasons, had fascinated me for years. On the screen she has been absolute mistress of the fleeting emotion. Especially in closeup, she has always been able to strike the exact emotional chord. Smiling through tears, one of her favorite pastimes, she could break your heart, this particularly true in her radiant youth. One never doubted in her films that Katharine Hepburn was one of the privileged class. She was entirely credible as a Main Liner, a judge, a physicist, a musician, or a princess, if only of Fairfield County.

I decided to go after her. It would be a stimulating period, to be sure, since one couldn't be Katharine Hepburn, the symbol of all that was strong, noble, aristocratic, and liberal, without being absolutely insufferable.

I saw us together as a team. There were some things I just saw in a vision, and this was one of them. I had once also seen something else and passed my vision on to someone at MGM. I had suggested that if he had any guts he would do a film biography of Gertrude Stein starring Spencer Tracy in the title role with Hepburn in a little mustache as Alice B. Toklas. It was inspired casting and therefore quite beyond the clods. It would have been memorable but, alas, it was not meant to be.

Believing in the direct approach, especially with those who are famous for their directness, I sat down and wrote Miss Hepburn a letter. She was a sitting duck at that moment and easily reached, as she was appearing in New York as Chanel in *Coco,* which, confess I must, was not my cup of tea. Katharine Hepburn couldn't have been a less likely Gabrielle Chanel, and when I saw her in a special preview for the fashion world I couldn't help but think that her performance might have been transplanted from any other play she had done, from Shakespeare's *The Merchant of Venice* to Shaw's *The Millionairess.* To be sure, I found her, as always, interesting to watch—but Coco never!

Despite my reservations, the house was now sold out and I knew she was going to stay put for a while. To my extreme pleasure, I discovered that we not only were in accord politically, but both loved fresh air and could not abide central heating. Practically the entire company of *Coco* was under doctor's care because of her insistence that the Broadway Theatre be kept so cold. I was now thoroughly sold on her, since guests at my house are clever enough to arrive as if they are on location for *Nanook of the North,* and I have lost several friends, a couple through anger and, in truth, only one from the flu. Yes, it all augured well for me.

I sat down and wrote one of my letters of petition. I offered Miss Hepburn not only my pen and my sword, my adulation and charm but posterity as well. It was made clear that I was not in the least interested in a Hollywood confession but an in-depth, full-dress biography of a woman whose impressive heritage made her a sequential if misplaced flower of New England. In any case, I offered to buy her a drink, be it hail or farewell. I received a hurried, half-handwritten, half-typed note from Miss Hepburn a few days later, informing me that though a book was out of the question, she would love to have a drink with me after the show one night. Would I contact a Miss Wilburn, her secretary, and arrange an evening at my convenience.

Before every book I have done, there has been the ballet. There are grave doubts, fears, even terror in the future subject. There is always the immediate refusal and then the courtship—one that makes the elaborate ritual of the peacock seem like the unpreliminary, easy-come-easy-go of an Easter bunny. This note from the actress was, I felt, the first stage in the relationship. I could tell she was interested. When I would meet with her my own gifts of persuasion would prevail.

Miss Hepburn had stipulated in her note that I call in the middle of the following week, so I did not change my plans to go off to Cape Cod for a holiday with friends in scrubbed, salty, white-clapboarded Wellfleet. Good things were in the air and my hosts, the Ernest Bragins, were delighted when I revealed that I was going to call one of their favorite stars for an appointment. After the usual teasing, I told them who it was and they both cried, "Perfect. You're made for each other." And I concurred.

I called on Wednesday and Miss Wilburn, who had been alerted, was warm and responsive. Miss Hepburn had found my letter most interesting and was looking forward to meeting with me.

"Mr. Dowdy," she asked, "is it all right if you have your drink at the theater or at Miss Hepburn's apartment? She never goes *out* after the performance."

I assured the young woman that whatever arrangement was convenient for the star was agreeable with me and my name was pronounced Dody. What night was convenient? It was arranged at last, and now Miss Wilburn asked if I'd seen the play. Not having enjoyed it and never having lied backstage to an actor, I thought it wise to forget the whole thing. I could not in honesty say, "Miss Hepburn, you were superb," and since anything less is destructive to an actor's ego, it seemed better to play dumb. I could compliment her genuinely if *post facto* on countless former occasions that had given me pleasure.

"Well," she now said, "it would be terrible for you to dangle until eleven-fifteen. There will be a house seat in your name. How do you spell it, Mr. Doddy?"

I had used my engraved stationery but why complain? I was wanted at the theater by Katharine Hepburn and going to see her concerning a possible book. I cut short my stay on the Cape and returned to New York in great anticipation.

What should I wear? I was sun- and windburned from walking on the beach, and with my graying hair, the grizzled look around the ears, perhaps a tweed jacket would be right. I'd play it informally. That was her style. Tweedy, yes. The sun had brought out my freckles. It was already starting, the osmosis, the mirroring of the subject, the fusion.

The first meeting, as I've already made clear, is of great importance. The chemistry must be exactly right. A wrong move can put the kibosh on the whole book. The presence of a dimple or absence of earlobes can doom the project.

Tweeds would be exactly right, I thought.

I arrived at the theater promptly one half-hour before the curtain and tweed-elbowed my way through the milling crowd in the lobby. The show was a great hit—because of its star—and it was still in the flush of its first weeks. It delighted me that these people had either paid the then high tariff of fifteen dollars a ticket or were trying to, while this aging bronze god in his Savile Row jacket was a guest of the star. I edged nearer the box office and caught the eye of the uniformed man asking for reservations. In the most carefully modulated voice, I stage-whispered my lovely credentials.

"Miss Hepburn left a ticket. The name is—Dody!"

The buzzing stopped around me and I was being carefully, enviously appraised. *How curious life is. Who who would have dreamed that Katharine Hepburn would ever invite me to the theater?* Certainly not Miss Hepburn.

"Oh, yes!" the man behind the cage said. "That will be fifteen dollars, please."

My tan faded perceptibly. My tweeds got a mite heavier. This was not a good sign. The New English are known for their thrift. I was already personally acquainted with it.

The seat was excellent, down front and on the aisle, and I rapidly adjusted. *It's a good investment. What in hell is fifteen dollars?* After all, I had pondered sending the star roses and had happily decided against it, thinking it was possibly premature, pretentious, premeditated— and expensive.

I am a slave of truth. In the few weeks since I had seen the play, Katharine Hepburn had made the part her own. Not able to become Coco under any circumstances whatsoever, she did the next best thing, that which came naturally to her. She made Coco become Hepburn. From curtain to curtain, this extraordinary woman did the impossible. Her energy, her style, her very will pulled the whole, impossible thing together. She was as sharp as a seamstress' shears and she cut the material to her size and pattern. It was absurd and wrong and she was marvelous, capturing the entire paying audience including me.

It was somewhat like seeing a dramatization of *Penrod and Sam,* translated by the Goncourt brothers and designed specially for the gifts of Yves Montand and Michel Simon. Miscast, misconceived, underdone, overplayed, it was nonetheless insanely entertaining and the audience rose as a man to cheer Miss Hepburn.

A crowd was already collected at the stage door.

"My name is Dody," I informed "Pop," who was guarding the door.

"Oh, yes!" he said as he allowed me in without asking for a penny. Things were looking up. *Bad dress rehearsal, great opening night,* I remembered. *All's well that ends well. It isn't how you start, it's where you finish!* I had a million of them. And it was true.

I was now led by "Pop" to a charming sitting-room and told that Miss Hepburn would be with me shortly. A sweet and elderly Irishman was sitting in the room, his bushy gray eyebrows bristling with good will, his merry eyes welcoming me. The vibrations were excellent. Evidently he'd been told of me.

"Mr. McKnight is also a writer," I was informed by "Pop" as he introduced us. When he returned to his station at the stage door, we made writer talk for a surprisingly few minutes for there was a sudden burst of energy and Katharine Hepburn—borne on the waves of applause still reverberating through the theater—made her entrance in black slacks. A white silk kerchief was expertly framing her glowing face. All the fraying edges were covered and all that was left was that perfect triangle.

The mouth was red, her eyes the blue of skimmed milk, the skin scrubbed red, clean of makeup, her teeth even larger than mine, teeth to be reckoned with. Here was Hepburn, nostrils still quivering, picking up a distant scent, her skin drawn taut over the bones of an Egyptian priestess. Her vigor cues one into alertness. It is infectious. Since she is always riding the crest, she is conversed with as a surfer might be interviewed as he sails and swoops and balances, every muscle engaged in that *pas de deux* with the sea.

She shouted hello to Mr. McKnight and pitched her hand in my direction.

"Hello there," she said in that familiar and nasal voice. She could have been greeting—so friendly and filled with bonhomie was her tone—a good neighbor, her vicar, the greengrocer, or another horse. She was beaming with the satisfaction of a job well done. I in turn was delighted that I could be honest.

"How dare you do that to an audience?" I reprimanded her—instinctively being both acerbic and avuncular. It was a pleasure to be able to commend her.

"They did like it tonight, didn't they?" she observed with as much accuracy as delight.

I decided to start our relationship off on firm ground, without any deception at all.

"You know, Miss Hepburn, I did see *Coco* before at preview—and I must tell you that my impression has been absolutely reversed. You were marvelous tonight. The entire evening was far and away a thousand times better."

She was pleased.

"That's because I'm not croaking anymore. I've been taking singing lessons and I've worked like a horse. You see," she shouted at no one in particular, "it shows!"

"I'll go further," I went on. "The air was charged onstage tonight. I had the feeling that nothing could go wrong. It was one of those nights. Everything seemed to fall in place and the whole company seemed to be charged with the same electricity."

"How marvelous. How keen you are!" She noticed. "It was a particularly special performance. *How he knows!*" she now added to the quiet gentleman.

It was obvious that I was on the beam and doing

everything right. She now looked straight into my eyes, frankly appraising me. The head jerked back in some satisfaction. She liked me. The first test was over. The rest would be easy. Her hand shot out at me again. *My God, the tweeds and the honesty worked.* "Put it there," her smile seemed to say. It was going to be a lovely evening. I grabbed her hand and shook it heartily.

"Good night," she said.

"Good night?" I repeated dumbfounded.

"Why, yes," she responded with flat logic. "I have an appointment with Mr. McKnight. It's been very nice."

"But Miss Hepburn, my name is Dody. Sandy Dody!"

The lady was puzzled.

"I wanted to talk with you."

"About what?"

"About us."

"About us?"

"Yes—about us."

"I don't understand."

"We had an appointment, Miss Hepburn. *I* don't understand. Your secretary arranged for me to see you tonight at *your* suggestion. I came in from Cape Cod to take you for a drink. All the way from Cape Cod," I added darkly.

"Mr. *Dody*. You did Bette's book. Oh, dear! So honest and *really* so good. It was a great job. My God, I thought you were an *actor*. Oh, my dear. I can't do a book—not with Spencer's wife alive. Never. No, no! *Here* we are," she suddenly shouted to some invisible minion. "We're coming." She looked back at me. "We have an appointment, Mr. Dady, and there really wouldn't be any point in talking any further. Bye." She pulled the old gentleman into the hall and disappeared into the street and the madding crowd huddled around her limousine.

I stood tweedy in my tweeds, gray of temple, green

of gill. I don't think I have ever been more angry. *Coco! I had to see this damned show twice and spend fifteen dollars. How dare she? Of all the high-handed, discourteous, insensitive, unbelievably gauche displays!*

When I got home, I sat down and wrote another letter. This was just the kind of thing I found stars most guilty of. This was Katharine Hepburn who had made a career playing sterling, sensitive characters who crusaded against boors who acted in this very way. Katharine Hepburn became famous being vulnerable in the face of injustice. The ringing sincerity of her film speeches, the courageous battles against all that was unfair, high handed, and insensitive were again all abstract symbols, banners— to be carried only in the land of fiction. Her very politics reflected the same commendable dedication to fair play. Once again, the silvery light of the distant star and the porous lifeless planet that once dispensed it.

It is evident that if one enacts nobility, one no longer need be noble. It is enough to play a crusader of people's rights. One needn't be considerate of another human being's feelings.

I remember, as a young boy, being taken by my father to a theatrical barber on Forty-seventh Street—Billy the Barber was his name. I loved it there for the famous men who were getting manicures from a brown-eyed peroxide blonde who was long in the tooth and wore a perpetual look of sneering disbelief, and a tiny, hunchbacked brunette with violet eye shadow and a fixed smile. The "girls" were always kind to me and kept me entertained while I waited for my father—who on this particular day deposited me in the chair for a haircut and said that he would fetch me in an hour's time.

Billy started removing all that marvelous hair I wish I still had, when Irving Berlin ran in unexpectedly. He was in a divine hurry and it was clear that Billy was the only man he would allow to shave him. I was already much impressed with the intelligence that Mr. Berlin had even taken Billy to Europe with him so he could always be properly groomed while on holiday. I used to wonder what happened to Mrs. Billy during these junkets, and whether she went along to give the songwriter a manicure. In any case I thought it was the height of style. I was ten years old but had been introduced to the composer several times and knew all of his wonderful songs, which my elder brother used to play and sing at home.

I now saw his swarthy, brooding face further darken with distress. He wanted a shave immediately and if it were true that he took Billy to France with him for that purpose, it did not escape me that he wanted Billy in New York. Billy held the comb and scissors up in the air helplessly and through the mirror I saw Mr. Berlin tighten his lips and shake his head ominously. "It'll only take ten minutes," he said, much agitated by my presence in the chair. I focused my eyes on myself again, and I looked like a miniature Hitler with a huge bang of hair weighing me down and newly mown hair covering the white and black striped stole that had been swirled around my shoulders. It struck me that Irving Berlin, because of this delay, might be kept from writing another beautiful song, so I jumped out of the chair.

"It's O.K., Billy. Please take Mr. Berlin if it's important."

I barely got out of the man's way in time. The composer lunged into the barber chair and a grateful Billy winked at me in relief. Mr. Berlin never thanked me or even met my eye. I didn't exist now that I was no longer an obstacle. The chair had become prone and a hot towel was steaming on his face, but it was a ten-year-old boy with half his hair cut who stood flushed with embarrassment. There wasn't even a seat I could rest in, since other customers were reading or getting manicures or shines. I stood, a skinny, freckled, half-tonsured child in a make-shift chasuble, some kind of prodigy cleric in a land of nonbelievers, doomed to suffer the insensibility of his elders. Today I would go into a softshoe and make a star spot of it. Then I was stung by Mr. Berlin's rudeness and my own inability to retire gracefully from center stage. The cynical blonde, Rose was her name, called me over to her as she arranged a stack of magazines on the floor for me to sit on. "Put it here, honey," she said.

Put it there, Rose. I will never forget you. The hurt that made your mouth twist in caustic resignation also made you feel a small boy's discomfort.

While I thumbed through a magazine, I wondered whether such lack of niceness was a part of being talented and famous, and I forgave him. Maybe only manicurists and barbers, elevator men and trolley conductors had the time to be kind. Maybe Irving Berlin at that very moment under the towel was composing "A Fine Romance," and if he had taken a moment to say "Thanks!" it would have broken his concentration. Maybe. I have always given him the benefit of the doubt. The muses do not encourage kindness.

I wrote Miss Hepburn a letter to be remembered and I sent it out before I could think better of it. As I admire Mr. Berlin's astonishing produce but wouldn't wish to spend five minutes with him on that famous desert island unless there was an orchestra with full arrangements, I will always be a devotee of Miss Hepburn's films, old and new, freshly effected by her shining nobility, but I had to relate realistically to her behavior. I was bored with understanding these people. I was reminded of Bartley Crum's remark many years ago that a man's mind can be so open that his brains fall out.

I purged myself. No ulcer-getter, I; though there are those who would suggest that I can give them. I ended my document with the opinion that I deserved the Oscar, the Tony, and the Emmy for my masterly concealment of the distress I felt at her discourtesy to a peer. I mailed the letter and slept, as the French love to say, on both ears.

Two days later I received a phone call from Miss Hepburn's secretary. She was distraught. "How could this terrible thing have happened?"

"Easily," I responded.

It seems that it was not the star's fault but her own. She had neglected to tell Miss Hepburn I was coming. It was an unforgivable mixup. Miss Hepburn was most exacting, absolutely punctilious about her engagements. It was an awful mess and it was all because Juliana was ill.

"Do you mean the queen of the Netherlands," I asked, knowing how the high and mighty are wont to cavort with one another.

"No, no," she replied. "Juliana fills in and she was ill. Miss Hepburn is terribly distressed and wants you to call her on her private line. Please do not give it to anyone," she added, drawing me into the cabal and supposedly flattering me. "She wants you to call to arrange another evening with her immediately. Please forgive me, Mr. Dody?"

The young lady couldn't have been more contrite; and mellowing, I thought that it was not without the realm of possibility that there had been just such confusion. How could I have been so unkind and gone into the whole star syndrome when we're all human? But we are not.

I called Miss Hepburn on her private wire at the hour suggested to me and got nothing but a busy signal. An hour later I thought I would give up or tear the phone out of the wall. There was an alternative, and I called the operator who gave me her supervisor. The number I was calling, I informed her, was still busy after six hours, and I feared foul play. Would she please check it for me. I was a doctor.

In a moment I heard a woman say, "Who is it? Who is it?" and I answered "The doctor. Would you please check the number?"

"Who is it? Who is it?" the voice screeched nasally and I recognized it.

"Miss Hepburn?"

"Who is it? Who is it?" she repeated in annoyance.

There are times one must give up.

"Who is it? Who is it?" she continued, like some mad bird limited to one call.

"It's your old friend, Sandy Dody," I said grimly.

"Oh!" she shouted, and plunged into the many reasons why she couldn't possibly do a biography. It was a nonstop flight of oratory which touched upon her shyness, her reticence, her sensitivity, her ancestor worship. Her adoration of her parents was such that she could not conceivably even speak with me about them without weeping. No. She couldn't do a book about her life. It was all too painful.

It was impossible to interrupt. She gave no leeway. There wasn't a break, no room for a breath.

"Now Bette was a different story," she continued.

"But Bette was equally sensitive about her life—at first," I managed to say. "It is one of my duties to make it easy for a subject. Bette used to call me her pagan confessor," I lied.

"But *she* didn't mind discussing her family with you. She didn't mind speaking of her youth and her relationships. Your book was first rate, splendid, but I'm not Bette and then I could never open those doors, not with *anyone* and then there's Spencer. You'd want all of that

224

and how can I? No, no, Mr. Dody. It's just impossible. I'm afraid it's not anything that I could do."

She had still to apologize for standing me up. I had to get her on the right track.

"But as I said in my letter, Miss Hepburn—"

"Oh, Mr. Dody, wasn't that a scream? I mean wasn't that really funny?"

"No, Miss Hepburn. I didn't think it was in the least funny."

"Oh, but I did," she concluded after careful consideration. "It was mighty funny. Ha! Ha!"

She actually said "Ha! Ha!" H.A.H.A. like a little girl away at boarding school writing home: "And then Miss Elmendorf tripped on the orange peel and fell down the stairs. Ha! Ha!"

I couldn't believe my ears.

"I once did the same thing to my niece," she recalled with glee. "Just plain forgot and got my dates mixed. It was so funny."

Then she returned to more serious matters.

"Mr. Dody," she continued, in what I decided to make her concluding remarks, "have you any idea how painful it is, how unbelievably painful it is for me to have lived my life in the public eye?"

I had seen her distress as she took tens of curtain calls, shedding years and fatigue as her name was hurled lovingly across the footlights like flowers. I reminded myself that at her age and with a financial security old Mrs. John Drew didn't have when she was forced to tread the boards to pay her bills, Katharine Hepburn need never work again. In her distress she will never stop; and it occurred to me that any further conversation would be pointless.

"Miss Hepburn," I quietly said. "I realize how painful the life of a great star has been for you and wouldn't

dream of adding to the great burden you bear so sacrifi-
cially. To give you the final triumph of immortality would
cost you more than you could pay."

We obviously brought out the worst in each other.

"And so," I added, "I am going to bid you good
day."

There was an unmistakable beat.

"I have your number if I change my mind," she said
quickly, and repeated my number, either from memory or
from a little book which she kept near her heart. "In case
I change my mind, I have your number."

"And I have yours," I added witlessly as I hung up,
always ready to kill a relationship for a curtain line.

It was a pity. There are the deathless ones and Miss
Hepburn continues to glow without my help. But there
was another who smiled upon me for a moment and then
passed on.

Miss Judy Garland

Late one night in 1967, Sid Luft called me from Hollywood. A mutual friend in Malibu had spoken of me, and he wanted to know if I was interested in doing a book on Judy Garland, which I certainly was. He was warm and friendly but it was a curious and unresolved conversation. When the proper time came, I gathered he would again get in touch with me. I made myself a sandwich and late as it was, put a Garland record on the phonograph and luxuriated in both.

Along with the rest of the world, I had the warmest feeling for Judy Garland. Since her childhood, I had found her endearing. By this time her star had reached its zenith, fallen, risen, and fallen again. Her health and her gift suffered the same extremes; but whether fat or thin, sick or well, up or down, Judy Garland was her own worst enemy now that MGM was out of the picture. Her comeback appearance at the Palace Theatre a few years before had been so dazzling an event and such a *succès fou* that news of it traveled round the world. Her Palladium appearance in London was equally sensational. Her miraculous return from sanitariums and scandal, the fact that this most vulnerable of child stars who grew up before the loving public's eye fell from grace and then rose to sing about it enthralled the public. I don't believe any other actress's personal drama was ever enacted so spectacularly twice a day. The public cried at her misfortunes and cheered her triumphs. You needed a program to know which it would be.

I caught her at the Palace and I can still hear her singing "Come Rain or Come Shine." She sang it as I've never heard anyone sing a popular song. Like Piaf she fused her life and her art. From that open-faced, chubby little girl who reveled in being alive to the sometimes bloated or sodden woman who more than once tried to die, from Metro's Lot One to the Metropolitan Opera House, there were many stages. Just when one was sure she was sung out, played out, on her way out, she'd bounce back. Her audience waited breathlessly to see Judy Garland survive life's vicissitudes. There were certainly those who feverishly anticipated the worst, even on stage, for there was no absense of morbidity attending her celebrity; but most people wished her well and held her in deep affection. And so she became a cult.

I wondered if I'd ever hear from her.

A couple of months later I got another call from Sid Luft. He and Garland were in New York. No longer her husband but still managing her career, he set up a few appointments with Miss Garland that were all for one reason or another canceled or postponed. I expected the worst. Was she drinking again? Was she ill again? I was happy that at that moment I was negotiating with the dependable Helen Hayes. When Mr. Luft heard this, he be-

228

came impatient. "Helen Hayes!" he exclaimed, making the dear lady into an expletive. "Why would you be doing her life when you can be doing Garland's?"

"In the first place," I replied, "she will make a great book. She happens to be the Theater, and in the second place, much as I love Judy, I may never meet her, much less be given the material for a book. Frankly, Sid, I can be following Miss Garland around from hospital to hospital for two years."

I met with Mr. Luft at the King Cole Bar at the St. Regis, where he and Miss Garland were staying. Miss Garland did not join us though she called downstairs and I was introduced to her over the phone. She was sorry, but her hairdresser had broken an appointment and she wasn't fit to be seen and could we arrange our meeting for later—dinner perhaps? Plans were made for that very night after theater—at 11:30 in her suite—and Mr. Luft and I returned to our table for two and discussed business. It seemed clear that were we to make a deal I would be expected to write the book for nothing.

"We have to support our kids," Mr. Luft confided warmly.

"So do I!" I ventured weakly. Was I to be punished for my bachelorhood not only by the Internal Revenue Service but also by the stars?

"You know," he reminded me, "there's lot of money to be made here. Ten per cent of Judy Garland is worth much more than fifty per cent of Elaine Barrymore."

"And fifty per cent of Judy Garland," I observed, "is worth much more than *ten* per cent of Judy Garland."

I almost always say clever things and then lose the deal. A string of glitteringly won battles have led to a lost war because the stylish battle cry is almost enough for me. *Fifty per cent of Judy Garland is worth more than ten per cent of Judy Garland.* It was really a marvelous response. But I wanted Garland so badly now that I could be had for a song, and Sid Luft knew it.

"You're shrewd!" he dissembled.

But I didn't feel that money was the problem here. There was, indeed, enough for everyone if all other things were equal. If Judy and I were right for each other.

First things first, I thought wisely. *This man Luft is a businessman and this ridiculous man-to-man conversation is a charade. He wants to get me for nothing and I am probably so doomed despite my gift of gab and my perceptions. Judy must want me and then my share will go up to a degree.* At any rate, the whole thing was academic unless Miss Garland and I liked each other. First things first.

I returned to the St. Regis and announced myself, only to find a message directing me to cross the avenue; the couple had suddenly and inexplicably moved to the Gotham. Perhaps unfairly, I thought I wasn't the only one with financial problems.

Mr. Luft greeted me in Miss Garland's suite. He was staying down the hall. Emcee for the evening, he introduced me to a nice-looking young man who was traveling with the star and who was eventually to become a husband. He was pleasant and kind and I was happy for the actress.

I had just left friends at an Off-Broadway theater and was gratified to see that room service had sent up a table groaning with napkin-covered trays that promised late supper. The sitting-room was pink and moss-green and I looked forward to the star's arrival on the scene.

I am used to the retinue attached to the superstar but I was quite unprepared for the creature who peeked round the door of the room to tell us that there would be some delay. She was birdlike, freakishly so, like a baby robin. One only saw the gaping mouth and the ravenous eyes. The hair was pulled back into a tight knot so that the tiny face was curiously naked. It was a sick creature, delicate to the point of brittleness, featureless except for those desperate eyes and cavernous mouth.

"Hello!" it said. "Miss Garland will be with you soon. Please have another drink."

The voice gave her gender. *They all have a sister, a cousin, a niece or an aunt, a slave who acts out the whole love-hate relationship with the star. It never fails,* I mused. I'm always fascinated by the loyalty and anger with which these companions guard and brutalize their treasures. But this one was the oddest-looking of them all. Was she doing Garland's hair, giving her a massage? No! The latter was impossible. This wraith didn't have the strength to brush her own hair, much less pound someone else into shape. The queer little head, bodyless, seemingly on a stick and shoved into the room as a grisly joke, still hung there, compelling in its ugliness.

"This is Sandy Dody, Judy," Sid said.

"Hello, Sandy," she said, "I'll be with you in a jiffy." And she disappeared.

A chill ran through me and I prayed I hadn't visibly shivered.

I was saved by the doorbell. A friend of her daughter, Liza, dropped by on some errand and none too soon. She attended to her business, joined us for a drink, and left to meet Miss Minnelli.

Shortly after, Miss Garland made her entrance. Judy could have been singing "Who?" with a line of white-tied, top-hatted and tailed young men behind her as she floated toward me, hand extended. She was radiant. Carefully groomed, dressed in a white, beautifully tailored pants suit, she was as bright and trim as a jeweled button.

That strange ornithic creature had coiffed and masked herself, applying the star's features. She had forged her own face, created it out of paint and powder and loving memory. It was un-Christian. Here she was—Judy Garland, the star, slimmer, older but superb. Her energy was enormous, her key pitched so high I wondered if she could sustain it. As slender as she was, there in the very center of her was a funny, pointed belly that reminded me of O' Lan's false pregnancy in *The Good Earth,* the promise of life that was, instead, the tumor that would consume her. It worried me all night.

She came on stage at fifteen minutes before midnight and a gin and tonic was placed on the coffee table. It stood untouched—at her fingertips for hours. That worried me as well. Mr. Luft had told me that she was in great shape, ready to work, in top form, all of which meant one thing, that the pattern of booze and pills had been altered. I hadn't believed it, of course, but I wanted to.

It was important this evening that she be at her best, and she was.

It was impossible not to fall under her spell. The sympathy between us was immediate and not in the least born of our mutual need, though that would have been all right too. Passing minutes brought an intimacy usually earned by years. Without question this was the warmest girl I have ever met.

Sid Luft, satisfied that plans had been well laid, was willing to let them hatch while he got a good night's sleep. He wished us well and made his way down the corridor to his own room, while young Tom Green replenished my Scotch. At about one o'clock, after several entrances and exits, he—now in pajamas with Gerold Frank's latest book under his arm—announced that he knew we both wouldn't mind if he excused himself and went to bed with *The Boston Strangler.*

Judy disappeared for a few minutes and returned in red—her second-act costume, looking even better than before and even more comfortable. As the Bolshoi dancers,

232

whose prowess and endurance are illogically increased rather than diminished by strenuous activity, so too Garland the singer, whose voice at countless concerts grew greater, her singing more effortless with each successive song, Garland the woman grew younger, prettier, and more like her film image as the night passed.

At 2:00 A.M. she casually put a couple of ice cubes in her untouched glass and I thank the heavens that my excesses are those chosen by a hypochondriac and not likely to kill me. I strengthened my resolve not to lunge at the platters until offered. Yes, her glass was untouched and she consciously avoided looking at it, as a puppy does with the chewed ball it fervently wants you to grab in play.

Supposedly Miss Garland was in great shape and on the wagon. But people without a drinking problem drink the drinks that are made for them. It was clear that Mr. Luft had suggested that the book, the advance, the first impression were important. The interview had to go well, its being the first step upward to recouping her fortune. It was the remarkable truth that Judy Garland was selling me as much as I was selling her.

The glass loomed larger and it was in closeup now, we the principals of the scene, blurred—the symbol at this moment taking precedence over the realities. The whole scene seemed to be dominated by that glass, the stream of chatter simply a musical accompaniment to its drama.

Judy Garland, that spring night, captured and broke my heart. I didn't have to ask her one personal question. The answers were presented to me one by one like gifts —generously wrapped in colored tissue and tied with a little girl's hair-bow. Our chemistry was perfect. I stole an olive or two from the bowl of melted ice, but my ascetic hostess ignored the food as well as the drink. She was concentrating on one goal.

Judy Garland was genuine. It was in her artless gaze,

her sweetness of nature, and the gallantry she displayed that night. That she was broke, between engagements, in poor health was clear. I had already told Mr. Luft that though I revered Miss Garland, I was forced to be practical. It was true that the book could put us all on our feet, but I had to make sure that if the lady lost her balance again that I would not topple over with her.

Judy was candid and bright and eager to please, with these shared memories of Louis B. Mayer and her mother, the latter surprisingly emerging as the less likable of the two. It seemed to me that she spoke, at that distance from the scene, most sentimentally of her early MGM days and, despite the seeds of horror sown at the time, accepted this price for the adoration of the world that was its harvest.

I felt that night that quite simply, this little girl who was born in a trunk realistically accepted the fact that she was doomed to sing for her supper. She never was given by family or bosses any reason to doubt it. For a woman as neurotic as she, I found this common-sensible acceptance refreshing.

Along with what proved to be a great will to destroy herself, there was—and I was rewarded with it that night —a joy in living and a lovely dimension that shouldn't have been unexpected, since her natural sunniness warmed all of her performances. A pathetic little bird she might have been, and slowly dying, but she never forgot her call and sweetly filled that night with it.

"Why are you doing Helen Hayes?" she suddenly asked. "We could work together. Sid was right."

"And I hope we will. As soon as I'm finished with the Hayes book we can start. You must know how eager I am to work with you, Miss Garland."

"Miss Garland? What is *that,* when you're going to know everything? It's Judy, Sandy."

"What is this Sandy business when I already know so much? It's Mr. Dody."

"See what I mean? We'll have fun and I think I'm going to give you a great book to write."

I took her slender hand.

"It will be. How could it not? Just tell me everything when we're working and trust that I know what I'm doing."

"I do already. Davis's book was absolutely terrifically honest and she comes out just great in it."

"Maybe, Judy; but remember it is easier for you to accept honesty in Bette's book than your own. This is my occupational hazard. But *I* want to protect you as much or *more* than you do yourself; not because I'm a darling but because I know what the public wants of you in a book, the way you know what it wants on stage and screen. *You're* honest as a performer; but you're an artist also and know what to be honest about. Some things are meant to be left out."

She now looked at me with a little smile.

"I really *do* trust you, you know."

And she reached for the gin and tonic, slowly cutting it down to size. It was three in the morning.

As stimulating as Miss Garland was, I was tired. I had written all morning, had been at my desk at eight-thirty, and taken care of some affairs in the afternoon. Dinner and theater had occupied me until I arrived at the Gotham and the next day was going to be a busy one.

"I'm starved, Judy." I needed fuel desperately.

"My God, go ahead and eat, darling. It's all for you. I'm not having anything—except some more tonic."

I joined her in the kitchen, where she fixed another gin and Schweppes. The food would keep me awake and, with her tumbler refilled, I loaded my plate with sandwiches, and we retired to the couch where like old theater buddies we curled up facing each other at either end, and spoke of Hollywood, mutual friends, cabbages, and queens.

The platter of sandwiches and relishes disappeared like a movie montage denoting hours passed. The time flew as we chatted and cozily sniffed each other out. We laughed a great deal and moved through the shadows as well. We got close, very close. The gin and Scotch didn't hurt but it could have, the berry and the grain—in my experience—simply intensifying one's impressions, not changing them. There wasn't a bad vibration. Judy and I were making it. But then I heard a hiss and I turned around—in all directions.

"What is *that? I* think we're fabulous!"

Judy jumped up giggling and searched the room for the critic or cobra. At last she detected the source. "It's the damned radiator!" she announced.

And it was. I never heard such hissing and sputtering. I offered to try my hand at stopping it but my hostess was already on her knees, her tiny bottom all that was visible.

"You can't reach the damned thing, it's so far—*ouch!* Oh, damn," she cried as the hissing stopped.

"You've done it," I yelled as I moved to help her off the floor.

"I certainly have," Judy agreed, and her face was contorted with mock suffering. "I cut myself on something."

Her wrist was bleeding slightly and I wrapped it with my handkerchief, asking her for some iodine and a Band-Aid. I will never forget the glint in her round eyes. They fairly glittered.

"Sandy, my darling. Can you see the papers tomorrow?"

"If this morning anyone had even dared suggest that I'd be doctoring Judy Garland's slashed wrist this evening—"

We were laughing wildly now. The cut was right near the vein and God knows it was an accident, but its strangeness did not escape either one of us and that's why we were laughing hysterically. I cleaned the wound and bandaged it. It was now five, and I suggested that we call it a day. Miss Garland would have none of this. She told me to make another drink while she tidied up.

I had drunk far too much and now finished the scraps of food that were left on the table. Pathetic little Miss Garland could outdistance an Olympic athlete. I boiled some water for instant coffee, saving a Danish pastry for dunking. It was clear that working with Judy Garland was going to be a twenty-four-hour-a-day job.

She returned in green—her third-act costume. It wasn't vanity, this psychological or physical need for her to change her clothes so often. She seemed unwilling to be anything less than immaculate. *Perhaps,* I thought, *she goes into cold sweats.* After all, who changes clothes at five-thirty in the morning unless its provocatively into nightdress? There wasn't a hint of such a thing. Miss Garland was now pretty as could be in a little dress that showed her beautiful legs to advantage and was not as kind to her sinewy, skinny arms. She had freshened her makeup, brushed her hair and, to my distress, was raring to go.

"If I play London, will you be able to come with me so we could work?"

I told her that I could and would go anywhere she wanted as long as the unmentionable question of money was first resolved by Mr. Luft and myself. "If Sid and I can get together, darling, I'm yours. I'm yours anyway, but ——you know what I mean. I'm yours if you'll have me."

Miss Garland assured me that she would have me, that she felt we were right together.

"It'll really be fun, Judy. I want to know your fears, your prejudices, your dreams, things you may not have bothered verbalizing before. The abstractions. By the way, did you every play abstractions?"

I then described my favorite game, giving her a simple and obvious example.

"I'm someone famous and—I never do this when I'm actually playing but this is a kind of sample—I'm dead. You can ask anything as long as it's abstract but I'll start you off. If I were a color I'd be—rust. If I were a dish of food I'd be a crisp salad with a good lemon dressing. As I said, when it's played well it's unnecessary to say it's a man or woman or theater or not—in this case it is a man *and* theater. O.K. I'm rust as a color and a crisp tart salad as food. If I were an animal instead of a man, I'd be a scrappy terrier who read when no one was looking—"

"What season of the year are you?" she interrupted, fascinated. She was sitting, her legs beneath her, the glass poised at her lips.

"Winter! A cold, dry, wintry winter day."

"I think I know, I think I know," she shouted happily. "One more question to clinch it."

She looked at me mischievously. She was so bright, that girl. At six o'clock in the morning she was spanking new and radiant.

"What vegetable are you?"

I knew she knew but I thought carefully.

"I'm one lone asparagus—vinaigrette."

"You're George Bernard Shaw—that's who you are."

And I was. And she was marvelously quick at catching the game.

"I've got to do one. I've got to do one. I *love* it."

"O.K. What color are you?"

"Wait a minute. I haven't picked anyone yet."

I waited while she bit her lips in excitement. She was a happy child as she slapped her thigh and told me she was ready for me. I asked her what color she was and to remember it had to be abstract.

"I know. I know. Didn't I get your Shaw? I'm pink.

A soft pink. Not one of those terrible ones from the five-and-dime, and I'm a summer day—a little too warm maybe but beautiful—sultry."

"O.K. What food are you?"

"Peaches—fresh peaches with real cream. None of that diet stuff. The McCoy. Yeah. Peaches and cream."

"What would you be if you were an animal?"

"An—well, it's the cat family. Wait a minute. Maybe an angora cat. No. no. I've got it. I'm a baby cub. I'm a cub. A lion cub. The kind you see that drinks out of a bottle like Elsa at the beginning in *Born Free* and everyone says be careful it's a lion and she'll bite you someday, but she doesn't. Yes, an adorable cub."

This girl was going to be marvelous to work with. I lost all fatigue as I triumphantly announced that I thought I knew who she was.

"But you couldn't. Not yet!"

"But that's the point of the game. You're playing it *well* if I get it fast."

"You told me you can't guess. You gotta *know*," she replied wistfully—obviously not wanting to stop.

"I'll *know*. Now what are you as a scent?"

"A scent?"

"Yes. A smell, an aroma."

"I'm the smell of an old-fashioned drugstore—a small-town drugstore. You know—the powder and vanilla and if I were a drink I'd be a spiked strawberry phosphate."

"You're Lana Turner," I yelled.

She looked at me in awe.

"Well, aren't you?"

"You know goddamned well I am," she answered unhappily.

"That was brilliant. It was *you* who was great. I couldn't miss it."

And I meant it. Her mind, challenged, was keen, her

239

imagination fertile. Judy Garland was an artist; and the book I could do and now felt I definitely would do would be a pleasure to write.

"We're on the same frequency, Judy."

"Obviously. This is fabulous. Lana! How I remember Lana years ago—when we all went to school together with that strange Deanna Durbin. That crazy schoolhouse on the lot. Poor, darling Lana. You got it before I could think of a flower. I wanted to do her as a flower."

"A gardenia corsage that was worn at the prom but fell off on the dance floor. Some lout stepped on it," I said.

"Together we could rule the world," Miss Garland remarked. "What am I as a flower?"

"Well, just as that was the Lana Turner the public made a star, the early Judy—the image—I would say, off-hand, was a sunflower, leaning over a country fence, towering over everything else in the garden—outsized and naive. It wishes it were a rose and doesn't understand its own power. A bewitched flower that has the power to hum and play with certain children."

Miss Garland leaned over and kissed me on the cheek.

At 7:00 A.M. there wasn't a topic we hadn't exhausted. I was now so tired that I felt a little sick. This enviable interview was slowly becoming a marthon. A man needed sleep. Miss Garland was fresher than ever and so was her gin and tonic. I announced with what strength of will I had left that it had been a ball and we had our whole future ahead of us and I simply had to get home so I would be in condition to face lawyers and agents in about three hours. I might just as well have suggested self-immolation.

"But you can't leave, darling. You just can't. There's so much we have to go over. Gable, Garbo, Mickey—and I haven't really told you about Deanna yet."

240

She laughed merrily and though I would have sworn that it could never happen, that the setting and the cast was such that it was impossible, I started to stifle yawn after yawn. I was almost unconscious with fatigue. It was a Chinese torture, the subtlest of punishments. Here I was, glutted with food and drink, glamour and charming company, and the only tariff was sleep. I was being robbed of sleep, without which no living creature can survive. My lovable, adorable, simply naive sunflower of a Judy Garland was insatiable, vampiric and I was fading.

"Judy, darling," I began, "I really and *truly* have to go."

But Miss Garland was now in a reverie. She freshened her drink.

"Isn't it remarkable," she now said, incredibly, "that with all the horror, with all I've been through, I never drifted into booze or pills?"

Groggy though I was I examined her closely to see if she was pulling my leg. She was not.

For the first time all night I realized how really sick she was. Even her energy level was manic. If she was serious, I'd have to do a lot of breaking down to write an honest book. At any rate my brain was befogged by weariness. There was no longer any question. I simply had to go or I would die at the Gotham Hotel of nothing more than exhaustion.

"Please don't go," she pleaded, "please!"

"Look at the sun, Judy."

"It's beautiful. I'll give you breakfast. You mustn't go, darling. *Please!*"

"But I can't break a date this important and—as is— I'm going to have to arrive with no sleep."

"Forget Hayes, darling. We're going to work together. I need you and you're right for me. Please don't leave. *Please."*

I felt as if I were suffocating. She was again the baby robin I had first seen, all ravenous eyes and gaping mouth, sweetly voracious, her very existence through the day dependent on that appetite and its immediate satisfaction. *You will disappear with the creature. This is the tyranny.* Not untouched by her plight but now actively guarding against it, I realized that our book could be a wonderful study and a challenge I had not immediately recognized and, in this weakened moment, could barely comprehend. I was giddy and only mistily realized the disciplines I would have to inflict on her and myself in order to accomplish the job at hand. It would be worth it but would cost me the rest of my hair, perhaps my sanity as well. I rose and started to put my shoes on.

"My God, you *are* leaving."

"Only to return, my dear. This is only the beginning, as your Pop Charlie Winninger used say. Honey, this is prologue time. If you let me survive the night we'll have a fine old time doing the book together."

"We will, you'll see."

"Sid knows where I am. I couldn't be happier, Judy. I really want to work with you."

"I've *got* to work with you."

"Then it's settled."

I managed to get to the front door. There was a long corridor.

"It isn't good-bye, Judy."

"I know. I'll talk to Sid later on, honey."

"I'll call you in a couple of days."

She stood at the door, suddenly frail and confused. I hugged her tightly and assured her that this was the first of many wonderful productive nights we would have. Then I broke away and started down the carpeted hall.

"Sandy," she called through the hall, "I *love* you. Do you hear me. I *love* you."

Her voice was shrill.

"Do *you* love me?" she now asked—offhand, as if it were an afterthought.

"You know I do, Judy," I answered.

She was now blowing kisses, her eyes glittering with tears. I had to remind myself that this farewell scene was being played by two people who had met for the first time earlier the same evening. I prayed that the elevator would come and conjure me away. She was not acting. This was real, but I was forced to rise to a pitch not too far below her own for fear of seeming cold and unfeeling; and I still had to refrain from any exaggeration that might describe her own excess and—as often happens with the drunk or mad—feed a trace of lucidity in her that would discern my condescension.

It was a tightrope, and I couldn't—especially in my sleepless state—keep up my balance much longer. Her intensity was so out of order that any acceptance of it was a presumption and any denial a cruel rejection. I was caught in that long corridor, unable to make a graceful exit.

When the elevator arrived and its door at last closed behind me, her voice once more rang through the hotel. "Do you love me? I love *you!*" It was a terrible wail and the elevator operator and I descended to the lobby silently, our eyes never meeting, like fellow mourners embarrassed by their anguish. I ran to the corner and turned south on Fifth Avenue, bucking the tide of office workers disgorged from the subway at Fifty-third Street.

I kept running, slipping through the waves of people, taking deep drafts of fresh air, delighting in the morning sun, which at that very moment was shining into a Gotham Hotel window and like an amber spot was seeking out a sick little robin who was waking someone up because she couldn't sleep and couldn't be alone.

243

We never saw each other again.

I wrote her a note and dropped it off later in the morning on my way uptown, and Sid Luft said on the phone that he was pleased that we got on so famously, and that—for whatever reason—was that. I went off to Mexico a short time after to work with Helen Hayes, and two years later, Judy died right around the corner from me in London—deep in Chelsea where she went like Elsie. I often wonder whether her gifted daughter made that connection when she sang of her in *Cabaret*.

Drunk or sober, Judy Garland was, doubtless, a problem—a difficult one. Perhaps insoluble. I would have welcomed the challenge. She had little of the enamel that usually protects the actor from himself, but only the breezy facsimile of brittleness. Rather than being short-lived, her light lasted longer than might have been expected. Curiously enough, without the despotic paternalism of the picture studio her vulnerability could not have survived the climate of white heat in which such stars are born. If we had both survived the sessions together we might have had a real book. I was wise, however, to have stuck to Helen Hayes, who can survive anything.

Helen Hayes

Helen Hayes is just about as controversial as a gold star in a window, an elm tree outside the house, and a pitcher of ice-cold lemonade on a July evening in Wichita Falls. She has one of those miraculously wholesome combinations of respectability and charm that few theatrical personages have enjoyed. When they do, they become folk heroes of a sort. Fairbanks and Pickford, George M. Cohan, Will Rogers are a quartet of Americans who have commanded the permanent adulation and affection of the broad base of the country rather than, though sometimes including, the cognoscenti. With Helen Hayes, they have all been beyond reproach, red-white-and-blue Yankee Doodle Dandies—all of them stars in Old Glory itself—phenomena, really. Aside from the talent that originally won favor, it is mostly the evocation of what Americans think is the best in themselves that attracted them to these men and women. Once so magnetized, nothing short of caught-red-handed-treachery can break the grip.

Helen Hayes is a bright little lady and conjectured that it was exactly her "lack of glamour," her plain-Janedom if you will, that made her astonishing career endure. She might, she wisely thought, be the triumph of the familiar over the exotic. Helen Hayes as *Coquette* was everybody's daughter. As Barrie's Maggie Shand she was, in *What Every Woman Knows,* everybody's wife and as *Victoria Regina,* she became prematurely, and with her great character makeup, not only everybody's mother but the answer to America's yearning for homegrown royalty. Part and lady blended, and Helen Hayes was never to be a commoner again, no less an ordinary or even extraordinary actress.

Helen Hayes became First Lady with all the royal prerogatives. Fans practically bowed and curtseyed and Miss Hayes practically demanded it. I remember the apogee of Helen Hayes's career, and it is small wonder that she kept her head at all, such was her immense popularity. Yes, Helen Hayes is America and has the constitution to go with it.

Bursting with health, she becomes grayer and plumper along with her subjects, but really doesn't change. She remains the same virtuous, plucky, and pretty little woman the country fell in love with so many years ago. Her face is known by everyone, her appearance anywhere insures a large audience, and her name on any letterhead lends a hundred diverse causes respectability. She is actually a theatrical extension of America. In *On Reflection,* she readily accepted my description of her as the Statue of Liberty in a Mother Hubbard. That is evidently how the country sees her. But 't ain't true, golly, land's sakes alive!

I had been asked by Herb Katz at M. Evans to go to

Nyack to meet with the lady in hopes of collaborating with her. I knew that if she liked me on first meeting and I was signed to do her life, I would have a hit at last. She was so universally admired that if I only did a fair job, we would have a smash. I had reason to believe that Helen Hayes would do all the promotion Miss Davis did not lend herself to. Now I had to pray that she did not recoil from my presence. If she did an Elsa Lanchester, I had best see a doctor or a dentist or Norman Vincent Peale or all three.

I was broke again, as usual, and felt that I had to give the opposite impression. Being broke is, of course, entirely different from being poor, which I have never been, despite the absence of a few meals in my youth. Poverty is a gray-brown place where nothing is ever beautiful and hope cannot survive. Broke is that buffer state between survival and plenty. Without any funds at all, one can live off of hors d'oeuvres and champagne—even getting the gout, once believed to be a sickness of the rich; one can retain a passport to the finest houses, hold meal tickets to the best tables, owe Bloomingdale's for the jacket and slacks your betters are admiring while you teeter on the brink of success. One may be in debt but one is able to be, and has friends who are not.

When one is broke one has prospects which the poor never have. Living by one's wits, however, becomes more difficult as the years and charm pass. Improvisations become tougher and tougher. I was broke again and no longer in my twenties—but forties. I needed this book.

What was beyond the legend of Helen Hayes—another staunch, honest, warm, wise, sympathetic, utterly feminine woman? To be everyone's mother is not to be a mother at all, but simply the distillation of motherhood. The fault might not have been with the stars, dear Brutus, but I had long been an underling and expected the worst.

I took the subway to the George Washington Bridge on a gray, drizzling afternoon and caught the bus at the Port Authority. As I watched the little towns go by and we neared Nyack, I passed the time planning my approach to Miss Hayes, which I knew was a ridiculous business. Unless one writes one's co-player's role as well one cannot depend on the proper cues. How can anyone plan a brilliantly cool entrance line if on arrival the house is afire and the hostess is being carried out? Of course one could have plans A to F but I have found that my reflexes work better than my memory.

Here I was, for all the world, auditioning again. Arriving by public transport while the great lady was probably playing croquet with her bishop and Maurice Evans, her neighbor and friend who lived across the Hudson in nearby Tarrytown. Mr. Evans and I had recently talked of doing a book, but the publisher's luncheons at the Plaza's Edwardian Room and low teas at the Players happily came to naught. Mr. Evans had a friend who wasn't sold on me and at times one must be thankful for small disfavors. The actor's *Richard II* years ago was a beautiful reading of a magnificent play and I will remember it all my life, but enough of his preciosity seeped into our meetings to dampen my enthusiasm for the work.

One always has to be concerned not only with the immediate reaction of the possible subject but of the subject's family, friends, and lovers. I didn't know who was going to be at Helen Hayes's house, but hoped it would be a private meeting that would allow a concentration of those charms I needed to exert.

We arrived in Nyack and I walked up to the bus driver and asked—as I was instructed to do—if he would point out the MacArthur house just outside of town. Unlike our New York drivers, who find your very presence in their buses an affront and any ensuing communication or the smallest inquiry justification for belligerence, the driver pleasantly engaged me in conversation, pointed it out to me proudly, and then wished me a lovely day as he went past his stop and dropped me at the house itself.

I wandered through the gate dividing the hedges and saw a beautiful old Hudson River house beyond. I saw no sign of life. With the bus gone, there wasn't a sound except bird call and the faint crackle of the intermittent drizzle stroking the leaves of elms and making them shiny. I assumed a look of importance and followed a path that I hoped would take me around the side to an entrance, which I now found. In an absurd gesture I must have felt would give me confidence, I rang the bell with the tip of my umbrella, almost falling back off the step in order to manage it. Regaining my balance I waited to no avail. This time I rang with my index finger, then my third finger and then my thumb. Was the bus driver pleasant but mistaken?

There was evidently no one home and since I knew that Miss Hayes would be dependable, this was not going to be the right place. The very entrance seemed unused. I now continued to make a circle round the house and came upon its back, which presented itself to the Hudson. I felt as if I'd wandered onto the set for *Mourning Becomes Electra*. I passed the graceful veranda and stairway, noting the French doors and elegant verticals. The Greek Revival austerity promised to be a setting for my American tragedy.

This was a fool's errand, and with my hacking jacket, tweed hat, and bumbershoot I was well cast. Could it be the wrong day? Completing the semicircle I arrived at a less imposing door which I gathered was the side entrance and tried my luck there. Again there was no response. Was the lady watching me through closed curtains, ascertaining my credentials? Now I began ringing insistently and knocking as well.

"Is there anybody there?" I called out, suddenly aware that the curtain had risen and I was opening a new play, establishing the character of the visitor and his relationship with the owner, and allowing the audience to settle in their seats before the action started.

I have always been amused at doors that never seem to be locked in plays. Someone impatiently rings or knocks and then just walks in. If people could really do that, we should all be living in empty houses; nonetheless I tried the door and—as in such a play—it opened and I entered Miss Hayes's life, annoyingly enough through the kitchen. Could it have been so designed? "Hello! Hello!" I said, as a protection against possible misinterpretation of my presence. Being shot as a trespasser was not the curtain I had in mind.

As I started toward the pantry on my quest, an old woman with glowing eyes came through the entrance gingerly. *My God!* I thought. *She's aged unbelievably. I haven't seen her offstage recently but this creature is ancient and barely resembles Hayes.* There was little reason why she should have. Miss Fleming was an aged retainer —something out of the *Cherry Orchard*—a governess of Jamie MacArthur when he was a small boy, living out her dutiless days with the mistress of this lovely house she had made her home for a lifetime.

I introduced myself and this spare Scottish woman vanished before my eyes, only to reappear to lead me out of the large country kitchen, through the handsome dining room, into a spacious and beautifully proportioned drawing room whose central French doors led thence down those veranda steps through the gardens then to the swimming pool, then to the tennis courts, finally to the beautiful river itself. The horizontal sweep of the room with its many windows was almost as impressive as the vertical thrust of the vista. It was a fine set, tastefully and traditionally appointed, and there, discovered stage right, back erect, bright eyes now raised graciously, was Helen Hayes.

She is a very pretty little lady, which somehow surprised me. Though the pastel picture of serenity, she exuded a great deal of energy. Contained, yes; she was releasing it by the inch like colored thread from a spool. I got the feeling that if she wished she could finish one of the unicorn tapestries in five minutes, smiling all the while.

"Miss Hayes!"

"Mr. Dody!"

Miss Hayes now cocked her head and allowed her blue eyes to focus on something more to her liking in the distance.

"Won't you sit down?"

There was a love seat not terribly far from her, but it wasn't terribly near either. Realizing my cap and umbrella were still in my hand, and since the Scottish crone could probably not be contacted for another one hundred years, when *Brigadoon* came to life again, I was on my own. As unobtrusively as I could—which is to say conspicuously—I now went to the entrance of the room and leaned the damned thing, cap atop it, against the wall of an anteroom, and returned to the settee while Miss Hayes, her eyes discreetly averted and concentrating on her tatting, allowed me to negotiate the trip. The vibrations were less than perfect.

"What a lovely house, Miss Hayes."

"Thank you. Of course I sold most everything at that auction a couple of years ago."

Considering the charming Victorian clutter, I found this statement startling.

"Did you buy it all back?"

"Oh, dear," Miss Hayes responded, rewarding my attempt at irony with the most perfunctory of smiles, "one acquires and one lets go. Like inhaling and exhaling."

I felt the house breathing.

"And what a view," I shouted too loudly. "To live on the water is a dream of mine." The voice was now too low, almost romantic. There are times when things just cannot go right and one should just forget it. "Does your property go straight to the water?"

"Why, yes," she answered in faint surprise, making the question a gaucherie.

Miss Hayes was in manner polite but distant, gracious but cool. If Bette Davis was Elizabethan and every inch a queen, Helen Hayes was Victorian and an empress. I had been granted an audience, and every word I said had to insure my return for another. Striking the wrong note could sound the death knell and, still it was not my style nor inclination to resort to merciless flattery, which, hideous as it is, rarely fails to work with actors. But Miss Hayes— or Helena Regina—struck me immediately as anything but typical. Obviously someone who kept her own counsel and was able to, she was to be reckoned with.

We went round Robin Hood's barn to discuss country gardens, English furniture, Periclean Greece, Bette Davis and her Lonely Life, the Arab-Israeli crisis which was about to burst into the Six-Day War, and, of course, theater. Although I had always admired Miss Hayes and remembered her with great fondness as Victoria Regina on Broadway and with equal pleasure as Vanessa, Maggie Shand, and Mrs. Arrowsmith on the screen, there were performances that were less memorable. In my younger years, particularly, I favored the kind of bravura acting and worldlier aspect of Lynn Fontanne, Judith Anderson, or Katharine Cornell.

She seemed so often to appear, even in her youth, as

a sugared doughnut that her radiance had escaped me. Wholesomeness with a touch of pluck and the ability to remain respectable while shouting "Heavens to Betsy" to the establishment does not attract the young and pretentious—both of which at one time described me. It wasn't fashionable in the smart set to like Helen Hayes. It just came naturally and one had to hide it, like a preference for chocolate milkshakes over martinis. It's a tough transitional period in one's teens. I had grown up seeing Helen Hayes and she was like a highly esteemed aunt whom my parents loved and whom it was almost always gratifying to see if you were not off to a hot date or a night with the boys.

I complimented her only on those roles I had enjoyed, but with my natural effusion made them pay off. I was mute on parts in which I found her wanting or miscast, as in the recently off-keyed Lady Teazle in *The School for Scandal*. It was difficult to avoid, since we discussed Ellis Rabb at great length, along with her unprecedented appearance in small, cameo roles with the ANTA Company.

Miss Hayes was such a star that her entrance as a maid in *Julius Caesar* could so interest the audience that the play would become a domestic drama. This is not to imply that she would not blend into an ensemble, simply that it was difficult. A star is a star for all her hiding behind a cloud of humility. She would almost have to unbalance a play by a trifling appearance in it. Still she had managed this admirably, I thought, in Pirandello's *Right You Are If You Think You Are*.

Remembering her from letterheads and public statements, I thought there would be time enough for political debate, and I steered clear of this topic. I kept recalling that Miss Hayes used to like Ike, whom the years and his vice-president managed to give the stature of Jefferson by comparison.

My audience was extremely formal that afternoon. We must have been chatting for an hour or so—with no offer of tea or, better still, a snifter—when I was astonished to see the remarkable Cathleen Nesbitt wander into the room. She seemed lost, and so she was.

"Oh, Helen, dear," she apologized, "I'm so very sorry, I'm looking for my room."

I stood up at the sight of this wonderful actress, prompting Miss Hayes to introduce us before she directed her house guest to the proper staircase along with a few suggested landmarks.

"I must say that I'm impressed, Miss Hayes. The place sounds like Windsor."

"Not quite, Mr. Dody," she answered unconvincingly. "Would you like to see some of it?"

And then, Miss Hayes showed me the ground floor and a bit of the grounds. Her carriage was ramrod, but heels and all she reached my fifth rib. Her experienced eye appraised her beloved rose bushes and she fondled one or two before she bluntly said, "There's a bus that leaves Nyack in exactly thirty minutes, Mr. Dody."

"Oh, fine!" I answered stupidly.

"Miss Nesbitt and I will walk you to town and get our exercise while we show you where it takes off."

"That would be very kind of you."

I then retrieved my cap and umbrella while Miss Hayes collected Miss Nesbitt. She asked Vera, her secretary-companion, who had been working somewhere else in the house, whether she could pick up anything in town and the three of us left, my evident dismissal softened by their company.

We made a lovely sight, out of something by J.B. Priestley. The scene could have been "county," the day certainly English what with the gray mist, Miss Hayes and I in our tweed suits and brogans, and Miss Nesbitt with her clipped speech and mackintosh, bringing out all of my insufferable Anglophilia.

We strolled past some pleasant houses and Miss Hayes, ever gracious, seemed relieved to be dumping me. It had not gone well, I mused. Helen Hayes, I decided defensively, was a bit of a cold potato under glass—reserved and lofty and ever so regal. Her faint but constant smile that afternoon revealed no more than total control over the situation. If I or anything ever got irritating enough, she would simply dismiss it. Such is the power of a queen. Rather than pleasure, the smile seemed to be saying "We are not amused."

All pinks and blues and grays, Helen Hayes could have been a sketch by Romney or Gainsborough. Behind her was always an invisible plum-colored drapery and beyond that her lands. Her attitude, the tilt of her head, bespoke her station and suggested that she was a power to be reckoned with.

Miss Nesbitt, for all her angles and points, her elegant looks gone to handsome hagdom, may have had a face whose two sharp profiles made a pair of shears, but they helped her cut quite a figure and one felt they would never draw blood. Surely as a proper guest and obviously knowing why I was there, she listened discreetly to our winding-down conversation about theater and books, but she exuded great charm and a welcome warmth.

"It's very strange, Miss Nesbitt, to meet you today. I just saw you at the Museum of Modern Art in the old *Pygmalion*."

"Miss Nesbitt wasn't in *Pygmalion*, Mr. Dody."

"Oh yes I was, Helen. How ever did you find me, Mr. Dody?"

"If I may say so, yours is not a face to be lost in a crowd—and that lethal reading of that one vicious line! How come?"

Miss Nesbitt laughed.

"I was visiting the set and the extra lady couldn't read the line. Gabriel Pascal asked if I would do it as a lark. I got into an evening gown and there I was."

"Cathleen!"

"Yes, Helen. I thought you knew. How fortuitous that you should have just seen me."

Was it a score for my side or not? I didn't know. I did feel, however, that if she were staying for an extended visit, her good vibrations, if she really had them, couldn't hurt me.

We got to town and there was the bus. My visit had been ominously short and most surely unprofitable. The day however had been unusual. I bought my ticket from the driver and then returned to the two ladies who—with all their gifts as actresses—could not conceal the fact that they had been dishing me. They smiled and wished me a good voyage and Miss Hayes added summarily that she really didn't know if she was interested in doing a biography, or even a book at all. She would think about it. It was no surprise.

"Well," I rallied, "not many men can say that Helen Hayes and Cathleen Nesbitt sent them off to the big city. Do you think I'll make my fortune?"

They smiled their assent. I bowed deeply and turned to enter the bus which, in the few minutes since my purchase of the ticket, now had a long line waiting to board. I waited politely for a short while and then turned to watch the ladies walking off into the sunset. But they were still standing a few feet away. I asked a woman if she would mind my place for a second and walked over to my hostess.

"Miss Hayes."

"Mr. Dody?"

"I once had a terrible scene with a young woman

and delivered myself of a particularly great curtain line, after which I stormed out of her apartment. The elevator wouldn't come and I was stuck in this tiny hallway, the whole mood dissipating while she stood triumphantly framed in her doorway. Machines do not always display a cooperative sense of timing."

Miss Hayes's smile broadened.

"You mean you wish we'd get out of here and savor your exit line."

"Precisely."

"Then it's good-bye, Mr. Dody."

And they picked up their cues and exaggeratedly bade me farewell. I remember looking back and seeing them gaily waving from a distance just before I was, at last, allowed to take my seat.

When I got back to town, I called the publishers.

"Herb! I was a dud. I don't know what the hell she thought of me. I was only there about an hour and a half and all that we settled was the world situation."

"Helen's already called me," Herb Katz now said. "She feels terrible. She told me that she did something awful to you."

"She didn't give me a drink—or even a cookie."

Herb was now laughing.

"Helen said that she was so nervous about meeting you that she gave a wretched performance. She said that when you arrived, she set the stage and was 'discovered tatting,' in a safe corner of the room like someone out of Jane Austen. She's mortified."

It was my first surprise concerning Helen Hayes. The whole effect had not only been contrived, which wasn't altogether undiscernable, but self-admittedly so, which, I must say, was. All of my insufferably pretentious views on everything from aardvarks to Ziegfeld designed to impress this celebrated woman were equaled only by her elaborate staging of our meeting, designed to place her at that advantage necessary to deal with this threatening stranger. Shades of my friend Louie. He had said "She'll be threatened by *you*." No one is immune. The pope wants to meet the queen of England and the queen of England wants to meet Jackie Onassis.

"But what's the upshot, Herb? There was just no way of telling what she thought."

"She felt that you were both so tense with each other that she would love to meet with you again—informally. If it's all right with you, next Thursday. Same time, same place—hopefully less stiffly."

"It's a date," I answered and I now called Louie.

"You're going to do the book, Sandy. Congratulations."

The following Thursday, Miss Hayes's poodle had a litter and we spent half the day lying on the floor with them. The weather was extremely mild and I had arrived in a sport shirt. The actress was also in something casual and we were approaching the whole business differently. All our external choices were easier. Our very speech patterns changed. The puppies helped too. You just cannot be too formal with newborn puppies around. It was a delightful day and this time, I was shown the entire place and given a drink.

"I'll have the pool filled in a couple of weeks. It's a pity you can't take a swim today."

And then when I looked at my watch, Miss Hayes quickly said that she had a gorgeous steak hanging around the refrigerator and if I wanted to share it and didn't mind a most informal dinner with some kind of improvised dessert, it might be pleasant. This was a good sign. But I never leave well enough alone.

I asked if she had any ice cream in the house. She did. And chocolate sauce? What good American didn't?

"My dear Miss Hayes, I will stay if you will allow me to make you the best *profiterole* you have ever tasted."

Miss Hayes now acquainted me with the kitchen and watched me in fascinated amusement. In five minutes I had the puffs in the oven.

"No matter where we are and what we're doing remind me in thirty-five minutes to spring them."

We now took a lovely walk around the grounds and then through her beautiful gardens, where Miss Hayes worriedly examined her famous rose bushes and pointed out the trees that her husband had planted and the quince Lillian Gish had given them. There was a story that went along with everything there, and I hoped that I would someday be able to describe the life and times of this—I now suspected—most unusual woman.

I have always derived great pleasure from watering gardens and offered to before dinner. That made me a man after this woman's heart. We were enjoying the last of the beautiful day outdoors when I suddenly raised my eyebrows and my finger.

"To the kitchen, Miss Hayes! Methinks the job is done."

When we opened the oven I expected the worst. Like bright children who won't show off their brilliance on demand, these puffs do not always reach the golden state of perfection in which we now found them. Even I was dazzled.

"Mr. Dody," Miss Hayes now whispered hoarsely, reminding me of the schoolteacher's wife in *Tea and Sympathy,* "when someday in the future people ask why I chose you to do my book, it will not be because of any literary gifts you may have or any personal persuasiveness. It will be because I never saw such glorious creampuffs in my entire life."

When . . . people ask why I chose you to do my book.

The way to a woman's heart. Of such intangibles! The steak was marvelous, the *profiterole* even better than it looked. Contracts were quickly drawn up that were eminently satisfactory and absolutely even-Steven. Miss Hayes and I signed them happily.

Plans were now laid for me to move up to Nyack for a few weeks. Miss Hayes was contracted to do a film in Hollywood in the summer, and always holidayed in Cuernavaca, Mexico, where she had a house. It was now or never to gather the necessary material. Before we started, she repeated her reluctance to write an autobiography. She wanted vaguely to do a book about the theater and her feelings about it, simply a memoir of her likes and dislikes. She had already done *A Gift of Joy,* which was just this sort of *pastiche,* and I plotted to change her mind—a calculation that did not escape her.

"I am sure, Mr. Dody, that you are going to do everything in your power to convince me but I do *not* want an autobiography. Perhaps just the early years, my childhood and the beginning with Lou Fields, but after that, I just couldn't go through the whole business again."

"Let's see what develops," I just as openly replied.

I was aware that her life had been a painful one in many respects. Both her mother's and husband's drinking had been burdensome. Their precious lives had become her responsibility. Her daughter Mary's early death was barely livethroughable even once. And these were just the few facts I knew about Helen Hayes. In talking I would discover other valleys someone as positive as she would not wish to revisit. Once more I was about to enter the life of another person. Someone I barely knew. Someone who would, despite the preliminary resistance, tell me not only enough for a book but too much for my own good. Like falling in love again, the initial thrill is destined to go, the exotic must become familiar, and the promise must be broken. But if we have hearts and if we have stomachs we keep trying.

I moved to Nyack with one valise and great hopes. I had met Helen Hayes twice, rather briefly, and was moving into her house. I adjust quickly. If I didn't, these books would have taken years to write. Miss Hayes gave me her late husband's comfortable quarters across the floor from her, and my view of the river and the grounds sloping toward it were beautiful. Charlie MacArthur's library was a fairly good one, and there was a fireplace aching to be used but for the early spring. As I settled myself I thought of John Barrymore and Carole Lombard in MacArthur's brilliant *Twentieth Century*. Had he and Ben Hecht written it *here?* I thought of *The Scoundrel,* which they had fashioned for Noel Coward in his own high style. A couple of weeks before, I had only known Miss Hayes as First Lady of the Theater. Now I was an honored part of her household. It was wild, and I was not unimpressed.

I put my toothbrush in the bathroom glass, my linens in Charlie MacArthur's chest, tested the excellent shower, immediately broke the "hot" tap, and met Miss Hayes downstairs in the bar which was Charlie MacArthur's pride that preceded his fall. It was a rathskeller type of bar, filled with short-snorters and posters and theatrical memorabilia and personalized photographs of fellow celebrities from Sir Noel to Harpo Marx. It was a gay and wonderful room that whispered of nights that began in a golden haze and never ended at all. Benchley had got loaded here, Fowler and Charlie Lederer, Sadakichi Hartmann and John Barrymore. But then who hadn't?

Elaine Barrymore, right in that chair, was pitied, as Helen MacArthur shared one evening the only thing these two women had in common. Charlie MacArthur's drinking was practically public domain. I had known about it for years but I didn't know whether his widow would be willing to discuss it. *That* might be the main reason for her prejudice against an autobiography. Living with an alcoholic and not mentioning it would be tantamount to the books of Matthew and Luke not mentioning Jesus. It seemed, however, completely incongruous that this woman, Helen Hayes, could be his widow. Life has a bad casting agent.

Yes. The bar had once been a popular part of the house but just as obviously it had fallen on sad days. Not that a guest couldn't get a drink there or that Madame wouldn't join him for one, but there was something there of the air of a hotel out of season. The refrigerator still made ice and there were still a few tins of macadamias and peanuts; nothing was really in disrepair but, like old Miss Fleming, awaited the mist to rise and find everyone young and gay again, with Jamie a small child to be tended, little Mary impishly alive and rosily healthy, Charlie writing and drinking on an exalted plane, and Helen needing age makeup for Victoria.

All this was there in the old wood and glassware and the lemon peelers, the strainers and other gadgets. Looking over everything with the dignity that only comes with the years were those young, beautiful faces staring at us from the walls. The Lunts, Beatrice Lillie, Leslie Howard. Frozen but not stiff in this bar were Fitzgerald's *Beautiful and the Damned*. Scott and Zelda and Hemingway were all friends of the MacArthurs. I drank a toast to the whole gang. I saw them and heard them. As a fellow ghost I felt privy to their gossip.

With Mary long since taken with polio and James a well-known actor with his own family on the West Coast, with Charlie dead from a broken heart and a tormented liver, Helen Hayes, then approaching her seventies, lived solitarily in this haunted, lovely old house. With an

Armenian secretary, Vera, with her Scottish retainer Miss Fleming, with romantic memories but always practical plans for the future, a worker since she was five years old, Helen Hayes was nowhere near retirement. Her energy was too great, her interests too varied, her need to prevail too strong. The chin was always up, the back always rigid, the eyes always clear and direct. I never for one second found "sugary" Helen Hayes sweet. She was salty.

I fixed her a bourbon on the rocks and then poured myself a double Scotch with a twist of lemon. We sat on comfortable leather chairs and watched the news on television. She asked if I was comfortable in my room and if there was anything I needed, but everything seemed to have been anticipated. Though I had virtually spent my days and evenings with most of my former subjects, this was the first time that I actually had moved in bag and baggage. There is a great difference.

No matter the time put in, one leaves and goes home. One can lead one's own life before and after the daily work, which is always exhausting. It is not so much a physical strain but an emotional one. One is always on the brink of disaster. As much as this work resembles psychoanalysis, it also has a great deal in common with dentistry. The patient's mouth is open, and you are always poking about near a nerve. If you hit it, it can hurt you more than it hurts her.

I have warned all my subjects from the outset that they are going to be annoyed with me and I cannot avoid it, that there will be times when I will purposely needle them to get at the root of the matter, that in order to do my job properly I'm going to have to hurt a little. I always say it and they always agree; but there is always the tension. It is only natural there will be, but the price is paid by both subject and writer—though the latter, like a doctor, has insulated himself to a degree over the years. But if he is at all sensible to another's suffering, the experience leaves him depleted at the end of a session.

That's where the diversion of one's friends and lovers refreshes one for the next try. I was in Nyack for four weeks or more, my notes, my library, and "The Late Show" my only relaxation when Miss Hayes retired for the night. If I were to get the work done before she was to leave for Hollywood I had a twenty-four-hour-daily job to do and no nonsense. I wondered if I could get into town for one weekend to change a couple of pairs of slacks and shoes. I wondered, too, about my laundry now. I had to speak to her about this.

My latest subject seemed certain that all would go smoothly and we would work well. We now toasted each other's success and she promised that the next morning, our first, she would be at my service. I knew she would be and wondered what was happening to poor Judy Garland and Sid Luft, who were appalled that I had chosen this course.

As we drank, Vera joined us and regarded me suspiciously. She was devoted to the star—her dragon and her moat. But I was not a marauder—only the lady's biographer. I don't think Vera liked me very much. We skirted each other whenever we were face to face, like boxers loath to deliver the first blow. The first night she was satisfied simply to glower.

After a good dinner in the bar, hostess and guest watched some television and then discovering that we both loved to play Scrabble, Helen Hayes lost the first of a series of games to me.

In the morning I scandalized all of Nyack by jogging up and down their Broadway in my jeans, and the town knew that their celebrated but ever so nice Mrs. Mac-

Arthur had another nut staying at her place. But though I was running in the streets I was still pussyfooting around the house. Miss Hayes, always polite and gracious, was at the same time formal. I was kept at arm's length in an ever so ritualized and unspoken protocol. There was something nineteenth century about my role as biographer in residence and hers as mistress of the manor. I recall at one point after she had asked, "Would you like me to tell you about my childhood in Washington, D.C., Mr. Dody?" when all I heard was my name. I knew that the secret of this work was the absence of barriers and I asked her, please, to call me Sandy. She smiled and did *not* at the same moment give me liberty to call her anything but Miss Hayes. There was just no doubt about her station, and in my attempt to equalize our positions I had now simply secured them.

I was now Sandy and she was still Her Majesty. I henceforth refused to call her Miss Hayes, though I could not call her Helen without her permission, obviously withheld. She now began addressing me all over the place as "Sandy," creating a situation from which I had to extricate myself. The imbalance was bad for our work, for aside from the rejection as a friend, I would have to suffer the implicit condescension. No, I could and would not call her Miss Hayes any longer, but had to find substitutions. When necessary, I resorted to an equally condescending "my dear" or warm "dear lady" or—in mock horror, "Madame!" This was the first of my subjects from the glittering Dagmar to the glowering Bette who did not immediately insist on the intimacy of first names. I thus discovered that for all her homespun Middle-American packaging, Miss Hayes was ermine-trimmed purple velvet. I later discovered that at the time of her triumphant *Victoria Regina* who reigned longer and more successfully than ever did Edward VIII, and with the help of the royalty-loving American public, Miss Hayes began to fuse with the redoubtable queen. It came naturally.

It would have been difficult if not absolutely impossible for her to do this with Catherine of Russia or even of Medici. But Victoria's was the perfect corona, the ideal fit. If Victoria had been an actress she would have been Helen Hayes. The combination of middle-class values and royal prerogatives, bursting health and formidable daintiness, unswerving loyalty and fidelity to one love that is equaled by her own sense of sovereignty and duty seemed to me interchangeable. Victoria was also far more peppery than saccharine, more jealous of her station than awed by it, and more vital and gay than her sometimes dour countenance would indicate.

Before I started work with Helen Hayes, she had asked to read the Bette Davis book, a copy of which was difficult to find for her and a copy of which I later found in her own bookshelf. Whether or not it was the first time she read it, she reacted oddly to it. After complimenting me—and though I had made not the slightest statement about Miss Davis—she told me that I would be extremely disappointed in her after such an exciting woman. There was a strange mixture of annoyance and wistfulness in her voice as she presented herself as a bland little lamb next to such as *La Lupa*.

Though the observation was as aggressive as it was plaintive, it was also inaccurate. Miss Davis has her public face and so does Miss Hayes. They are at opposite poles, the North and the South, and on inspection both are similar —if not necessarily snowbound. Despite their choice of masks, most suitably designed for comfort, Elizabeth and Victoria were not that different. It was a matter of angles and curves, not so much of character. Both loved their crowns, I believe, above all else, which is as it should be

with queens. Both were women of great strength and dura-
bility. Both were passionate, one loving her work more than
any one man, the other adoring her one man throughout
her life and between the acts and edicts. Both were stubborn and loath to admit defeat or fallibility.

Helen Hayes will be as surprised as Bette Davis to hear
that when the chips were down and the masks loosened for
easier breathing, these ladies were to me remarkably alike
—each being what she must be at all costs but with the
techniques best suited for each need.

Miss Hayes, the daughter of a sweet, loving, and mild
man, is a more conventional woman and gladly has brought
her respectability to what was once a profession a notch
above the streets. Miss Davis, the rebellious daughter of a
brilliant, insufferable man, loves to shock a world made up
of fathers but in a sense continues his reign, albeit a more
enlightened one. But she is blood-proud. Miss Hayes, a
sport—the queen no one expected to be queen, just like
Victoria, snatched from obscurity to rule a growing empire
—took her work seriously and needed the gaiety of her
talented but light-hearted consort. When he died she could
never replace him. He was the love of her life, the leavener
who lightened the burdens of her duties. But a queen remains a queen no matter her grief and as the widow of
Nyack, Helen Hayes now lived in a kind of grandeur, her
highness robbing us of intimacy, her manners impeccable
but her confidences superficial and apparent. I wasn't even
her John Brown, much less her Disraeli.

After a morning cup of coffee, it was my habit to jog
into town and back and then wander around the gardens
preparing my questions for the day and awaiting milady's
appearance. We would then, depending on the weather, sit
on the veranda facing the Hudson or return to the scene
of our first scene in the drawing room. The work, though it
was going well enough, was, as I said, simply factual. I was

getting a picture of her early childhood and the background in which it was set. Born with the century, she was able to tell with her prodigious memory of colorful times. She had still to bare herself and I wondered if she ever would.

On the third or fourth day at her house, I awakened early, went downstairs, greeted and circled Vera a few times as I prepared my coffee, and then sat with the woman and tried to be friendly. She was civil. I was obviously an interloper to be suffered and short of changing my will in her favor I was not going to reverse her judgment of me. With every subject there is someone with whom you have to deal and invariably he or she is more difficult to please than your collaborator. I later heard that Vera didn't believe I would ever do a book. I don't know what she thought I was doing in the house. At any rate, on occasion I got her to laugh and tried desperately to relieve her mind. When she once asked me if I remained friendly with my subjects after the work was done, I told her, not at all inaccurately, that I barely ever saw them again—unfortunately. This might have helped a little.

We chatted a little longer than I had expected and Miss Hayes had not come downstairs. I returned to my room rather noisily thinking I might awaken the lady. Not a sound could be heard behind her door. I wondered what the bedroom was like, never having seen it. After fussing about my room and deciding not to change my tennis shoes and also deciding as I looked at my reflection that I was a rather superannuated Marchbanks, I entered the hallway humming "Oh What a Beautiful Morning."

"Sandy!" I heard my sovereign call.

"Yes, Miss—my dear," I answered to my annoyance.

"Would you mind terribly if we worked in my room this morning. I don't feel too well."

"Why of course. What's wrong?"

"Come in, Sandy."

And I entered milady's chamber. It was the perfect set for her—a beautiful proportioned room filled to brimming with bric-a-brac and an international lifetime of acquired clutter. It was the sleeping chamber of a personage, a setting for a levee. Now I cannot swear this but I seem vividly to remember that in addition to the charming rosetted and beribboned peignoir there was a similar confection on her head. I only know that Helen Hayes propped up in her queen-sized bed was a queen. Pretty as could be, she evoked several images, the first Miss Austen's Mrs. Bennett, feeling the ague on a damp English day and having to forgo a shopping expedition with her brood of chicks; this surrendering to Charlotte of England but dissolving to the middle Victoria writing her German cousins of the foul weather at Balmoral. Affairs of state in the form of many papers were spread over the comforter. She was, indeed, a picture of bustling regality persevering in the face of mundane exigencies.

Miss Hayes, propped against all this lace and linen, far from looking helpless or ill, was more formidable than ever. The bed was a throne. One felt that by simply touching a tapestried pull, the palace guard would appear to protect her from the slightest gaucherie.

"I thought very carefully about something you said about my father yesterday and I found a quote that is most apt."

She looked up at me, her head cocked to one side, her eyes again looking beyond me—at her muse. She was acting again. How could she avoid it so costumed and surrounded with props?

"You don't mind, Sandy, if we have coffee up here and work. I really feel as if I may be coming down with something."

"Not in the least. It's such a lovely room. I must, as Miss Austen used to say, 'take a stroll about it' later and examine all of your *bibelots*."

After arranging for a pot of coffee, I sat at her window, the sparkling river to my left, Miss Hayes floating on a cloud of pillows and papers and laces. I was tempted to put a silver saltcellar on her head in imitation of W.C. Fields's magnificent, blown-cheeked imitation of her in *Victoria Regina*. A napkin and a saltcellar and the madman became Helen Hayes. It was quite a trick and *Vanity Fair*'s famous photograph of it spurred a whole generation of dining theatergoers to try it, without his brilliant success.

Miss Hayes was all flutter and bustle and eager to discuss her childhood and quote some poetry which she loved. She had bits of paper with notes on it to recall events or impressions and she seemed to be relishing our labors. It must have been about nine-thirty when we began talking and the morning progressed nicely. Even royalty is a little less informal *in camera*, and with all the trappings meant to awe, the setting somehow smoothed the way and, at one point, in an effort to break through her fluent but censored narrative, I attempted to jolt her into reality. I asked about her daughter.

I am always, the first few days, a little cautious about my questioning, but it was time I approached, no matter how gingerly, the depths. I did not plan to probe deeply this morning but I wanted to feel my way. Eventually this would have to be discussed. With glistening eyes, Miss Hayes, with much too steady a voice, told of her adored child doomed to die before Dr. Salk's miraculous cure. I was touched by her simple recital; and now my eyes were glistening too. That was our first communion. Better far than wine are tears shared. It happens eventually in this work and brings you closer—encouraging more such moments, one feeding on the other. Davis allowed them to flow. With Hayes, I felt a need for containment. The moment the story was out, the actress retreated to her ribbons and laces and became a bit too gay. She is a sturdy little soul.

I studied this vision, this valentine of a woman, while and after telling her terrible tale, all of it understated and stark, the only gimcrackery simply surrounding her. Her reading warily hid her undying agony and in so doing intensified it. I realized that Helen Hayes was the strongest of my subjects, stronger and more enduring than Bette Davis. This woman could survive anything because, real as her feelings were, she could manipulate them. Her emotional administration was masterful. Helen has the detachment of the artist and the need to embroider over the genuine article. On her own admission she has always found it necessary to outline her suffering or joy—in bold leading like a stained-glass window. It is not enough that she is happy, she must indicate happiness. What a terrible poker player she would make, although her sense of mischief might encouarge her to confuse her opponents by indicating the opposite emotion or even "play" at having a poker face. This I would love to see.

Helen Hayes's emotions are layered and she possesses, oddly enough, what queens possess—the ability to cushion grief, perhaps to numb herself against it, momentarily enabling her then to convey it after the necessary preparations and with the dignity due such heroic anguish. This is a technique for life as well as art and I suspect that Bette Davis has never learned it. She is not as disciplined as Helen nor as wise nor even as cultivated. She is simply more spontaneous.

I felt that Miss Davis was being consumed by her flaming passions. Miss Hayes could bellow them with her breath but could dampen them with her tears. Here was the ultimate actress who had learned a technique for suffering.

Like Judith Anderson as *Medea,* who had to rely on her brilliant technique for most of her run because the ecstasy of her opening-night performance if repeated eight times a week would have destroyed her, Helen survives on the carefully observed simulation of her own suffering. Once removed is thrice insured. I suspect that Rose Kennedy is another so blessed—their Church doubtless helping both ladies, but oddly being strengthened itself by these rocks.

Helen Hayes then survives on the carefully observed simulation of her own genuine suffering. Bette Davis succumbs to hers—eager always for the emotional experience. Miss Hayes, understanding better her heartache and her need to evoke it, was mostly honest and cooperative—but only rarely breaking through to reveal the unrehearsed actress. But this, too, was Helen Hayes. There was a reserve as characteristic as Bette Davis's extravagance. As such I had to respect it, but a change was in order if I were to have a book that would satisfy.

It must have been a good four hours later when Miss Hayes looked at her watch in stunned acceptance of the passing of time.

"Heavens! I *never* do this. It is three o'clock and I've done nothing in the garden, haven't even dressed or been in the kitchen and I'm sure I've given you absolutely nothing."

Mea culpa, mea culpa, mea maxima culpa!

"Nonsense. As a matter of fact it's been an excellent session. By far our best."

"No!" she insisted, "I've been an absolute *lump.* Just lying here. I get you to come up all the way from New York and then lie here like a dead fish."

"Nonsense! I tell you it was very good. Do you feel better?"

"Oh, I'm fine. You've quite made me forget the sniffles. But I'm wretched that I was such a dud all day."

I was to learn that Miss Hayes, who has worked her

entire life, feels guilty about the night's sleep she takes. She feels guilty about many things. Her faith, doubtless, encourages this compulsion to blame herself for earthquakes, droughts, and the shortcomings of others. I am certain that Helen Hayes needlessly blames herself for the loss of her daughter, her husband, and her mother. It is her nature. For a tiny woman, her shoulders are strong.

I was organizing my notes and her papers when, in a burst of energy, perhaps fed by the hours loitering amidst her pillows or—and I prefer to believe this—because she was so stimulated by our work, she now suggested that I wait for her in the garden while she dressed so we could take a hike. She had much of Nyack to show me and she now felt capital.

"I shall wait for you in the garden—third rose bush from the left of center. If we synchronize our watches . . ."

"Sandy, I do hope I didn't thoroughly waste your precious time."

She continued to rattle on guiltily about her early lethargy which I had never noticed. She is the kind of woman who can be as active in repose as on her feet. It was obviously most unusual for her to give in that way. I watched her gathering her papers together, pink ribbons and bows all bobbing, and I thought of the bar downstairs and my own quarters that belonged to the most irreverent and incorrigible Charlie MacArthur. While Madame La Reine twittered about I suddenly remembered the photograph of Harpo Marx over the bar, staring madly at the beholder while he picked his nose, and I was suddenly struck by something.

Why in hell am I pussyfooting around with this woman? She probably hasn't been treated so respectfully by anyone except her priest and her gardener in ages. What was this nonsense, this cue I had picked up? Yes, the work had gone pleasantly enough and I'd got some fair material

273

and one moment of shared emotion; but we were still employer and employed, the countess and the bellhop, the queen and the footman. It was ridiculous, this calling her "Miss Hayes" and practically curtseying. The lady interrupted my musings.

"Imagine!" she went on, "three-thirty and I haven't budged. Are you absolutely *certain*, Sandy, that the day hasn't been a total waste for you?"

It was now or never.

"My dear," I now observed, "not only did the work go well but if I may be frank—"

"But of course . . ."

"You were great in bed today."

There. It was done. I'd had enough of all this bowing and scraping. So, obviously, had she. Her arms now were flung over her head, scattering some of the papers. Her head fell back on the pillows and for a split second I thought she had died of *lèse majesté*. But no! She was laughing as I'd never seen her laugh.

"Oh, my dear," she sputtered, trying to catch her breath. "Oh, my dear."

She now looked at me for the first time with real warmth.

"Get out of here, you nut. I'll be downstairs in a few minutes."

"Yes, Madame," I laughed as I went through the door.

"And for heaven's sake, call me Helen."

It was the first of many laughs Helen and I shared. It really shouldn't have been a surprise to me. For all her old time religion and imperial manner, Helen Hayes is an irreverent, impish Hibernian and not without the loquacity and pugnacious bent of her countrymen. Though her name should have given me the clue, it hadn't, and it came to me that I had never thought of Helen as Irish, though if I had been asked I probably would have realized it. Great stars transcend their origins unless they willfully or help-lessly exploit them like a Harry Lauder, Barbra Streisand or Sammy Davis, Jr.

Helen has all the gift of gab, lightness of touch and antic charm of the Irish. The sky-blue eyes and heavenward nose don't lie either. Nothing is really permanently sacred to the penetrating eye and the quick tongue.

It had taken me a few days to get it through my head that she couldn't have had such a maverick husband and such satined, sabled, and fabled cronies without having far more than meets the eye. Helen proved to be great fun and she has, in my opinion, done herself in by allowing the legend of the upright, foursquare little high school principal to color the real picture. It isn't that it is a false impression. It simply isn't the total one. I found her fine company and she wore extremely well, the most complimentary thing I can say about someone with whom one has to work under close and intimate conditions.

I became very fond of little Helen Hayes, though, truth be told, I rarely found her sweet or compliant. Or lacking in guile or even arrogance. It takes just as much shadow-making substance for her to have become First Lady of the American Theater as it did for Eleanor Roosevelt to become First Lady of the World. Helen's drive is every bit as great as Bette's and as channeled. They differ only genetically. If Bette is a leopardess who must rule her jungle acres, Helen is an angora cat determined to win every goddamned blue ribbon in the show—or else. The quick little creamy smile can fade with the tender paw fast transformed for scratching. These women are both survivors, both committed for life to the fulfillment of what they believe their destinies. Both have accomplished that but—and I know them both like books—I believe that Helen has done the better job.

For all her little eruptions Helen is cooled and at

peace. She has, I observed, a remarkable oneness with the whole. One sees this when she is in her garden or the ocean or the woods or standing on a pyramid. Helen Hayes is ecclesiastical. She's aware of the rhythm of life and sways to it.

While Bette Davis strikes me as elemental, violent, at odds with the other forces, Helen Hayes works in concert with them. She is wiser than Bette and one can see her instinctive knowledge, even in her childhood pictures, even in her little five-year-old face. One sees in Bette's early photographs will and defiance. Lightning is in her. Indeed, it struck as she was born, illuminating her entrance.

I was much amused, as time went on, that Helen could have feared that she would be dull after Bette. She is a far more complex and interesting woman, her subtleties beyond most who react only to the violent phenomena in nature and in people. It will be the storm, the heat wave, the blizzard that attract their attention as well they must. God knows Bette Davis is exciting. The broad stroke is not to be sniffed at. The bouncing diamonds of rain on water, the clap of thunder, the silver torrent are all Bette Davis. As actress she is all these things. But Helen is weather, without which. She seems to know this. Helen is the mysterious norm rather than the phenomental aberration. Also not to be sniffed at or lived without. There are more minutes in her day and it is my guess that being more in harmony with the whole *gestalt,* her star will endure longer. Bette Davis endures as a great name, which is different. Of course, with the proper charge she will always light up the sky anew; but Helen Hayes quietly twinkles away, retaining her ascendancy, never slipping into the desperate and questionable areas of darkness near the horizon. Perhaps it's her inner life. She is intelligent and she is more than that. She is wise.

I must add that for all her artistry and more dignified

tenure as a star, she has rarely achieved the summit as Bette has, though a recent viewing of her old MGM film *The Sin of Madeleine Claudet* reveals a powerful passion that was subsequently tempered to create the Helen Hayes we all know.

Lightning is spontaneous. It is not wise. It is.

I was at Helen's for about ten days when, in an act of generosity far greater than grateful ecstasy at being plucked from celebrated obscurity, with ANTA needing money desperately, Helen agreed, after happily appearing in cameo roles, to star in a revival of George Kelly's *The Show-Off.* Helen liked them over at ANTA and now for the first time in her life decided that her semiretirement could wait while she plunged into a role with more "sides" than *Hamlet.* It was the longest role she or probably any other woman ever tackled.

She received the script and after reading it asked, for the fun of it, if I would cue her so she could get the feel of it. We sat outside. I remember watching the occasional river traffic and sipping a cool drink while she studied the part for a few minutes. Then she gave her first "cold" reading of it. I was convulsed. This role was absolutely up her alley. As loose as could be, Helen made me laugh so that it was hard to play with her. My reaction was so real and so infectious that she started to soar. I am glad to say that Helen is not a dressing-room actress. Anyone who saw that performance, especially on opening night, knows how hilarious she was. I will go as far as to say that, in my lifetime of theatergoing, at least Helen has, in her most enviable career, never been as great. Even the cognoscenti had to stand up and cheer. Helen is getting better and better.

I was very pleased in one way about her planned appearance. Anything that would bring her more prominently into public view would be good for the book; but I wondered now when we would be able to work together. Rehearsals were going to start immediately and I was expendable in the face of this new development. Helen didn't seem in the least worried, and I knew that she was happy working with me, so I just bent with the wind. It seemed highly unlikely that Helen would have any time for me now since ANTA planned to take the show out of town and play it in Hollywood before its fall opening on Broadway. The problem seemed insoluble since the West Coast opening, the tour, and the fall return were also complicated by Helen's stint in the film *Airport* and her annual holiday in Cuernavaca. It then came to me and I stopped worrying.

When Herb Katz and George de Kay, our publishers, asked what was going to be—though they were certainly willing to wait until Helen was good and ready to continue—I told them I had a feeling that it was going to work out just fine. I saw no reason why she couldn't arrange our continued work in Mexico. Her breathless descriptions of the place struck me curiously like feelers. We were having fun and loving our work and there really didn't seem to be any visible reason why we couldn't love it in September as we did in May.

I find it difficult to imagine this kind of ghostwriting, and the séances that precede it, being at all fruitful without the willing and sympathetic cooperation that has always existed with my subjects. Cut-and-dried sessions would certainly yield like material. The more enjoyment shared by the partners the greater the chances of success. Our publishers agreed that were Helen to suggest it, they would invest most happily in any further expenses.

It worked out perfectly. Helen did ask if I could spend a month or so in Cuernavaca and, even better, knowing my shared love of travel and rubbernecking, asked that I pick her up in Hollywood so that we could drive down there, stopping at various garden spots like Guadalajara so she could show off the beautiful country. She now worked out all the particulars. With Vera driving, Helen and I and the pups would leave California some time in August. I couldn't have been happier with the plans.

Helen went off to the coast and Evans arranged for me to follow her, not believing my refusal of plane reservations. I do not like flying in planes and it is easy to explain. It is sheer cowardice. I am the only man alive who would prefer and enjoy crossing the country on a burro. Herb and George managed a ticket on what is no longer the Twentieth Century, and tripping over the filthy and torn red carpet that once was rolled out for the likes of Garbo and Chaplin and Huxley and Hearst, I joyously, with gift-laden friends, found my roomette on the train, located the bubble car that would give me my view of the wild, woolly West, and then wobbled to the white-linened and shiny-crystaled dining car, planning to order in the morning their grill-scarred toast and yellow corn-kerneled scrambled eggs, oatmeal and cream, and matchless coffee served to you by dark, handsome, elderly men of breeding who pretended that they had never heard of the civil rights movement.

I looked forward to this cross-country junket and the adventure of eventually seeing my star in her show and then lying amongst the enchiladas gathering the great tales of theater, the Algonquin set, and early Hollywood from a triumphant, relaxed and loquacious Helen. I had only visited Tijuana and Nogales and was eager to know this beautiful country once briefly but so Warner Brotherly ruled by Bette Davis and her Brian Aherne.

Unlike my other subjects, Helen now was extremely active at the time of collaboration. It's true that Elaine had her orders to get out and Bob was singing a couple of nights a week at the Metropolitan, but our sessions were to all intents and purposes practically worked out. With

Helen, I was to find that I was never in repose. As I've said, I adjust quickly, but this little lady surely set a pace.

With her active social life and busy work schedule, there wasn't very much we could do in Hollywood except get to know each other better—which was as important as anything else—and iron out some of the original wrinkles in our agreement. Helen was still talking in terms of loosely strung anecdotes with "perhaps a bit of my early life" and I was still after a real memoir which I honestly told her she had a duty to write. It was unthinkable that such a star as she should not record her impression of her life and times. I would see a flicker of hope and I was biding my time.

When I took lovely Tracy O'Dwyer to see Helen in *The Show-Off,* she was everything I had imagined she could be after that first cued reading up in Nyack. There was nothing patronizing, not a suggestion of the queen stepping down to laugh with the commoners, not a scintilla of the serious actress having a lark. Helen was what she started out to be, before the critics and the legend makers got hold of her and made her a personage. She was a knowing, funny, painfully human woman—the genuine article. It was the performance of an Abbey Player at that great company's height. My God, she was funny.

And what a pleasure it was to go back and be able to say so. An added delight backstage that night for Tracy and me was our sharing Helen momentarily with the author's niece, Princess Grace and her Prince. She was coolly lovely in pale yellow and, as I remember, I also met there the striking now-departed Agnes Moorehead, whom God had created with some help from her in glorious Technicolor.

Being starstruck and pleasure-mad, I enjoyed my rather glittering stay in California prior to our trip, but I was becoming worried since my notebooks were still empty. I began treasuring our moments together, like a mother knowing her soldier son is leaving any moment. As I greeted Helen I would ask her a personal and profound question, praying that before we sat down and half of Hollywood walked in she might give me both an answer and a climate of feeling from which I could work when I was by myself.

Days passed and weeks and I met her son, James MacArthur, whom I liked despite his unspoken reluctance to give me anything but the most apparent reactions to Nyack, Miss Fleming, his father, his feelings about his sister's death. It struck me that it must have been horrendous for a sensitive little boy, who knew he was adopted, to witness the loss of Helen and Charlie's blood child. It struck me that it would be a burden he might well carry for the rest of his life despite the MacArthurs' sensibility. Of course I never verbalized this. Jamie had been and was virtually their son but I tucked the subtlety away; it was a note to be struck gently but firmly once we were safe in Cuernavaca. I couldn't help but observe very carefully Jim's reaction to Helen. There was awe as well as love. They were bound together by a hundred ties, but I felt a hint of protocol, of the reserve the crown prince has for the queen mother. I half-expected him to call her ma'am instead of mom! I do believe, though, that they would do anything for each other.

Certainly Helen had no other reason but Jim—once Jamie—for her now latest plan, to do a segment of Ron Ely's *Tarzan* series being shot in Churabusco, on the outskirts of Mexico City, with her son. Maurice Evans had appeared in two sequences with, from his point of view, great success; and evidently the star and his director were attempting to transform the great old chestnut into a *marron glacé*. It seems that Jim MacArthur was going to appear in one of the installments as a young doctor, and the producers decided that Helen's appearance as his mother would be a feather in everyone's Quetzalcoatl. But now I was worried further. When in hell were we ever going to have those vis-à-vis necessary to write a book? The ghost is expected by everyone—perhaps because of his designation—to do the impossible. Bette was the only one who recognized my needs and satisfied them from the word go, albeit because she had little else to do at the time. She could have socialized, God knows, but she didn't. She was a good girl in that department. Helen was busy being a working star.

I had lovely, elegant little lunches poolside under an awning with Helen and we played at work a few days at Lari Mako's exquisitely appointed and well-run house, but I ached to get away. The time was nearing and Vera, who seemed to find it harder and harder to be civil to me now, decided that she couldn't drive us all the way to Cuernavaca with the puppies because she couldn't drive the wee things back to Nyack herself. Or some such reason. I, I suspected, was the dog responsible.

Helen shifted plans quickly. She and I would fly down a week later, giving us time to say farewell to friends and relax a bit before the trip. She and Lari gave a party and Edna McHugh—with whom I was staying—and I had Helen and Lari to Edna's handsome Malibu house for my hostess's gourmet food and a swim in her wonderful Pacific Ocean; and I suddenly stopped and realized that I had to fly. It was not too terrible a moment. They wouldn't dare take Helen Hayes. This was clear, and if she held me all the way, to which she laughingly agreed, I knew I would get there properly. It simply was not Helen Hayes's fate to die in a crash and so I was safe.

Her presence, a half-bottle of Scotch, and the fact that Helen was captive made the flight in this airborne confessional both an enjoyable and profitable one. She couldn't go anywhere, and we had one of our best and longest sessions. I jumped madly from topic to topic in an hysterical effort to get as much done as possible before we landed and she was again assuring me, as she made plans to show me *el museo* or *la mercado de las flores* or Cortes' palace, that she would settle down and fly right very shortly. Helen was a challenge. It is as much to her credit as mine that under the most impossible circumstances—climbing pyramids, hanging off trolley cars, riding an elephant, playing three-handed gin with the chain-smoking Countess Tchernitchew, a Cuernavacan lady to be reckoned with, swimming alongside each other in her lovely pool overlooking the slums, visiting her endless list of friends who wined and dined us in a luxury I have rarely seen, walking the *calles* during fiesta, listening to mariachi bands, attending communion, fighting Montezuma's revenge (*I*, that is, and with the help of tiny pills left near my bed by Alfred Lunt on his last visit), rehearsals and retakes and loopings and conferences and restaurant-going and opening nights, sightseeing and shopping jags that we got as much done as we did.

Like me, Helen adjusts instantly. With all her disciplines she can emotionally recall on cue; and because I had no choice, I was able to prod her and record all that she told me, sometimes writing in an automobile going over mountains on roads so bumpy that the notes were unreadable, impossible to decipher. There were often miraculous answers to sensitive questions never to be repeated with any hope of response, much less civility. I am grateful for my memory. There are one-time topics to be pursued only at the ideal moment, in which the weather, her mood, your charm, and the conjunction of stars together create a never-again-to-be-got receptivity. Ask these questions again at the wrong time and the whole shebang can be canceled. Such is the danger of some approaches.

Even if information is not used, your receipt of it has given your relationship and work texture. It has given you a key to locked doors which open and, at least, reveal the forbidden.

It is rare that these men and women do not know when they have lent you that key. If the relationship is good, each wants you for that second to have it; but one must not make too much of the situation at the time. It is much like giving oneself to another in semisleep. One can even exact a denial later but one doesn't shatter one's chances or the moment by identifying the act and thereby ending it. It is a fragile moment, to be recalled from a distance rather than ogled at the time. These artists are usually disciplined enough and frightened enough to sense when the writer is trespassing. I have never underestimated my confessers—especially Helen.

I now knew enough to worry plenty about the future. Now that I was mining treasures I couldn't be sure of my claim. Helen's legend was greater than reality, and this I had always to consider. In a moment of flashing insight and brutal honesty, she had told me that she even felt guilty about Mary's death because its tragedy had added still another dimension to her fame and the admiration of her great audience. How could she not use it? How could she disassociate herself from such a subsidiary dividend? *Helen Hayes is so gallant. What a dreadful loss.* The alcoholism of mother and husband while she was building her career (certainly not without their help) was bound to evoke pity in others. *How can Helen stand it? What courage, what character!* What emotional blackmail. If she wept even judiciously the whole country would shake its head and cluck its sympathy. If she squared her shoulders and accepted the inevitable then she was a Christian martyr. Since Helen is strong, martyrdom seems her fate. Not of her own choosing. Helen has far too much sense of fun, but the world is made up of labelers and labeled.

I suspect that Helen Hayes, for all—and because of —her understanding, must have been hard to take. Husbands and mothers, along with all others who are not as strong as they would like to be, may cling to their protector for dear life, but I fear they resent her as well. After all, the strong, no matter how gentle, show up the weak for what they are. They may even unwittingly weaken them further. Still nothing can be done. The strong can be nothing but strong and, in an occasional effort to be attractively weak, they invariably make things worse. As for the weak, we all know how destructive they can be when given just a bit of power. Helen, indeed, was as strong as Bette, and though her power was pastel, it was just as formidable.

The lady's loyalty to both of these adored people was irritatingly impressive at first. Helen would not go beyond the facts she knew were public domain and I couldn't crack her reserve concerning them. She could hardly have discussed Charlie as a teetotaler or her darling "Brownie" as Grandma Moses and so, after some of the textured tête-à-têtes, I was able to imply those things which Helen now tacitly accepted. As long as we didn't discuss it further, she understood, as every good actress, the need for dimension; but it took me quite a time to crawl into her heart and really unburden her.

I too had my own self-imposed restrictions concerning Helen Hayes. Were I to have discovered some dark area, scandal, some shocking character defect that would alter the definitive and official portrait of the lady, which of course I did not, I would have been forced, not only by the actress's blue pencil but, by my own common sense, to avoid revealing it—this time—no matter how obliquely.

The clever ghost can slip through locked doors but the really clever ghost must know when not to. There are some subjects the audience prefers remain inviolate.

Bette Davis's public image allows for more leeway than Helen Hayes's. The public has so accepted Bette as a virago that if she were to be involved in a crime of passion she could doubtless continue her career even more profitably after the verdict. Now a courtroom heroine, both defendant and her own lawyer, Bette would only have acted out to the limit the role with which she is comfortably identified. Helen under the same unlikely circumstances, would be guilty, mostly, of disillusioning the country, and her eventual return to favor would be as slow as was the wholesome Ingrid Bergman's when that lovely lady rushed the season and anticipated the present moral climate by acting like a passionate, committed woman before it became acceptable.

One's mask must be chosen for comfort as well as effect since one may never be able to remove it. Like Thomas Mann's character who found that the mask he wore for years had adhered to his face, becoming one with it, neither of these actresses—Bette nor Helen—is any longer anyone other than her advertisement. But each, remembering her original motivations, suspects she is not. And each is caught in her own trap. Dear Bette has got to be passionate, forthright and driving twenty-four hours a day. God help her if she's ever mean instead of cruel. God help her if she ever wants to take a nap. And poor Helen can never in her life for even a relieving moment ever be ignoble, self-pitying or even say shit, no matter how provoked by the Fates. No wonder she has always loved rascals and clowns and iconoclasts. She can be human by proxy.

After those first few formal days, though she often

retained a reserve, I never once felt ill at ease with Helen nor ever found her stuffy. Irreverence in others was not ungratifying to her, articulating as it did her own doubts and affirming her slightly reproving but smiling acceptance, her own expansion of spirit. Interestingly enough Helen had confided that she had always adored rapscallions and longed to bask in their rapscallionness, only to find that unfortunately something in her always brought out the best in them. The most antic and irreverent of scamps would become a gentleman in her presence. It has been her curse and she is helpless to reverse it. Certainly her husband accomplished what she desired to excess, but Helen paid the price for marrying a faun.

Helen had fallen in love with a brilliant, beautiful young man and he had fallen in love with her. You can't beat that and she hasn't tried. The sweep of her stately and symphonic career could hardly help but change his tune; but Charlie MacArthur remained a troubador—in person. He "spread merriment" in the world's salons—instead of writing. He loved the beautiful people and he would always be off with these charmers.

"I am studying them!" he would say. "I am recording their frivolity." The very thing Helen adored in him was to prove unadorable in time. Charlie never grew up. Helen was never young. Work was to Helen more than an ethic, more than fulfillment. It was a necessity. Work was her habit. Work was her life. Charlie's life was his career. Though the best of his work reveals his undeniable gifts, he reminds one of Wilde's observation that his talents were employed in his art, his genius he reserved for life. Charlie MacArthur threw himself into the pleasure of life and worked overtime at it. Reacting to his own father's cruel piety and humorlessness, Charlie lived for pleasure, lived for the moment, from *bon mot* to *mot juste* like a bee sucking—leading the sweetest of lives—a maker of honey, with a sting that may hurt others but usually is fatal only to itself.

His drinking, one assumes, sent him reeling from the reality of his own limitations—not perhaps as an artist but as a working writer. The talented aren't always given drive but they are given a sense of responsibility if not the will to exert it. Artists with the gift never throw it away without suffering from their profligacy. If only the lazy writer could enjoy his leisure; he simply spends it. Not many, if any, have the gift to throw it away carelessly, stylishly. If only. We carry instead the original hope, the promise we are breaking. Perhaps, after all, the driven man we pity is better off. He may someday regret much but never the squandering of his birthright, the wanton murder of his own seed.

As we are known by our choices we are likewise known by our excesses. Some drink to escape, some eat, and some love themselves to oblivion. Then there is the refuge of work. Of all of them, it is work alone that is salvageable. Everything else, for all its press relations and undeniable satisfaction, disappears with the doing. One luckily passes food and drink with dispatch and what is quicker spent than passion? Yes, *all* things pass, but work, like well-planned sex, produces a product. Work can allow one to enter—no matter how fleetingly—the future, to meet and seduce the unborn, to do what men have dared to dream, to live beyond the grave. This untransferable ticket is given to a few. To lose it or destroy it is more than irresponsible, it is catastrophic.

Helen's little boy, her husband, her Charlie, mislaid the ticket the man gave him, and he was lost. It wasn't enough that he always had Helen's private train to take him anywhere. He took it but it was not satisfactory and what might originally have been a Dionysian love of the grape and the guilt of the goat for not smelling like a rose caused Charlie's drinking to become more and more destructive. The human body as well as the soul can take just so much ravaging. The middle-aged Charlie was more vulnerable than the young one. Every party Charlie went to, "to gather material" for plays never to be written, gave him one more hangover from which he would eventually never recover.

Wayward he was, Charlie; but Helen worshiped him and from the beginning had welcomed his suit. Against the counsel of her friends and his, with everyone in New York warning Miss "Prissy Prune" that she was flirting with disaster, Brownie, her mother joined the army and delivered the supposed deathblow. "He drinks," she had the loving cheek to observe.

When Charlie gave Helen an engagement ring from Cartier, Brownie gave Helen a band of rubies and emeralds. She was losing Helen and was becoming a member of the wedding. She certainly couldn't have believed that Helen was marrying for the ring and would now break off her relationship. She did not like Charlie and warned Helen that she'd heard he was a "satire," which was true enough, and he would leave her, which was not. Brownie, to preserve the status quo, wanted Helen to stay the socially insecure girl she was. Charlie, in one of the marvelous paradoxes of human relationships, wanted his little girl to become the strong woman who would not only take care of herself but of him as well.

I wondered if I could say this all later and planned my juxtaposition of simple sentences again, should it prove necessary. How often the honeymoon between writer and star had allowed, as honeymoons should, for license later revoked.

"She knew her love by his way of talking. She knew her love by his way of walking." As Helen told me, happy is the one who knows his fate and accepts it.

I've often pondered Helen's amazing reversal of rôles with her mother, starting, so she confessed, with a bitter momentary confrontation with Brownie over Daddy. Helen was furious that her beloved, passive father had been made unhappy, and forced her mother to apologize. In doing what little Helen wanted, Brownie, though surely a strong influence, the strongest in her daughter's life, still relinquished the reins in some departments. Because of her problem, she had even earlier been mothered by her child. Helen's childhood had been glittering but painful with this alternately gay and sober and ever so vital woman. Far earlier than Bette with Ruthie, Helen healthily resisted her stagemotherly guardian, without whom her career would not have been but whose past battles and court intrigues that insured it (as with Bette's mother) seemed to entitle her to a continuing regency over her queenly daughter.

Once again, like Bette, Helen—inheriting her mother's drive along with her own genius—eventually freed herself from loving tyranny. But Helen, interestingly enough, and after all her suffering, clung to the familiar and repeated the pattern, marrying an alcoholic. Could she, I thought, have relished the role of Mama? And is it such a sin, answering, as she must have, the mute call of a little boy? Men with wit say clever things and women of strength protect their loved ones. The wit may be lethal and so may be the strength, but as my Aunt Rose used to say, "That's the way it goes." As actress and writer, they must have been aware of the undercurrents of their love.

Helen told me of a play that both she and Charlie adored. It was by Marcel Achard and called *Auprès de ma Blonde*. It was adapted for the Lunts by Sam Behrman, who called it *I Know My Love*. The script addressed itself to the kind of love whose grand passion belongs only in grand opera, where it could proudly sail on the crest of cadenza-filled arias over heroic acts and tempestuous scenes.

Contained in art, the lovers can soar mightily, evoking tears and bravos from the spectators. Life is sloppier and such a love, though undying, can be killing as well—for others as well as the killers. The lovers are helpless in their love, powerless to break their bondage. Achard saw children and friends destroyed in such a consecrated love. In the play, the husband—in an effort to release himself from his wife—takes a mistress. He hopes to destroy the marriage, but instead, the mistress meets her doom. The unit cannot be destroyed. There are loves that are ordained, if not in heaven, somewhere beyond our reckoning. This kind of love, expostulated the playwright, makes demands impossible to be met, evidently, by anyone but a tenor or a soprano. This was a passion to be sung and played by actors and not lived by mere mortals.

Helen paused after she told me about the play. We were driving back to Cuernavaca from Mexico City, driving above the clouds nearer to heaven than I'll probably ever get. As high as we were, in the distance we could see a range of peaks that were silhouetted against the purplish dusk, one behind the other subtly fading in intensity, a study in perspective, a diminuendo of grays vanishing into mist. One knew that they did not cease with our inability to see them. Both Helen and I were silent as we stared, our driver, thank God, looking straight ahead, doubtless sated with the wonder of this place.

Helen's voice was quiet. It sounded as if it had voyaged far.

"And that, my dear, is the kind of love Charlie and I had—and we didn't know it then. God help us!"

I knew I mustn't speak. She was in reverie.

"There were moments when I thought it impossible to go on, impossible to witness his suicide, an absolute stranger doomed to watch this terrible thing. The blackest predictions of the Church and our friends all came true but we could not change it any more than we could our natures. I would say I was through. Yes. I did. I would actually say I was through, it was finished; but it was never true for one second. Far truer was my announcement that when I said I was through and finished he must remember that it was just blather and he would have to shoot me if he wanted to get rid of me and God help me, that was the real truth of the matter."

For better, and now, I knew, for worse and worse. Helen had left the Church to marry this divorced man, was spunky enough to defy her pope who, too, was helpless to fight the inevitable, simply able to warn against it. Helen's love sustained her through her years away from the Church if not from churches. But this was an added burden she had to bear—and did. I looked at her as she looked across me at the moving landscape.

I heard a sigh escape her. It floated out and I almost saw it, visible, like a wounded, gliding bird vanishing into the twilight in its eager return to a nest already destroyed. The car was silent for a long time but for the scratching of my pen. Helen had got as near the nerve as ever she was going to; and up there near heaven, I prayed that when I returned to New York, I would be able to capture that sigh and what caused it, and that in reading what I would write she might not regret her confidences. We had had our moment of magic, and I was determined to preserve it.

A second later, Helen was describing a small town outside of Mexico City that she had to take me to while we still had time before shooting started on the *Tarzan* script. And would I like to escort her to the palace to meet the governor who was visiting? The scene was over and she could replenish herself. She has an emotional tidiness that is enviable. Everything is tucked carefully away in paper-lined drawers easily removable and replaceable. Nothing gets wrinkled or lost, and if there's a skeleton in the closet, it's scrubbed, polished, and in rattling good condition. Helen's recuperative powers are formidable and her disciplines and organizational abilities beyond my understanding.

When Jim came down to Cuernavaca, he arrived before schedule at the studio to spend some time with his mother, and we all had pleasant times together, moving as a threesome to Mexico City, where Mr. Ely and the management not only gave me my own apartment but a daily stipend as well. Traveling with Helen Hayes was not in the least unpleasant or unprofitable. She was perfectly willing and ready to put me up somewhere in Mexico City at her expense, but the studio, with typical panache, would hear none of it. An entire floor in an apartment hotel off the Reforma was assigned to us and we, each of us, had a private flat—as charming as could be. Jim and I shopped for some groceries and booze to have around if we ever needed them, and then began a social life in the big city as pleasant as that we'd had in Cuernavaca.

At the opening night of a Dolores Del Rio play I sat astonished by the preserved beauty of the Mexican star, if not by her talent. Her performance consisted of arranging her serape in endless patterns, sucking her lovely cheeks and glowering sultrily as the plot swirled about her. But she was gorgeous—no more than a woman of thirty. Helen leaned over and in a voice of mock tragedy whispered, "We are *exactly* the same age." When I turned in shock, she was staring wildly at the stage, her eyelids fluttering in an ecstasy of grief. I almost laughed aloud and Helen, continuing her loony act, put her finger to her lips. She never once uttered a negative word about the performance, and compared herself only unfavorably to her old MGM colleague whose mother and Brownie used to be pals.

But Helen was blessedly sequentially older and, in my eyes, far more human looking. We had discussed this in examining her own Grandmother Hayes who, as most of our grandmothers, was an old lady and comfortably there when she was needed. In denying the seasons, women and men are in danger of all expiring in the spring of senility. There are no contrasts, just different stages of youth, young youth and old youth, the latter so near the lifeless, faintly smiling, almost sleeping renewal of embalment that I am given the shivers. Helen in her spryness—perhaps an unflattering adjective—has more life and fun in her than all the hand-painted harridans that hobble about, nothing but bones and tucks and stitches. My eye, at least, is always refreshed by many sights, and one of them is the face of a life that has been fully lived. There is a cycle that has been denied, and I am sick of living things cut off and pinned back in their supposed prime. Frozen women. Bonsai women. Ancient women who insist on dying young. I was most impressed not only by Helen Hayes's sweetness of appearance but by her regenerative energy.

I will always remember one evening when she was planning a dinner party at one of the best restaurants on the Calle Hamburgo. She was having her director, Edwin Shery, her star, the handsome Mr. Ely, their wives or whatever, Jim, and me. Our reservation for their matchless *boeuf Wellington* was for eight o'clock. The day on location went slowly. There are days in which all goes wrong, lights, animals, actors not acting as well as they should. Tarzan was finished for the day and promised to be at the restaurant on the dot. I was interested to see the gentleman dressed, believing mistakenly that so covered he would make the rest of us men look somewhat less odious by comparison.

There was retake after retake and it seemed unlikely that Helen was going to be able to greet her guests, since we had to return from Churubusco, dress and shower and then hope the company car would be available and we didn't have to depend on a taxi. The assistant director made one call to both Ron Ely and the chef to postpone dinner until nine o'clock, and now we weren't sure even this could be managed. It was going to be a photo finish, we decided, as Helen, Jim, and I drove back to the city. By the time we arrived at our hotel it was twelve minutes to nine. Helen's eyes got bright. "We're going to make it," she said. "Let us synchronize our watches." We were now in the elevator on our way to the top floor.

"The restaurant, we have to figure, is about eight or nine minutes away," Helen announced. "That means that we rendezvous here in the elevator in exactly three minutes." The elevator door opened and Helen shouted, "Ready, get set, go!"

The three of us rushed into our separate apartments, laughing in dead seriousness. I am highly competitive and decided that I would impress Helen with my famous coordination and speed. I flung dirty clothes in all directions, put on the shower, mentally chose my costume for the evening and then, half wet, started dressing. I have made quick changes in the theater and it is remarkable how long three minutes can be. It was a broiling-hot day and shower or no, all this activity was making me hot again. I was buttoning my shirt when an hysterical Jim ran in. "Well!" he yelled as he tried to tie his tie and lace his laces simultaneously, "I'm through."

"You don't look through," I yelled back, grabbing my jacket and remembering my notebook and glasses.

"It's almost three minutes, Sandy. I've locked my door. Lock yours."

We were tripping over each other and out the door and we both raced to the elevator as we patted down our hair. *I knew it. I really shouldn't be unkind and lord it over her, since she lost another game of Scrabble to me and I wouldn't let her have "tonique"!* I rang the elevator bell and the door opened immediately. There, as soignée as you please, stood Helen, bathed, coiffed, and in a lovely evening dress. In the sweetest of voices, and with eyebrows raised, she asked, "What's been keeping both of you?"

And we made the restaurant on time, preceding our guests, who, on their arrival, saw a triumphant Miss Hayes, after a hard day's work, superbly groomed and looking like a million while Jim and I in mismatched socks and ties and weak from exhaustion were happily having our first drink of the day. Helen's only comment when we all laughingly recounted her victory was, "You didn't think you were going to beat an old pro like me." Let me say here and now that it is a pretty tough thing to attempt.

Life on the set of *Tarzan* was as unreal as the story. Until you've seen Cheetah straddling Helen Hayes, his hairy arms and legs lovingly around her, his head upon her breast; until you've seen Jim and me within camera range but stealing through the "brush" waiting to catch an earnest and petrified Helen if she was thrown from the biggest elephant in captivity; until you've seen my old friend, eight-feet-tall Geoffrey Holder, who turned up on location as the evil witch doctor, cavorting with a painted dwarf with an accent like the Cisco Kid while, notebook and pencil in hand, I persevered in my work; until you have seen wise, naked Tarzan telling spunky but bitter Victoria Regina that she must allow her son to bring civilized medicine to the Dark Continent despite her sacrificing husband's death at the hands of the heathen and then, knowing why I was there, confiding to me that he used to date Marilyn Monroe, you just haven't ever been in Never-Never Land.

It was, I must say, a most amiable company in every way, and Geoffrey kept things lively with his choreographed gang of feathered natives. I have photographs I've still to show his gorgeous, magnificent wife, Carmen de Lavallade, of me tied to a stake trying to look petrified while Geoffrey plans to both choke and then cook me for supper.

This entire period was unreal to me, with the colors and tastes and sounds of Mexico, the dazzling sunlight, and Helen's lovely house and sweet servants. There was something of the mirage about Calle Victoria. Yes, that was the name of the street where she lived. It was all unreal and I wondered if the notes would curl up and turn to dust on my return home.

One morning shortly before the end of my stay, Jim and I were eating our *huevos rancheros* out on the patio when we both bolted upright at the same time. It is rare that one can see the distant, breathtaking peak of Popocatepetl; the horizon is usually veiled in haze. But there it was, snow-capped, like Fuji—somehow holy—the kind of vision that made the primitives believe that the gods lived there and the civilized certain that if they didn't it was only because they had moved away. Helen was still not up but the sight of Popocatepetl is not to be slept through and that is understood. We ran to awaken her.

"Mom! Mom!" Jim shouted as we knocked on her door excitedly. I had only heard about this mountain and seen countless paintings of it.

"Helen! Helen!" And we roused her. She emerged immediately, ignoring her toilette, and now all three of us sat, surrounded by hibiscus, in wonder at the sight before us. It was curiously like hope. When again, at any second it would fade from view, one knew, having seen it once, that the dream was real—that dreams were somewhere a reality. I managed to steal a glance at Helen, who was almost devotional, and I recall clearly feeling very much one with her and knowing of a sudden that the notes, illegible and arguable though they might me, would some-day make a proper book. I wanted her to be pleased. She had been married to one writer and knew all the others. I cared whether she liked my work.

It was late September, the filming was over and with it the make-believe. The idyll was soon to be a thing of the past. Leaving Cuernavaca, bags packed, tans already fading, bowels already righting themselves, we traveled as from Shangri-La over and through the dizzying mountains into Mexico City on our way back to the world of Do It Now, where people age and anger and reject each other and die. I had a new problem. Helen had to join the ANTA company in Ann Arbor and was only flying as far as Chicago, so I was assured safe passage only to the Windy City. After that I was on my own, and so I refused to fly on to New York. I made my arrangements to go home by rail—planning to take the Broadway Limited from Chicago to New York—as Helen shook her head in impatience at my terror and my outdated travel plans.

"I tried catching the Nineteenth-Century Limited but it's not running until the next day."

"You're a nut!" was Helen's last word on the subject.

And that is how I traveled from Mexico City to Chicago in three hours and, misinformed by the travel bureau near Chapultepec Park, traveled from Chicago to New York via Canada, I swear, in almost twenty-four. It is almost impossible, but I accomplished it, arriving alive, it is true, but exhausted. I had survived my travels. Now I had to write a book.

Again it was those initial pages, that first indication to the subject of the style and eventual impact on the reading public, that give the writer pause. Such pause that several weeks can go by before one dares start—though the reasons masquerade as environmental readjustment, jet lag (rather difficult to buy as well as sell when you have traveled by Lionel train), the need to digest before spewing out, a need for a new eyeglass prescription, and any number of other obvious dodges. But the moment eventually comes when one has to sit down, tack the notes all over the room, and then face the music.

Every star has started or has had a mother who has started an outline of a book, and it is wise not to ignore it altogether. It is always handwritten on blue-lined yellow sheets—and I always use a line or two she will recognize as her own and therefore love. This happy acceptance of the familiar now placed like a gem in a real paragraph always includes a great deal along with it. Since one's earliest years are, as I have earlier explained, the least controversial, probably because, with everyone's help, the child is the center of the universe, I have rarely had too great a problem with the first chapter. Dagmar was a special case because it was the present. She hadn't for years seen her reflection in anything but smoked mirrors and bottoms of Baccarat wine goblets. All the others were looking back from success and fame and a now much discussed awareness of themselves.

Helen had a letter she had scrawled to her grandchildren as a sort of preface. She had told me to ignore it if I didn't like it. It was a lovely gesture—the note—and it ended with a poem. I incorporated the three lines and the best of the letter into several pages that I felt sounded like Helen Hayes. The publishers agreed it was right and I then started the first chapter. I tried to get the lilt of Helen's speech, which certainly was not Irish but oddly had some of the rhythm. Her speech was filled with airiness. She could be quite high-flown in the best tradition of the

Irish, and then suddenly it was all jigtime. Graceful, then curt; eloquent, then colloquial. The queen wisely speaking to the populace from on high, but with the common touch.

When I had about fifty pages, a sample enough, and the best I thought I could do, I showed it all to Herb, who thought Helen would approve. I sent it to her in Nyack and awaited her reaction. She had not too long before refused to accept the work of a well-known writer. I had, once I was ready, sat on my bottom and not moved until I had these fifty pages ready. This was the moment. I did not hear anything for a couple of days and conjectured either that she had been out of town and hadn't read the work or that she was trying her best to let me down easily. On the third day, I just kept writing, went to the theater with friends, and retired fairly early so I could rise and shine at dawn.

After midnight I was in bed reading a book Brownie had written in 1935 about Helen. It was laundered and starched, but not at all bad in an official and expurgated way. When I am writing one of these biographies I sate myself with material about the subject so that I feel more and more like her and the style becomes less and less conscious in its need to reveal character and background. When it becomes second nature it flows. I was rereading MacArthur and Ben Hecht as well, and refreshing myself on the overvalued Algonquin set. The smallest of clues could solve the mystery of the marriage, his drinking and paralysis, her productivity and survival. Through her *Letters to Mary* I was presently struck by Brownie's niceness of nature. These were "letters" to her granddaughter and doubtless the inspiration for Helen's. I was reading about "Mommy's stubbornness" when the phone rang. It was Helen.

"Sandy? Helen! I hope I didn't wake you but I've been

trying to get you to say, dearest, that it is *beautiful!* I love what you've done with Mother and the whole family. You really understand—and it's written with such grace and wit—I do wish I were that witty—and . . . well, it still sounds so like me it's spooky."

I cradled the phone and decided I would sleep with it in my arms, a lover, a deliverer.

"Helen—how very dear of you to call . . ."

"Well, I knew how you must be waiting for the other shoe to fall."

"You mean the ax!"

"I want you to know how thrilled I am. And how glad I am to have entrusted you with my life. Now, you're not going to make it a biography, dear, are you? This much is all right but . . ."

"Please trust me, Helen."

"I do, dear, completely."

I now threw myself into my work, arriving at that point in the book where Helen and her mother were living in New York and Helen, a small child, was appearing with Lou Fields. It was time to send another fifty pages or so off to her and into the mail they went. I knew she would love these even more than the first, since they had to do with those initial years in the theater; and I felt I had revived old Broadway and reopened the Empire Theatre for a whole new generation to enjoy.

I had done my homework and incorporated Helen's anecdotes into the history of the American stage. Lou Fields, John Drew, the Castles, Charles Frohman, William Gillette, George C. Tyler. The little rivulet, Helen Hayes, had joined the main stream, adding her own special current, both feeding and being fed. But the little girl, was growing up too early, gaining painful knowledge to be used in her art. It seemed to me an excellent second section.

It must have been a week later when Herb called me. His voice was that of a doctor helpless to change the bleak diagnosis.

"Helen is talking of calling off the book, Sandy."

"What? Calling off the book?"

"She hated what you did. *Hated* it."

"Hated it?"

"She can't stand the writing."

"Can't stand the writing?"

"I know you're in shock, Sandy, but you keep repeating what I'm saying."

"But I don't understand."

"She can't be talked to right now. Don't even call her. I'll let you know what's what."

"What's what?"

"Don't dare repeat this, but Maurice Evans told her that he doesn't like it and—I don't know, Sandy, I think we have to sit tight and let her get over the shock. I think it might be the way you treated Brownie. Who knows? I don't. We'll try to rework this part, after we get some more idea of the trouble."

I knew Helen far too well to allow this third-person business to go on and I called her. She was as cold and remote as she could be. The first Helen. Helena Imperatrix.

"But what is wrong, Helen? I don't understand. If there's anything you disapprove of—"

"My dear, it is hopeless," she replied.

"But I think you should explain."

"If you could see my mother this way after all we've discussed. Well! It's no more Brownie than the man in the moon."

"What isn't Brownie? This is what I got from our talks."

"That's why it's impossible to go on, Sandy."

"But Helen!"

"Perhaps, after I feel a bit more relaxed and have a few moments, I may send you a few pages of my impressions of Brownie. I rather thought you had them, knew them, felt them—but I'll try [and she sighed deeply] in the meantime—I just don't know, dear. I feel just as badly as you."

This of course was not true. I had an immense investment in this book—in time and money and now prestige. If Helen Hayes dispensed with my services at this point—and this, despite all my battles, had never before happened—I wouldn't be offered the job of writing the life of Gabby Hayes.

It was a bleak, cold January day and I walked over to the Morton Street wharf with those pages and, wrapped up against the wind, intermittently watching the ice floes move toward the harbor, I reread the second section and couldn't imagine what was wrong and then it came to me. Helen's problem was not her husband, but her mother. It had been the same damned thing with Bette after Ruthie died. Helen had read a story she had related to me but evidently did not want broadcast and now resented me for telling it. I was being punished for her supposed disloyalty.

I had written what I believed a moving scene. Indeed it had moved me while I was writing it. The whole segment in question filled about a page and was sparer, leaner in style than anything I'd ever done. I had found the dynamics so powerful that I allowed the story to write itself.

One day, Helen—her glowing eyes focused somewhere over her right shoulder, deep in the past—had told me a hair-raising tale. Since she was not Scheherazade and not being paid to entertain me, I could only infer that the story was to be used. It was a moment in her life that ended one chapter and began another. The tale had so impressed me at the time that I had put down my pencil and gaped at her. We were in Mexico, and I remember the way she turned her profile toward me as she gazed out over the rooftops toward the hidden Popocatepetl. She had swallowed hard, and my stunned silence was applause. She had continued with a few more details which I didn't have to scribble on my pad. They would remain with me always. By placement, with utter simplicity, I had transcribed that moment in our book.

"It is an absolutely dreadful scene and embarrassingly overwritten," she told me.

"Overwritten! I didn't even use an adjective."

"You managed it without one and quite a feat it is. But more important, it just isn't true."

Helen, evidently in a mellow mood, had confided a moment so personal as to have been untellable as well as unprintable. The first she could only resent and deplore; the second she could forbid *or,* when she saw it in black and white, she could feel that it was too damning to her mother (which was not true) *or*—and this was the danger I had usually been careful to check against—she had simply, for attention and dramatics, been inventing, and now had to shift the ownership of patent to me.

Often a subject would confide some tidbit, once in the rhythm of confession, declaring it however off the record. This was always respected. Too, I often sensed when a sensational revelation would prove unusable and always discouraged the confidence (only, of course, after my curiosity and love of scandal had been satisfied). This was not such a case. It was pointless to belabor the fact that I hadn't fabricated the scene. She, as well as I, knew whence it came. Nonetheless, Helen Hayes was suddenly extremely busy and unhappy and cross and very unfavorably disposed to her Boswell.

I was stymied. I just sat at my desk staring at my carbon of the section that had so offended her. The offending moment had affected, like a virus, the entire three chapters. And there was so much that I knew was good there. Helen hated it all. Like Dagmar at that first reading I did of her introductory chapter, she hated around the topic that was taboo—lashing out at the man who dared so to blaspheme. Therefore everything became terrible. If one would not hire a black man of a group of auditioning actors, but will not be branded a bigot, one simply rejects the whole group in order to camouflage the particular.

There is an honesty that abides in truth and there is an honesty that compels one to reveal the lie. We are only human after all. The church which demands the most of us expects the least. Helen was confessing again—sidewise. She did this most charmingly another time, when her dog ate my scarf—or chewed it to such a fare-thee-well that it might just as well have been devoured. I had come indoors one chilly night in Nyack and hung it, as was my wont, on a hook near the door. It was a beautiful scarf, ancient madder tie-silk on one side and cashmere on the other. I had bought it in London and I adored it even though it couldn't walk. Helen insisted it did—that its disappearance had nothing to do with her little poodle. I seriously doubt that Vera threw it in the river. There was simply no other explanation when all three women and I hunted in vain for the beautiful muffler. Helen stoutly defended the dog, who was not without taste. A year later I received a gift from Helen. "To make up for your lovely English scarf." Not a confession perhaps. But I know Helen. Her conscience couldn't take it. Someday, she would tie up this loose end also. Helen was that neat.

It became more and more clear to me that my dear lady had been carried away that dusk in Cuernavaca and had exaggerated an event out of all proportion, and its playback doomed her to purgatory and me to hell. And that is where I was at this point. Helen was through. Her reversal was remarkable. I had been happily entrusted with her life just five minutes before, and now I had been accused of threatening it. One would have imagined that I had set out to destroy her family, and that is exactly what she had begun to believe I had done at her instigation.

I sat in my study that January, now perhaps self-inflictedly grippy, in a stupor and in a fever. I was incapable of doing anything but study the same damned scene over and over. Had Sandy the Sensitive atypically toyed with what he had already recognized as an exposed nerve? No. I had not, unless the mere mention of Mama's name was going to create a like eruption. How did one avoid it? At eight years of age Helen could hardly be living alone in New York. Not even serious, capable little Helen.

I now looked back into Helen's Washington childhood again. Having always known that her mother was going to present a problem, I wrote—as well I had to if Helen Hayes's story was going to make sense.

> . . . I see now how Mother's demons helped shape me. They were hardly joyous companions for a small child but her weaknesses made me strong. As the years passed, her problem grew. It was her hell. It was my crucible. I was taught to accept responsibilities, to be leaned on, not clinging. I was taught by my mother's demons to stand alone . . .

This statement of fact, which is in the book, was meant not only to explain something of Helen's subsequent character but also serve the rest of the book as a blanket, never-to-be-repeated-reminder of Essie Brown's, Brownie's, Helen's mother's losing battle with drink. It is never even hinted at again, except once and then obliquely in relation to Charlie. It didn't have to be. Such an approach was more tasteful for Helen and far more acceptable to her public as well as herself.

It is true that the scene in question preceded this, and —more's the pity—was not only cut but could easily have been deleted without all this brouhaha.

Now I still wanted to please Helen—to save the book, of course, and my sanity, as well as my apartment. My face needed saving also, but I can honestly report that I have my own compulsions and one of them through arrogance and vanity is to finish what I have started, and when I'm paid for something, to earn my money. Though I had to watch my step, I didn't have any intention of losing hard-earned ground.

I walked up to the publishers looking like Ichabod Crane, now also wondering what might have been happening in Helen Hayes's life to have justified this over-reaction to the past. I had learned, living with her, that if rebuffed or rejected or disappointed by someone, *everyone* could suffer her displeasure. Conversely, a princely gift or adoring press—any courtly affirmation of her station— could end in that second Thursday of the month becoming a national holiday. Everyone's mood reflects a stimulus and affects his actions but with Missy Hayes—as one might expect from an actress and a woman of temperament— she could be transformed, by *lèse majesté* or what she considered vulgar exploitation, into first a snapping shrew and then the Grand Recluse. Obviously I had been judged guilty of both sins.

"Why are you so pale?" Herb madly asked as I fell into his office. He looked thinner to me. He was certainly going to be poorer.

"I've just been bled," I answered, "by a doctor who tried everything else to cure my mysterious malaise. What's with Hayes? She's thriving I'm sure."

"We've simply got to get rid of that stuff in early New York."

"Where shall I set the scene—in Istanbul?"

His expression indicated that I had better save what I thought passed for wit for a script acceptable to Helen. I really could easily have been walking around with pneumonia. I was dizzy and as congested as Fifth Avenue.

"I received a few pages on Brownie from Helen, Herb; and she's reversed herself completely. That was a good scene and don't tell me it wasn't. This stuff is sheer nonsense. And I won't use it. The book is not going to be a fairy tale. Whatever I did, I've obviously sent her round the bend."

"She'll come through. I know Helen. But you've got to be patient. Right now she wants to dump the whole book."

"I've taken her pages," I said, "and worked some of the essence into a rewrite. I sent it to her and haven't heard yet."

"Helen said that it was better, but she feels the whole business is hopeless."

"I don't believe it," I groaned, holding my head. *She never even got in touch with me.*

"Nor do I, Sandy."

"I am going to go on with the book," I said.

"Good!"

"Don't humor me, Herb. I know I'm delirious now; but I've got to cut the knot, like Alexander. If I can get past that spot I'll be all right. The book is in me and Helen will accept it eventually."

"Of course she will," Herb answered, his voice trailing after his attention, which was now on other matters. *If I die it could almost make a headline—in the* Enquirer, *at least. Writer dies of rejection in publisher's office. With the Hayes angle, it might make the* Post—*even the* Times, *although with their present proofreading and my luck, my name will still be misspelled.*

"I'm going to cut the knot," I raved on.

It came to me that if Mama's drinking could so affect Helen, what was going to happen to the love of her life when I started on him? My head started to pound and my eyes now refused to stay open.

"Go home!"

"Do you think I'm contagious?"

"Only your laugh," my witty editor answered.

I staggered out of his office and past George's door as he waved and smiled a too-kind smile. It was obviously the end of the Helen Hayes project.

A couple of bitter-cold weeks passed, and I did a great deal of walking once I beat the bug that was in me. Down to the Battery where immigrants had landed from Ellis Island in babushkas and velvet jackets and boleros, all with great hopes for the future, and not one of them had ever been rejected by Helen Hayes, the First Lady of America. I took the boat to Liberty Island—a writer who had so angered the lady whose statue I was now going to visit that I would never even be offered the life of Emma Lazarus. I walked miles to my favorite Frick Museum to hear Bach played as I studied those Corots. Johann Sebastian, Jean Baptiste, and Henry Clay himself were all dead, and therefore free of the kind of disgrace I would soon suffer when everyone knew. How in hell was I going to explain this defeat so horribly snatched from victory?

The plum had turned truly into "Miss Prissy Prune," her own self-deprecating description of herself. I had advertised Helen's gracious nocturnal call raving about the first fifty pages. *Could I make a novella out of them?* Could I take an ad out in *Publishers Weekly, Variety* and the *Manchester Guardian* announcing that though I had been working with Helen Hayes, I had decided to drop the subject for reasons I was too gentlemanly to reveal? Or even think of? Could I tell all of my friends, who were silently bored with my chronic financial mortification and hoped this partnership would relieve it for their sakes as well as mine, that I was loath to make money, that the idea of Helen's book becoming a success would shatter my security, that I would no longer know if I were loved for myself or just my money?

I have always said that if I were elected President of the United States, Congress, in special session, would immediately pass a law declaring it a seventy-five-dollar-a-week job with no expenses paid. Now I had the perfect explanation. Helen, going on seventy, was pregnant—another Act of God baby—and just couldn't go on with the book. God was the father. I the unholy ghost. And both our reputations were intact. I was going mad in an effort to save my sanity. But there was no way out, I decided. Except one. I had to finish the book at all costs, despite all of them. And I had to make Helen approve it. There simply wasn't any other way.

Admittedly—and writers will all tell you that at best their work is solitary—this was the loneliest time of my life. Drained from the flu, I bought a lot of fruit and juices and as much food as my refrigerator could hold and locked myself in with my notes. And started writing. My only escape from my depression was oddly the very work that caused it. It is an inexplicable truth that I could write as Helen with a love for her family, and as alter ego while I so resented her rejection of me. I will never be able to explain my involvement in her life—in all the lives I have written. I believe it takes not character but a kind of madness.

Surrounded by notes and a great big picture of Helen in *Dear Brutus,* and being in no admiring state of mind, I slipped like a phantom into her psyche—or perhaps allowed her spirit to flow through me. Usually my ego, in the hope that the work will be lauded, carries me, but this time it was hopeless, and it seemed I could do nothing but enrage her further. Despite this I illogically started to enjoy myself. Telephone calls from Connie, Martha, and Helene, Louie, Ernie, and Joan, and my brothers Jerry and Peter, to assure themselves that I was still alive, were my only breaks in the work. My other recreations included taking a morning and midnight walk—and the seven o'clock news.

There was no contact between Helen and me and Helen and the publishers. Not that I knew of anyway. I was now compulsive and drove myself. On Lincoln's Birthday (Old Abe might have been assassinated by an actor, but he was never rejected by one) I was taking one of my daily walks in the West Village when I came upon a lovely antique valentine in a shop window. Helen loved valentines and had a collection of them. This particular one fortuitously had a tiny openable book set in all the old lace and gingerbread. I simply wrote, "I remain faithful" beneath the flap, signed my name, sent it to Nyack and went back to work.

Valentine's Day was the perfect time for me to start writing of the meeting between Helen and Charlie. As I sat down it started to snow and as I sat in my multiwindowed study surrounded by huge falling flakes, I tried to recreate that day a half-century ago at Neysa McMein's studio, where Marc Connelly had taken Helen to a cocktail party that changed her life forever. I felt absurdly romantic and the writing went as smoothly as it had gone haltingly the days before. I felt Helen's presence in that room, in my chair, her fingers on the typewriter. It was not the testy, forbidding Helen but the once-young girl wanting to be a woman. I felt the same kind of excitement I always feel when writing a play and the character takes over. I felt the same kind of excitement one feels falling in love.

Helen's entrance into the New York scene, the absurdity of her presence, kitten that she was, in such a den of lions was fun to write. For a shy little ingenue to be in this setting with everyone vying with everyone else for attention, glittering if not golden, to look back and down from such a height as hers and remember the socially inadequate young thing was dynamic. She was in such terror and I chuckled to myself as I found us writing,

> Everyone was on—shining and outshining. I sat terrified that I would be asked the time of day and I would have to coin a *bon mot* in reply. This was not a room in which one could answer, "six-twenty." What a bore! I suppose "everything is at sixes and sevens" might have given me high marks, but it has taken me thirty-five years to think of it and this crowd was not in a waiting mood.

I was carried away. There was no stopping this abandon that dared in the face of Helen's rejection to fantasize and prolong the ecstasy. I had now turned into Helen and what came out was right. Was I remembering something I'd never heard and seen? My notes were sparse. A list of fellow guests, some good descriptions, a general impression. But I was *there*. And I was now delirious. I continued.

> I would occasionally cock my head with knowing amusement or lower my eyes in tolerant acceptance of the madness that prompted Dotty (Parker) to say "Really!" with such pith or provoked Harpo to insist, "You're slightly, Dotty." I didn't know what in tarnation they were all talking about.

Tarnation? Don't tell me Helen wasn't with me in that room. It came straight from her. *Goddamn it. She has to like this stuff. She's writing it.*

And then there we were at the nub. There was this "beautiful young man . . . with hazel eyes and . . . pointed ears—a faun." There he was, Helen's love now insanely mine, offering her peanuts and wishing they were emeralds —a twentieth-century legend. The beginning of the love story the other side of which I knew and would have to write also.

I kept writing steadily. To know the end at the beginning, to see Charlie and Helen then and now and in between, to know at the inception its demise, to see the whole is awful. No wonder God is wretched.

How odd it is to be all around the place. To see someone yielding and aching with desire, dashing and virile— both so romantic—and then to see the sodden and the rigid and the agonized. My God! That darling, frightened little girl is making my life a hell! What happened to her? What happens to all of us? How marvelous to be a writer even if no one will ever read you and Helen rejects this too.

Helen Hayes is less sentimental than I. This has always given her strength. I'm absolutely maudlin but I mustn't show it in this scene. I was reveling in our romance. Clap hands. Here comes Charlie. He saved the day. I was swept up by their romance.

From this moment it was clear sailing. Even with Charlie's boozing. I handled this exactly as Helen might if she could write, with all the love and understanding and veiled contempt. I felt her ambivalence, but I knew on balance where her heart lay, and I believe it was all there. I felt something in Helen from that third day in her Nyack bedroom when we had become equals. I still feel it through all the horror. It is a curious closeness—an empathy. Something told me that if I finished the book I could sell her on it. Something told me that Helen and I were meant to do this book and damn it, we were going to.

For the first time in many weeks I received a note from my alter ego. It was noncommittal but it was sweet. "I, too, remain faithful!" Helen answered. *All things considered,* I thought, *her mood would seem to be softening. All things considered,* I felt, *everything will work out. Just keep living her life.*

Marriage, children, the ascending career, and then the perfecting of craft. Acting, theater, anecdotes. Hundreds of pieces of paper. My God! Avoid her mother at all costs but write Charlie honestly. Mary! That's going to be a hurdle when I get to it. I can't avoid her at any cost. Mary! I'll be sticking a knife in Helen's heart. *How do I do this? But I must.* How does one open the wound and not deserve her revenge. *I can't worry about that. She had a daughter and she died. What the hell am I, a Christian Science practitioner?*

With Mary done, my next jump in the steeplechase was the Church. Excommunication. *Jesus! For a nice little lady, she's handed me more goddamned problems.*

The publishers liked what I had done. "You've taken off!" Herb said.

"And I may crash," I answered.

Herb and I always speak in dialogue. He told me that Helen was in town working on a television broadcast. She had not called or written me. I decided to take her to dinner.

She was staying at the Westbury while she taped *Arsenic and Old Lace* with Lillian Gish. She agreed to see me and suggested the restaurant at the hotel. I brought her some violets and we dined at a corner table. She was just distant enough to keep me worried but close enough to make a pleasant dinner companion. She was impossible to fathom. We talked of many things as if we were simply friends. Then I decided to speak.

"You know, Helen—I'm continuing the book."

"Oh, my dear," she said.

"And I will show it to you only when it is completely done. You know how much I want you to get the book you hoped for."

Helen put her hand on mine and got that maddening expression of comic saintliness. She was still determined to play it both ways. She patted me with one hand and strangled me with the other.

"You really don't think you can pull it off, Sandy? I'm hardly likely to change my mind."

She shook her head. But the line's credibility was lessened by her affectionate reading.

"You really believe that you can salvage this? That I will suddenly accept it all, that you can change my unchangeable opinion? It would have to be a miracle!" she added opening and closing her handbag in an act of finality.

"Then a miracle it will be, Helen."

"Good luck, my dear," she said in the tone of one who has just been promised the Indian rope trick. She now held her purse tightly and her eyebrows lifted in expectancy. Not for the miracle but for the table to be pulled away so she could be freed from the banquette.

I walked down Madison Avenue and decided that Helen Hayes was even more complex than I had imagined. I still felt she was acting and went back to work. When I got to the end of my notes, I finished with a summing up, which I concocted of a little God and a lot of Charlie, sprinkled with a generous supply of Helen's salt and pepper.

The book was done and I took it to Herb, who is not only an excellent editor but was, I felt, the detached eye that would seek out the fly in the ointment, the monkey wrench in the works, the overalls in Mrs. Murphy's chowder. I knew, however, that as ticklish as this business was, I must under no circumstance not be outrageous. In a sense Helen had to feel in me and my work something of Charlie. Once more I had to break down this reserve and cut through her naughty haughtiness. She wanted that and I didn't want to disappoint her. If she wanted an Irish free-for-all and it ended in a good book, I was her man.

Plans were made to send her the manuscript. She was apparently in excellent spirits again. The climate was right, and this strange woman who had loved and hated my work and me along with it, but with whom I had somehow retained through it all an uncomfortable intimacy, now invited me up to Nyack.

"To help me in the garden," she said.

"I can't wait until you read your book."

"Herb is raving about it—but I can't see how he couldn't, dear. After all, he's not going to say he doesn't like it, when it's so important that I aprrove. Really, Sandy, I really want desperately to like it—but—"

It was certainly a game, something I hadn't thought possible. For all the world, Helen acted as if my presence at her house was purely social. As always, we enjoyed each other and her awakening garden. Maurice Evans took us to Tarrytown to visit the famous Mr. Perkins and his roses and I was to be astonished by his weeping copper beech through whose curtained branches one entered a set for *A Midsummer Night's Dream*. The monsignor dined with us at Nyack and Helen and I took long walks. And we scrabbled and she lost. And then she said,

"I will take the manuscript upstairs, Sandy—though I dread it—and I will not emerge from my room until I finish it. Make yourself breakfast and do all the running and playing you wish. I promise that the next time I see you

316

I will have, God help me, read the whole blasted business. And—good luck, dear."

She now smiled genuinely and I felt that at least she wanted to love the book. She went off to bed and I took a walk into town where I found a telephone.

"She's got the damned thing in bed with her," I reported to Herb. "Do you know how to pray?"

"For God's sake, let me know as soon as you can."

"She's being a sweet potato," I ventured, knowing this had nothing to do with anything.

"Good luck. How's Vera?" he now asked, to lighten the mood.

"Sepulchral as ever, but not at all unpleasant, which may be a bad sign."

"Call me as soon as you know."

Helen was well aware that her decision was as important to us as Dred Scott's was to him. She had now gone to her sanctum to lock herself in until a verdict was reached. She was jury and judge. With the manuscript, I had included as a grisly joke a pair of scissors, a large blue pencil and—if she were really furious with me—a rolling pin. There was—beneath all the lace curtains—something, on occasion, of Jiggs's Maggie still in Helen. I knew that she would laugh, and I was amused to realize that she was quite capable of using all three of my gifts with pleasure.

The ancient Miss Fleming was rarely to be seen in the house, since she spent most of her time in her room, only wandering into the kitchen for hot water or some porridge and, I believe—aside from her naps—going to sleep at dusk. When Helen retired that night and Vera returned to what I believed might be a box of her native soil, I went down to the bar for a nightcap. I wandered through the darkened house, a ghost seeking peace. But there was none for me. I rifled Helen's picture file near the bar for old photographs that scanned her entire career, and then raided the icebox. I was so restless that if there'd been a family safe, I would have gone through it. And then I went off to bed, passing Helen's door and seeing the crack of light that meant that she was deep in what Herb wanted to call *Beyond the Legend*—a bone of contention between us. At this point I bleakly observed that without a book one didn't need a title. Yes, she was reading it and I wished to God I could have watched her face.

The sun was shining into my room when I woke up. I quickly shaved and showered and ran to town and back. I had to be in good shape for our next meeting. After coffee, I wandered down to the river and then returned to the pool and lay on a grassy mound overlooking the little dock where, in their heyday, the MacArthurs used to board their little boat and, picking at caviar sandwiches, Charlie would sail his wife down the Hudson and drop her off at the theater on matinees of *Victoria Regina*.

There was no sign of activity in the north wing. The cleaning woman arrived and then the gardener came and went, and then there was some official visitor who disappeared into the house, doubtless led into milady's chamber, and then let out again.

I lay sunning myself, the book I had started in bed lying unopened near me. I was no longer able to concentrate on it. There was another book that was occupying all my attention. *What is she up to? Was she crying with Charlie and laughing with the dogs?* Was she delighted with the way I handled the little anecdote about little Jamie and the German shepherd outside the Dorchester Hotel in London? Could she bear to put the book down—even to brush her teeth?

I heard a bark and thought for a second that I was imagining it, so vividly did I see that scene of love between a child and a dog. Turning over on my side I saw Helen's poodle, Chiquita, running toward me. She always heralded her mistress's entrance and my heart leaped. As I patted the ground and shouted an excessive greeting to the animal in some vague belief that my proven love for the beast would insure Helen's approval of my book, I saw Helen walking down the long stairs through the garden. She had the manuscript under her arm. I became half-crazed with love for the poodle and now allowed it to jump all over me. *Dear Sandy. His love for small things is so endearing that no matter what I think I will stand behind him and his work to my death.*

Peripherally I saw her walking toward me and wondered if her choice of costume would give me a hint as to her inclination. She was all in white . . . *Well, better than black,* I thought, *although in this weather it was unlikely in any case that she would have chosen it.* Lynn Fontanne, in her unending crusade to make Helen chic, had warned her against wearing white. *Did I use that? And if I did will it save the day?*

"Good morning, dear Helen."

"Good morning."

"It is a *glorious* day. Crystal clear, the loveliest of breezes."

"Sandy!" she began, ignoring my weather report. I wondered how many test openings she had tried before settling on this. "Sandy, Evans can publish this if they wish but it will be under *your* name because—under no condition—will I have mine attached to it."

"But—"

Helen had started calmly, quietly, with this absurd, left-handed offer to permit us to print her life in third person written by me. It was an impossibility and we both knew it. She would never countenance such a publication, and Evans and Fawcett, who had already contracted for the paperback rights of her personal memoirs, would hardly be eager to pay all that cash for a book she would not be willing to promote. Still, I thought this was an odd way to reject a book.

"I don't understand," she now continued, warming to the subject. "It's just impossible. I even hate the beginning now."

"But you loved . . ."

"I just can't dear. I just can't. It's awful. Simply awful."

"What about the end?" I asked idiotically.

"The end? Oh, my dear. I never got to that. I never even finished the book. I couldn't *even* read it. It's unreadable."

What else had she tried? But Helen had the most curious expression on her face. The faint smile was almost sensual. Satisfied. Secretive. I didn't understand that smile.

"Are you joking, Helen?"

"Would that I were," she answered, tossing her head. "Oh I wish I were, for your sake."

Her lips now tightened and her brow grew lined.

"I warned you I didn't want an autobiography."

"But if anything is disturbing you . . ."

"But it's everything. I just don't like it. It's all for naught—oh, dear, there's the monsignor. I promised to see him. I'll be back in a short while. I'm sorry, dear. I just *hate* it."

I saw that fleeting, feline expression again and I knew what was happening. And if it was only my imagination then—knowing Helen as well as I did—I had nothing to lose anyway.

Monsignor or no, Helen had not moved. She was staring at me, and it came to me that I hadn't picked up a cue. It is true that I weep only at art. In life I reveal nothing I do not wish to reveal. I have never understood people who immediately indicate their every feeling and thought. One sees their emotions passing like a parade across their faces. I am not in the least attempting consciously to hide these reactions but was I, early in life, forced to wear a mask of protection? With the exception of laughter, which bubbles up and sometimes has to be repressed, and a lost temper ofttimes hard to retrieve, my feelings do not pop to the surface until I beckon them.

I was shattered by Helen's verdict. Why wouldn't I be? Much more than financial considerations were at stake. It was a crushing blow and though, like a blush which comes involuntarily, I am certain that some shocking events have drained me visibly, I am in such times if anything rendered immobile. My fist does not go to my head or hands seek each other out in desperation. Perhaps pride has kept me in moments of sheer terror from showing more than mild concern.

Of course I was shattered by Helen's verdict. I was desolate. Still, I had been acting as if we were bickering about some easily lost or gained bagatelle, potshotting at each other from like positions of power. Instead, the lady was informing me that a year's work had gone for a pittance, that I was broke again and without prospects and very far from eighteen years old. That stylish joke of insolvency had grown stale. I was deep in my forties and I was ruined. I should have turned pale or had a heart attack or revealed something other than a high comedic disbelief in this woman's stubbornness.

I was shattered but, idiot that I was, I hadn't shown it yet. *Can it be that Helen is Candida and I that superannuated Marchbanks?* More important, am I now so part of her life that I must pay the dues? Everything seemed clear. Thank God I was Dan Dody's son.

I allowed my face to fall. I acted dignified grief. I looked out over the river wishing my jawline were more severe, all the better to point up my agony. I bit only the inside of my lip, believing in underplaying. I became what I was, the rejected writer, the crushed man, the man made a desperado, the man in need of a strong woman. It was as clear as anything would ever be in my life or hers that Helen had mothered her mother, her husband, and her children. Why not me? I held the tragic pose, unable even to face her, and I heard her voice. It was very low and very gentle.

"I'll be back as soon as I can, dear."

I watched her go, her poodle following her, dependent on her and in turn adored and cared for. *I have just played one of the most important scenes in my life and I co-starred with Helen Hayes. It is an Act of Mercy. The scene is laid on the lawn of a Hudson River house. It is midday and there are no shadows cast. Only a famous actress and what had better be a promising desperate writer. It is Chekhov time, and I had better play it her way or it's truly the final curtain. Why do I always forget what I have learned during all the months of talking turkey?*

She may have confessed once more with the good monsignor, but she was back in about a half hour. I was still looking out over the Neva, lost at sea, in need of rescuing. Stripped of everything but pride—bloody but not bowed. In order to be saved I had to be drowning. Where was the challenge unless I were screaming for help?

I am so talkative that simple silence could create the gloom from which I was now recovered.

"I don't understand how these publishers . . . and you say the typist . . . could be so affected," she began.

We must all help one another.

"You mean, Helen," I asked in a depression, "that you were not pleased with the handling of Mary?"

"I never got to it, dear. Perhaps . . ."

"May I read it to you, Helen?"

"I'd really rather not but—well, go ahead dear."

She lay down on the grass and posed graciously as I quickly found the part I had done on the loss of both Mary and Charlie. Though there were a few years between their deaths, there was certainly a causal connection as well as a literary need to double the power and minimize any bathos.

It is true that there are emotions so strong, grief so swiftly identifiable that the bare fact stated simply touches the heart. I had seen my own cold grandmother stand at my mother's bier, expressionless, her first tear—a tear of iron—adhering to her cheek. I was fifteen, and never forgot it. I had lost my mother. I had neurotically dreaded the moment for years and though I lost her early, it was natural that I lose her. But my grandmother stood over her own child. In an unreasonable survival of her young she suffered one of nature's obscenities. I never forgot this woman's suffering, nor forgot Helen's glistening eyes that day in her bedroom.

In two paragraphs, Mary was gone, and with barely an embellishment. One page later, Brownie—already in the hospital—and Charlie were gone also. I think it was good, tight work, understated but not underwritten. And I topped it with a marvelous tale that Helen had told me months before. She had recently tried to place a bouquet of violets on Mary's grave after a big snow that made it impossible to reach. Undaunted, Helen—in one of her wild and woolly moments—took careful aim and pitched it over the drifts where it landed smack on target. She was—in the grim setting—reminded of her sweet father and the early days in Washington, D.C. when he used to take her to baseball games, to see his idol. That pitch, she thought, was worthy of Walter Johnson. The whole macabre scene struck Helen as funny and there in the cemetery she began to laugh and she knew that gay, ever-young Mary would have laughed too. It was their first laugh together in years. Fini.

I read the two pages quietly. I was auditioning all right. When I was through, Helen was looking away, but she was crying.

"Well," she said hoarsely, gruffly, "no wonder they were all touched. I mean . . ."

"Helen," I now said, my voice quivering with emotion, "please finish the book and then—then if you still feel the same way—well, I guess—I don't know—but I guess if you're not pleased and that's all that matters—then I'll just leave."

I decided on a feeble attempt at humor.

"I can always *jump* into the river—and swim home of course."

Helen looked back at me. Her head was raised high, her nostrils twitching. She sat up and then turned her pretty profile to me. Her back was arched. She could have been a Seurat.

"Let me read it from beginning to end, dear. From cover to cover and then we'll see."

I had been right.

"Oh, Helen," I heard myself say. "I know you're going to see what I was trying to do. Please read it as a unit. And if you don't like something, of course, I'll take it out or change it."

"We'll see, dear. Now let's relax and have a drink. It's almost five-thirty, and I think we both need one. And then, maybe we can have a game of Scrabble before dinner."

There were no words. How could one play Scrabble with someone being destroyed? Obviously I wasn't going to be destroyed. Helen, after all, was no monster. I knew now that I had passed my audition as actor, as writer, and I hoped as friend. I foresaw the next few days. Helen was going to demand changes. Helen was going to become Bette and I was going to have to remain calm at all costs. If I lost my temper, I could blow the whole book. The reprieve I felt unspoken was only a preface to a greater challenge. Could I survive the coming changes?

I took a walk after dinner while Helen was doing some telephoning. That booth in the general store was becoming my haven. I called Herb and told him what had happened. I swore that all would be well if I could take the gaff that was about to come my way. I would probably be there for several days while she wielded the scissors and the blue pencil. She had already knocked me out with the rolling pin.

The next morning, Helen greeted me in the kitchen. She was brimming over with good will.

"It will take a few days," she said, "but we'll work it out together."

Together! My God.

"And then we'll see," she added, in case I had become too optimistic. "Have you called Herb? He must be terribly distressed. Perhaps," she said, spreading her favors, "you'd better let him know that we *may* work it out."

There was now not a question in my mind about the book's eventual acceptance. Only my sanity. I could only imagine—with the stakes as high as they were—how this Albertless Victoria would salt and then nurse my wounds. *She should have played Florence Nightingale at some time in her career. All that spunk and energy and the desire to help mankind.* I knew she was going to tie my hands and bandage my mouth but Helen was not going to let me down. It was now my job to see that the book we would definitely publish would be a good one. If not there was really no

325

point. No. She definitely wasn't going to let me down. It occurred to me that if I had had a drinking problem, my fate would really have been sealed.

There was no end to the surprise package called Helen Hayes. She sat with me in the dining room, each of us with a copy of the manuscript spread out over the lovely table, and I could have been a child being examined by a stern but excellent tutor. This was evidently the latest role. Every solitary page had to be approved by her and I had to sit there and defend every comma. There wasn't the slightest question now that Helen was making it tough for me and I could have, at moments, gladly choked her. My temper, so often sweet and so often short, I knew could be my downfall. I could hear my dear Martha's booming voice from New York. "For once in your life, boob, keep your mouth shut. Do you hear? Shut! Of course protect your book but remember it *is* *her* life and you'll throw the whole damned thing away if you go into one of your fits."

But it was tough to follow this excellent advice. Helen was pulling all sorts of nonsense out of the blue. Suddenly there was even some cockamamie business of the house possibly being haunted. I haven't even retained the details of this outrageous last-minute red herring which I had to reject out of hand. She brought it up, eyes lowered, a trifle embarrassed a few times and then stopped when I refused to react. She may not even have been serious.

The first flush of suggestions she had sent to me concerning the terrible period that ended our honeymoon—when she first called off the book—was the most sensitive area. Surprisingly little was cut. It was here most of all that I had to control myself. I had no alternative here but to accept her changes. It is to Helen's eternal credit and a tribute—not only to her husband but to all writers—that she allowed me to incorporate her changes in my own words, thereby retaining the uniform style of the book. She understood, like the adult professional she was, the necessity of not usurping this authority. Helen did understand writers—all too well.

As time went on, it became clear that I would live with this threat. In actuality, very little would be changed. Some of the alterations were perfunctory and merely a formality designed to prove who was boss.

Depending on her mood, she could be unnecessarily rude and even mean-spirited, getting her own back with some petty dig at me—for some infraction or other. Some seemingly harmless flourish would get her Irish up and I would hold my tongue. Like Hemingway's Anselmo, I would not be provoked. By the same token, in a happier frame of mind Helen would compliment me graciously. After first informing me that I had written far too much about the dogs and what did they have to do with anything, she not only retained every solitary word but burst into laughter at one point, saying, "Heavens, you really took off here, didn't you? Charlie would have loved that, it's so antic."

With editing, as with most things wisely accomplished, one gives away small things to keep the large. One saves one's ammunition. I would seem conciliatory when I was only being indifferent. There were things I would fight to the death for and others not worth the energy. There were numerous bits I could rationalize away to save the peace and even more, the book, but there was a dimly remembered page where Helen tried to bully me into a change that was totally destructive. It was wrong for the book and wrong for her, and she didn't seem to see it. I could hardly believe she could be this blind or stubborn or stupid. I didn't know which. But she kept insisting on the change and things looked ugly. It was time to fight. I kept calm but my impatience showed. I would not give in this time. I would have been a tasteless moron if I had.

This was what I had saved the ammunition for. I simply refused to change a word, once more demanding that she see the sense. But Helen had some materiel as well —and nuclear.

"It *is* my book!" she exploded.

"And as writer I know what is best!" I countered.

The glint and flint in Helen's eye I had seen in Bette's. God, how alike these women were. It's the love of battle, that look. Now our eyes locked in combat and on that gray day, in what had become for me that oppressive prize ring of a dining room, we sparred and circled each other, the champ and the contender. One fighting to keep the crown, the other to stay on his feet until the bell rang.

Helen made the decision. "You'll really fight to the death for that, will you? All right!" And she checked the page through as it was. I hadn't stared her down. She simply knew that I was right.

Though I kept Herb informed, it was just about three or four days before Helen had approved much of the manuscript, all but the last six or seven pages. The rest was now cleared by her. I had survived it. These last pages, my epilogue, I loved—as a father loves the child of his late years.

"I suppose you think this is brilliant?" Helen asked with the kind of aggressive good nature that, in time-honored tradition, barroom strangers can quickly transform into violence.

"Yes. I do—as a matter of fact."

Her distortion of mouth and nose meant to imply eternal disagreement.

"I don't. I've got to get into town and at least you've

got ninety-nine per cent of the book now. I'll have to study the last few pages carefully. Maybe," she said coyly, "I'll write a few and see what you think. I'll let Herb know."

It is difficult to relinquish power, as well as the "remains."

I handed Herb the script and we fell back in our chairs. The climate was terrible but the weather did hold.

Helen maddeningly postponed decision on those last pages for a week or two and then, without ever having looked at them again, on her own admission, she called in her approval. She was in a flurry of activity again and whatever needs she had were elsewhere satisfied. The first part of the book was already at the printer's. Now—as I daily proofread it once more—the work was sent in its entirety.

The last day in Nyack, I had wandered down to the edge of the property below the neglected tennis courts and gone wading in the river. Sitting on a rock, looking at myself in the water, the title of the book came to me. *On Reflection.* Helen was very happy with it and told me to tell the boys that she wouldn't O.K. the book unless they used it. Vera drove Helen and me into New York and charmingly, graciously wished me luck with the manuscript.

I had it and was grateful. And so was Helen. She generously admitted to me that she might have been carried away when she spoke about her mother and other things.

"I guess I was showing off, dear. I guess I wanted to impress you. Some of it just wasn't true, what I told you— and, well, I couldn't let it go through and perhaps I got a little difficult."

Helen is a bit of all right.

The
End

Until Dagmar's final exit she continued to keep in touch with dramatic notes announcing alternately her impending death and transfiguration. "Darrling! Sviatoslav Richter and I—" . . . "Sandya! I am very ill. When I get back from the house party I am invited to on the Costa Brava I will go into the hospital to see if the gall bladder has returned for another chance." She always wanted me to "type" another book for her.

As for Helen, she sends me Christmas cards from distant places. With good wishes and affection and blessings. All of them genuine but distant.

Mr. Merrill sends me season's greetings also. On Robert's twenty-fifth anniversary at the Metropolitan I dropped by and left a note of congratulations in his dressing room. Marion wrote a sweet note of thanks, asking me to call for an appointment. "I wish you'd call and tell us when you can come to dinner." But when Arno Press called last year to suggest a lovely reprint of our book—unsalable everywhere else—I happily accepted on condition that Mr. Merrill, my partner, agree. The Merrills refused without telling me because they were planning another book using our material as a selling outline. Ah, well!

Elaine has disappeared into Haiti, perhaps a victim of Baby Duvalier. When I wrote her on some business over a year ago, she played dead until I discovered she was negotiating with Ray Stark on a film deal that did not include me. She denied it and then added, "Did he really say I wanted too much money?" She thinks and moves in circles too rarefied for the likes of me.

Miss Davis was given a day at The Players not long ago and this created an awkward moment since I am a member whose connection to the actress was not unknown. Ordinarily one would have imagined I would be at her table. I decided to attend anyway. Bette arrived for all the world like Margo Channing. She looked just fine and very stylish, and the great respect in which her talents are held was made obvious by her reception.

It was quite proper that Bette be so honored, although on request for one of her films and without me to advise her, she sent on a print of her worst picture, *The Catered Affair*. Life is getting shorter, and as she was greeted at the door I could not resist the melodrama implied in our reunion.

"May I kiss Bette Davis?" I asked in close up.

"My God! Are *you* a member of this club?"

And then she turned her other cheek for kissing.

"Yes, I am."

"We—must have a—chat later."

And we did. Bette showed me her grandchild's tiny picture hanging from her neck. She was aglow with her.

She spoke of the children, whom I'd liked so much, and then she looked at me.

"Are you well? I mean doing well?"

"Yes, Bette, quite well."

"Goot! Goot-luck-to-you, Sandy."

"Good luck to you, Bette."

Good luck to them all. Despite the prickles and the thorns, the fire and the flood, the famine and the pestilence. My Four Horsewomen of the Apocalypse, with a vocal by *"mine* son, the singer." They all gave this too tender a soul a body with which to enjoy the tortures and pleasures of this world.

Yes. I certainly used others as they used me. I was doing an unnatural thing, writing someone else's autobiography. And though there were professional hazards I recognized, guarded against, and even understood, I couldn't accept them.

After hearing the worst why did I keep expecting the best? In order to do my job well, I suppose I had to get caught up in the magic of these actors and thereby got caught in their trap. How could I expect Bette Davis to be Margo Channing, Robert Merrill, Germont, and Helen Hayes, Harriet Beecher Stowe? And if they could have been wouldn't they still have had to scratch themselves and change their underclothes? Only in art are the unessentials disposable.

The truth has always been to me what should be—not what is. I had no right to expect my heroines to act heroically. I wanted these hard-working actors to be gods.

Elaine shared this madness with me and she had to suffer her alliance to such as John Barrymore. He wanted to be a god. That was our sometime gain and his all-time torture. It is the man with a taste for greatness who achieves it.

I wanted my gallery of doers, my gifted ones to be larger than life. And only Dagmar really was. It was Dagmar Godowsky, with no achievement whatsoever, who proved the futility of my quest. It was Dagmar alone who *was* a great invention, heroic if only in her frivolity and therefore a warning to others, an excess that advertised moderation. Unlike all the others, Dagmar was the work of an artist.

What must I have done to them all? It was I with my adoration who made impossible demands on them. I who ravaged in an effort to ennoble.

I'm sorry, fellers. But you asked for it. It was indeed a collaboration. Let the next star—be she the latest Señora Peron or the shimmering if bemused Vanessa Redgrave—write her own damned autobiography. The good and the bad, the beautiful and the damned, the boll and weevil can write their own epitaphs. I've had them all, and I've had them up to here.

I would be only too pleased to ghost the wedding announcement of Prime Minister Menachem Begin's eldest son to Yasir Arafat's beloved daughter, the Ayatollah Khomeini's deportation papers back to the eleventh century, and most important, a presidential speech that would rouse our countrymen from the torpor and self-indulgence that is transforming us into declining Romans. I simply could not endure the agony of one more star.

Herewith I kill the golden goose. It laid some plated eggs anyway.

Helen was not one of them. Dear Helen. The first of the Irish queens who has survived everything including her counsel of imps and her own coronation. It was she who gave me my greatest lift.

333

When the dust had settled, and in fairness to her, long before the book was a best seller that earned her gratitude, Helen looked at me squarely.

"What kind of work is this for a writer like you? Why don't you write me a play, Sandy?"

I just might try that, Miss Hayes.